UNDER ANGEL

a memoir

COREY!
THANKS SO MUCH
FOR BEING A
PART OF THIS
CRAZY STORY!
LOVE

DAVE KEHNAST

PINA PUBLISHING 🍍 SEATTLE

PINA PUBLISHING 🍍 SEATTLE

Text copyright © 2023 by Dave Kenhast
Cover design by Jon Hahn © 2023 by Dave Kenhast
Interior book design by Susan Harring © 2023 by Dave Kenhast

For information about special discounts for bulk purchases contact:
sales@pinapublishing.com

Manufactured in the United States of America
Library of Congress Cataloging-in-Publication Data Kenhast, Dave.

Summary:
"Anything you need can take you to dark places in its absence."
In *Undercover Angel*, Dave Kehnast takes readers on a vulnerable, raw, gut-wrenching jour-ney into the heart and mind of a sensitive, often love-sick teenager in his explorations of marijuana, LSD, alcohol, and ultimately opiates and heroin. This harrowing journey brings us among junkies and thieves, prostitutes and police, heartbreak and love, and to Japan and back. As Dave navigates the Dantean realms all addicts face, he ultimately comes face to face with his inner child and inner warrior—and the unlimited possibilities that emerge from the power of hope and surrender.
This rare look at the experience of addiction from the inside out shines a light on the connec-tion between childhood wounds and addiction, and the unpredictable nature of recovery. All those seeking to understand the nature of addiction, whether in themselves, those they love, or in larger society, will come face to face with their own woundedness, the ways we try to ease our own pain, and ultimately empathy and hope for those who find themselves on this path.

ISBN:
978-1-943493-70-8 (paperback)

[1. Addiction. 2. Recovery. 3. Heroin. 4. Drugs. 5. Surfing. 6. Spirituality. 7. Alcoholism. 8. God.]

This book is dedicated to all of the millions of people who are facing, have faced, or will face that which feels insurmountable, and to those who have even decided that what they are facing is impossible to overcome.
I understand why you would think what you do about your situation but please don't give up.

Acknowledgments

Where to begin? There are so many so worthy of thanks and were it not for their existence, this work would never have been possible. I'm going to attempt to include them all.

My Higher Power, whom I choose to Call God. Dr. Bob and Bill W and all of their friends, particularly the fellowships in Chicago and North County San Diego.

My kind, caring, compassionate mother and father, Gerrie and Michael Kehnast, whose unconditional love sustained me through the darkest time in my life, which was equally dark for them. My amazing brother and sister, Andrew and Lauren Kehnast. Thanks for being so great and also so unconditionally loving. I hope that all of you know how remorseful I am.

Mike Sullivan for speaking sense to me through all the chaos and pain and for getting me into Cornell.

Cornell Interventions for bringing me back to life.

Max Shields and Paul Simms. You guys were there for me during all of that crap and you loved me. Thank you for all that you are and for your lifelong friendship.

Andrew: I miss you and I love you. R.I.P. dear friend.

Melina Macpherson. You sat and you listened and you laughed and you held space for my soul. I might not have made it had it not been for you.

Katrina Miller Stevens: You have always been there and I know you always will be. Thank you for the gift you have been in my life for all these years.

Everyone at Accomplishment Coaching and all of the brilliant professional coaches I've had the honor to know, especially Jodi Larson, Rodney Mueller, Marita Bolles, Halli MacNab, and Christopher McAuliffe.

Thank you all so much for your stand. I know that each of you saw my greatness buried beneath all the muck.

Hans Phillips. You see things in a way that no one else does. It has helped me to see them as well.

Dr. Dasha Zabalina, PHD. Thank you for believing in my writing and for being one of the most trusted members of my soul family.

Adam Sachs, you have in so many ways made this possible, more than just about anyone else.

John Tebbens, thank you for helping me get back on my feet.

Val Irvine. Thank you for your patience, your hard work, and your partnership, and for believing in me and taking this on.

Everyone at Pina Publishing. Thanks for believing in this project.

Abigail Gazda. I'm not sure you'll ever quite know the inspiration you are to me. You model and exemplify vision, integrity, and more than anything, hard work.

Alex Bayer: Your friendship matters to me more than you know.

Nikaya Kipp: You're an amazing force for love, good, understanding, compassion, and empathy in my life. Thank you.

Tamara Emerson: You introduced me to the life I have now and I am very literally eternally grateful for you.

Lisa Randall: What can I say? You're one of the other interdimensional soul-traveling super freaks I adore. This would not have been possible without you.

Linal and Carlos: You guys loved me, believed in me, and always saw the possibility of this story. Thanks for who you've been and for your stand.

The teachers who made a difference for me. Randall Hendee and Kath Bergen, in particular.

To all of the amazing people in Glen Ellyn: Megan Savitt, John Hess, Mike Keating, Bree Benson, Courtenay Gordon, Wendy Dunk, Josh Youstra, Alyson, Jennifer, and Jon Sieloff, Kristin Sima, Jeff Burke, and too many others to think of.

Tyler and Zicker and Craig: thanks for putting up with my shit all those years.

To Kevin Remmert: Thank you for the gift of surfing you gave me.

God bless everyone else at the Sherwin: Amy Remmerrt, Heidi Malm and Dan Hefter, Fred Morton, Larry Fox, Nina Mueller (R.I.P.), and Laura Lerner, just to name a few.

All of the badasses in Fort Collins and throughout Colorado who were in so many ways integral to the story: Abe Brennan, Garin Daum, Vinnie Fasano, Karl Alvarez, Kelly and Pete Hevenor, Stacie Stevenson, Jay, and Jacki Whitlen, Josh Grey, Meredith Flynn, Sherman Dippel, Robin Jones, Kevin Desilet, Chris Whalen, Mikel Semen, Rick, and Chris Van from Jay's, Angie Thomas, Samantha Salyer, Etc. Again, too many people to name.

Thanks so much to each and every one of you for existing inside of this dream with me.

FOREWORD

Seldom do I meet people that resonate at the frequency that Dave does—the type of vibration that sticks with you long after the interaction has passed.

When I met Dave for the first time he lied to my face, mainly because he was trying to be someone that he wasn't, someone he thought I wanted him to be. Someone that he thought he needed to be able to change his life. It wouldn't be until years later that I would learn how significant that moment was for Dave. I don't want to disclose more because this is Dave's story to tell, and your story to read.

Fortunately for both of us, even though I knew he was lying, I could see something else was there. Hopefully, the reader will also experience that same "something" through his words in this book. There is a passage from the book *Siddhartha* by Herman Hesse that I always appreciated where he is describing Siddhartha allowing himself to get cheated a bit by people that came to see him as something of a positive well-intentioned behavior. I think this first experience I had with Dave reminded me of that.

There is an authenticity that you rarely find in people that Dave possesses. His vulnerability can be shocking sometimes, which draws you further into the narrative. You want to take care with this soul who has experienced so much and lived to tell the tale, to see him continue to impact lives in a positive way to this day is inspiring.

As I reflected on the 15+ years that I've known Dave, it was fun to remember the many different ways our lives have crossed paths. Our encounters have spanned different decades, different regions, and different jobs, and it's always easy with him and never complicated. He is reliable and funny and has a magnetism that comes through in his words. He is passionate about his life, his sobriety, and his spirituality. When I started the agonizing process of quitting alcohol myself, he was one of the first people I told. When I caught my first really long wave, he was one of the first people I reached out to. When I needed an extra guy to make some money while I was between jobs, he was the one to carry the other end of the couch. When I turned on the news and saw this winter kayaker saving a stranded dog on Lake Michigan, he was the guy. When I'd be walking down the street, it wouldn't be uncommon that he would bike by. When I didn't believe in myself and I needed someone to tell me ten years ago that no doubt I would be successful in professional pursuits if that was my intent, it was Dave. After a really rough altercation with my seventeen-year-old son in Chicago, the first and only time we ever got physical, I was a complete mess and just had to walk…and of course, it couldn't have been more than ten minutes in and I hear the skateboard wheels rolling behind me and man did I need it to be Dave to tell me I wasn't a failure as a father, and it was. I have this feeling I'm not the only one and maybe you the reader will have a similar connection through his stories of addiction and hope. Maybe they vibrate for you with the same intensity that Dave does and has in my life.

There is something that connects him and me, regardless of time or distance, and we couldn't be more different or live different lives. He gives generously and expects nothing in return. I have always appreciated the difference that is Dave, and I hope you do too.

~Jon Elhardt

TABLE OF CONTENTS

Setting the Stage

Childhood

Adolescence and Early Drug Use

Colorado

Back to Glen Ellyn

Morning Drink—At the Shrink—The West Side of Chicago—The Honeymoon—Japan Part Two—Teach Abroad and Get Paid—West Side Jail—Rehab (Getting the Meds, The Guys, Hilfiger Man, The Girl on the Smoke Deck, Chores, Girls, Frank, Getting Out)

Incomprehensible Demoralization

Newport Nightmare—Fill-Ups—Cook County Jail—James' Resurrection—The Abscess—Probation—Cat Shit—A Spot off of Laramie—Drinking Mouthwash—Boo—The Restaurant— A Spot off of Lake—Staying Sick—The Bed—Cubs Game— Eating Shit

Rebirth

Detox—Ain't Too Proud to Beg—The Pool—Cat Fancy— Undercover Angels—It Came Shining Through—Getting Swoll— The Mattress on the Floor—The Good Times—The Fracture— Freedom Rings

A Life Beyond My Wildest Dreams

Rogers Parker—Serving the Homeless—Smitten— Happy Birthday—The Job—The Sherwin—Jim Called— California—Andrew's Celebration—Hope

Setting the Stage

Hope—Heroin—Spiritual Warfare/Angelfight—Japan (Waking, Complimentary Cocktails, Adjacent Room, But First a Bath, Nighttime, Phone Call, The Dolphin, The Mall, Homeward Bound, Texans)—Why

Hope: /hōp/
Noun

1. A feeling of expectation and desire for a certain thing to happen.

Hope

It's all about hope, the memoir I'm writing, or I guess that I've written if you're sitting here reading it. The hope we cling to especially as people are dying; the hope that brings souls back toward life, reinhabiting bodies they thought they had moved on from forever. The hope that unfortunately, more often than not lets us down, leaving us angry and hurt, cursing at God—the kind of thing you *can't* count on, which is exactly what makes it hope in the first place.

"This diagnosis is considered terminal; you may want to get your affairs in order," a doctor might say, whether it's cancer or dementia or Parkinson's, predicting your almost certain demise, "but there are rare instances of spontaneous recovery and remission that medicine cannot explain."

"Shoot," you might think, "I'm going to die," and then maybe you'll pick up a Bible and start praying, and possibly, just possibly, you'll manifest a miracle as the result of the prayers that it told you to pray but that you can't prove even worked in the first place. *Do any of us ever have any proof of the unseen?*

A friend of mine recently passed. Cancer. It was awful. She fought for nine years, each time not giving up—being *hopeful* when tests came back clear. Tied to concoctions in ominous, clear-plastic drip bags, having accepted them as a regular part of the flow, *hoping* the cancer was gone, that it wouldn't return; occasionally resting, assured for a moment or two. *Hoping* she'd beat it—that her children might have a mother to be at their weddings; that she wouldn't die young, before her mid-forties, forcing a six and nine-year-old to search for the meaning of life without their mom. In her last days, as I was praying and sending vibrations from my early morning Kundalini Yoga practice, and as she was hanging on longer than expected, I let the word and its energy into my field, into my conscious awareness. I started to think, *She just might live.* I hoped she would make it, an indulgence of sorts, entertaining thoughts of seeing her again on trips back to Chicago. She'd be smiling, have a full head of hair, and her children would be by her side—growing and becoming adults with her guidance. Her husband would smile, bum me a smoke, and we'd share a few courteous words like we always did. For a few minutes each morning, I let her live. I breathed life into the fantasy. I even convinced myself, for moments at a time, that she'd make it.

But she didn't. She rotted away, in front of her husband and kids. An unfair and horrible death. Hence, hope and how I've described it above. Mostly you're screwed, so why bother?

But then there's me, a driveling drunk who was spared. A junkie who somehow heard God screaming down through the chaos. Go figure. None of it really makes sense, except that I guess that it does. Does it?

Heroin

*Heroin is hell. But it doesn't end there, because heroin is beauty and heroin is love. Heroin is your first kiss and heroin is death. Heroin is truth, lies, pity, and God, and unattended 12-step meetings. It is perfect, and serves a purposelessness like no other by making good people go insane and do despicable things their mothers taught them not to. It defines deals with the Devil and makes feelings "go away" to other places, to be squashed down into compartments and hidden in dark, abandoned palaces that only God has the key for. I still love heroin for all that it is; because I am here, because it was destiny, and because there's a story with a living ending that has made me a man. I want to call it "Her," like it is the sea, a vessel, or a country worthy of recognition. But despite all of its **influence** it is still not worthy of anything proper. Dope remains filthy in its essence and covers the dirt that all junkies have filling up their insides, making them bearable in otherwise despicable lives of ruin.*

Spiritual Warfare/Angelfight

"Stop it, now," Michael commanded the demon, "he's going to die and you know it!"

"Micheal I'm sick of your shit you goddamn, do-gooding menace," the demon shot fervently back.

"Not this one, Asbeel. We've worked out a deal and we're taking him home to the Light."

"Fuck you. This one's ours. We both know his preference for darkness. Remember his nights in the Fort? The drugs and the whores and the rock and/or roll? We both know the place he belongs. Now, if you'll excuse me."

"But this one's good, like purely, and you know it. You're really just trying to kill what you know that you can't."

"Piss off, Mike."

"You know, He's willing to let this all go in exchange for the simplest apology."

"He can go fuck himself."

"Have it your way. I guess you choose war."

"Piss off. Here, have another sip, sweet David" the fallen one whispered.

I slid the coin in the machine.

Japan

Waking

I remember the smell, and the taste of the crackers and water; they had some sort of bite, bitter and un-American. I wrestled the blanket and covers and grasped at the pillow; it squirmed like a brown paper bag. *Where are you and what have you done?*

There was a vague recollection while laying in bed. I'd been on a plane and then taken a train. I remembered the mist in the mountains. I remembered the valleys and sea of Japan. There were also the others, my colleagues. They had been at the airport and been on the train, but all of this felt like a dream as I lay on the bed.

I finally got up and remembered the parts that the sleeping had helped me forget. It was such a peculiar, dark phenomenon that I had made manifest. I'd been in another dimension, floating around with the ghosts; and now here I was back on Earth, in this *room*, in Japan, "prepped" for the job I had gotten. It hit me at once and a terror struck deep in my bones. This could have been prison or death.

It was 2006 and I'd left Colorado, thinking Chicago would cure me. I figured I'd smoke a few bowls while I got things in order, and it worked; I'd gotten a job! There was also the heroin dream, dreamt up by something much darker than I could imagine. And now here I was in Japan.

Just the two of us....

Complimentary Cocktails

I'd planned it all out: Xanax, Klonopin, Adderall, Ambien. I had all the pills in a pouch. I knew that the dope would wear off and that I would be sick.

My Blanket/My Safety

I found a blanket; it was hiding inside of a closet, nicely folded and sitting pristine, like God wove its patterns together especially for me—a present from a great aunt or someone who I'd never met. It was white and pink and green, and baby blue, soft like the wool of a lamb. I sucked on my thumb with my finger on top of my nose, pressed it up to my cheek, and carried it with me for years—a safe little home in itself. There was also my Garfield. He was my friend. Both of them shriveled to pieces.

Kevin and Jim

One morning in early fall, I ran into Kevin and Jim by the playhouse out back. They'd barged into my yard like they usually did, making me scared and uneasy. They weren't very nice and had crewcuts and shirts from the Catholic school, both of them stronger and bigger than me at the time. "Hey, David," Kevin said as the squirrels ran along on the branches above.

"Hey," I answered nervously.

"What are you doing?" he asked, sort of moving toward me.

"Nothing," I answered. There were orange tracks in the playhouse for Hot Wheels cars sitting in piles on the floor. I saw them through the window as I looked away and then realized they saw them too. They seemed like they both might be thieves.

"Oh, nothing? David's doing nothing..." he teased, mocking me as I stood there, confused and afraid, and both of them laughed like the mean little boys that they were, and then, very suddenly, Jim unzipped his pants, exposing his penis, and started to pee on the window. Kevin was laughing and egging him on, and I watched as his pee trickled down. Both of them thought it was funny but I knew it wasn't. And I knew that I couldn't defend the house they had defiled. Both of them knew this as well, as they both were much stronger and bigger. He zipped up his pants and they left and went back to their yard, both of them laughing, at me and the pee on the window.

I went in for lunch. "How was playing?" my mother asked.

"Jim peed on the window..." I didn't know what else to say.

"He what!?" she reacted. She always had such animation to all that she said.

"...of the playhouse," I continued, and then there was silence. My miniature mind knew that something about them was off, but how does a child explain this?

"Go to your room for a bit," she ordered and I obeyed, feeling like I had done wrong.

Jim didn't ever come back but Kevin still came to our yard, but now he was different, *friendlier*, or at least pretending to be, donning some sort of peculiar Cheshire smile. I think he was seven or eight, a year or two older than me.

Jared and Jeremiah

In fifth grade, for my eleventh birthday and after I'd failed at making the travel soccer team, I got my first real skateboard, a black Sims Jeff Phillips with Ugly Stix rails and all of the other accessories. Its wheels were green; the boards were so heavy back then and it rode like a tank.

"I got a Jeff Phillips!" I called Jeremiah after getting back from the skate shop.

"White or black?"

"Black. It's super cool!"

"What kind of rails?"

"Ugly stix."

"Badass. Meet me and Jared at Lincoln."

I went to the school. The spring was warm and damp, with leftover rainwater dotting the landscape. We'd all gotten boards for our birthdays and were cruising around on the blacktop, doing powerslides through puddles and other easy tricks. There weren't any launch ramps just yet.

I was riding along, popped up a curb, and then heard something snap on my board. I had broken the "bird" at the bottom. I picked up the broken, black piece and yelled across the asphalt to my friends, showing them both what had happened. I wasn't upset, more like bragging; this was my first broken part!

They laughed, all of us laughed, a little at first, and then both of them paused as the sun set beyond the horizon.

"Hey Dave, is your *dad* gonna buy you a new one?" Jared then said antagonistically, taunting, a little at first.

"Looks like Dave has to take another trip back to the *skate* shop," Jeremiah chimed in sarcastically as both of them joined in the fun, laughing at my expense. And I was all of a sudden, *not* laughing, and they still were, now a little bit harder.

"Looks like it wasn't that great of a *birthday* after all."

"Looks like *Dave* needs another adjustment…"

"Shut up," I responded, defensively. I could feel the Incredible Hulk.

"You must have gotten a *defective* one, *Dave*…" Jared said, taunting me more. They were both very clever and smart, and both started pointing and laughing a little bit more.

"Maybe *Dave's* just a defect himself," Jeremiah jeered in my direction.

They laughed together from across the blacktop as I stood in the shadow of the wall of the school, holding the part in my hand. At first it was funny for me but then everything changed. They'd read my emotions like wolves and were suddenly laughing much harder than they were before. I started to scream like a baby who was scalded with water.

And then that was all that they did, nothing but pointing and laughing.

"Hahahahahahahaha!"

 "Hahahahahahaha!!"

  "Hahahahahahaha!"

I thought that my head would explode, that my brains would go flying, staining the pavement with globules of sickening gray matter.

Psst.

That feeling felt like it went on for hours. My heart broke to pieces that birthday when I turned eleven. They were laughing as hard as they could. I wanted to set them on fire.

My head turned to stone and exploded. They laughed and then laughed and laughed more, as hard and as mean as they could, all at another who cried.

"I HATE YOU!!!!!" is all that I had against what amounted to a very simple strategy on their part.

Point and laugh.

Point and laugh.

Point and laugh.

They finally got bored and went home. I left, crying and punching myself. What kind of monster was I?

One on One

But one on one they respected me, all of my friends, they always played nice during after-school play-times, with parents around and when we were alone. Jared invited me over a lot. He had a pinball machine, and we spent hours in his basement bouncing the ball around with the flippers, trying to score and to keep it moving, always outdoing each other. His house had a park in the back with dirt jumps and trails through the woods. We rode through for hours, jumping and flying our bikes through the air. I always loved launching off jumps, becoming weightless, then landing in the soft dirt, happy, stoked, and then going back for more. I loved to go flying and rode my bike better than most, and then skateboarding bloomed in my heart. I loved having wheels beneath me and places to soar. I was free from my friends and the world as I flew through the air.

Jeremiah's Affliction

One day he woke up in pain—the most awful kind, his stomach screaming in the way that only stomachs can, informing him things weren't working the way that God had intended them to. One day he wasn't at school, and then that day turned into a week, and then multiple weeks, and then months. *Something was wrong.* I was curious and sad. I was worried. I missed him.

The experts believed he might die. I'm sure he was frightened to bits. I imagine the ones in his family had all *felt* as well. His siblings looked up to him in the way that younger siblings do, and he was seen in no other way than a firstborn is seen by his parents. Their family was loving, and each of the children was smarter than most of the rest.

When he came back he wasn't the same. His cheeks were puffed up like he'd been to the moon but the rest of his body was thin. He had on a blue sweatsuit and there was a faint bluish tinge to his skin that sort of matched it. His hair was thinning and he'd developed some acne; and it was in seeing him and knowing that this was the face that he saw in the mirror and that it hurt him to do so, that I knew that he felt things in the same way that I did. This was why we were friends; we felt mostly the same about things. I didn't know I had a gift. I didn't realize that I was swimming around in his body with him, inside of the eyeballs that looked outward and into the mirror, seeing what looked like a ghost; and that this was empathy I was experiencing, *feeling the feelings **he** felt.* This feeling *I* felt—a reflection of his—was the good part to all of the bad. The anger was one thing, and this was another, but all of it lived on a spectrum.

I didn't have words to describe it, or the language to make it make sense.

Down to the Dungeon

I always was small, but all of a sudden, it seemed like I'd become *real* small, like an actually really small person who would stay small forever. In fifth grade, I fought and was scrappy, but then all of a sudden I seemed to be suddenly weak. In the wrestling units which would soon be a part of this growing-up experience, there would not be another adolescent child who I'd be able to beat except for one whose name was Doug and whose faculties, both physical and mental, were *diminished*, to say the least. This wore at me in ways that only a weakling understands, and I took on the role of a jester and made people laugh.

"You are going to be six feet tall, someday," the doctor proclaimed each time I saw him. He looked at the bones in my hands and predicted my height but I never believed him.

I carried my books, more than I really could manage, wrapped up in covers I made out of brown paper bags, down the block and then onto the bus for the first day at Hadley.

I got off the bus and then looked at my friends up ahead, Jared and Jeremiah, and a few other kids I didn't know, waiting beneath the foyer. I approached, happy and relieved to see them, but Jared quickly closed in, "What's up, Dave?" he asked, sarcastically, smirking. He'd been nice during summer, riding our bikes through the trees and exploring the woods, but he quickly closed in and then pushed all my books to the ground, laughing as Jeremiah followed suit, knocking them down as I'd hastily just picked them up. I scrambled, on my knees on the ground, and struggled to get them in order. And there on the blacktop, with the school busses running in the background, it seemed like the childhood I knew months before had existed in some irretrievable time and place, and there was a distinct knowing that it never would return.

I finally stood up, slouching with shoulders hunched in, and forced out a nervous, odd laugh. There were also some girls and they suddenly seemed like they mattered.

Psst.

My first class was with Mr. Miele, a peculiar, perverted old man. He had coke-bottle glasses, a bushy, black beard, and the glasses fogged up when he spoke. He gave out long homework assignments, sometimes three hours a night, and I tried to keep up with it all but it was all too much.

"I can't!!!!" I screamed, banging my head on the table, and punching myself in the face, sobbing. My father was out selling beds, staying away from the home. My kind little brother and sister would hide in their rooms. My mother stood helplessly watching then went to her bedroom.

She flipped through the channels. I was alone.

The lunchroom was loud; there were all sorts of kids, most of them bigger and stronger who I didn't know. They sold pizza and french fries, and all sorts of sugary snacks. The ladies who worked there were mean, yelling at all of the kids, and blowing their whistles.

The Fight

"There's a fight!" A boy named Ron informed me enthusiastically as I walked into the gym and toward the locker room one morning. I rushed in, in excited anticipation to see what was happening, as I'd heard that fights were a part of junior high life. It wasn't at all what I expected. There was a boy I knew from years before, whose name was also David, and who'd been my best friend in preschool, being beaten and punched by a bigger and much stronger boy. He drooled and he cried like the child he still was and was crawling around on the ground. There was blood dripping off of his chin that was mixed with saliva. He coughed and gasped, and begged the cruel, bigger and stronger boy, whose name was Jeremy, and who lived beyond Ackerman in the lawless part of town, to stop. Jeremy was wiry and strong, wore a black shirt, and had hair that was long in the back.

"St-ah-ah-p..." He begged and cried, weakened and traumatized from the beating, and spat out words through the sweaty, agonizing pain he was in.

My heart beat, filling my body with terror, leaving me searching for air. The saliva got thick in my mouth and I almost threw up. *What if I said the wrong thing?* Things were all of a sudden very different.

"You fucking pussy!" Jeremy screamed and laughed. "Huh-huh-huh," he grunted, his face pressed up to the suffering boy's bleeding mouth and nose, pounding his injuries with insults and gore. David coughed. David cried. His eyes popped from his head and squeezed out tears as the crowd cheered on, indifferent. It was loud like the Colosseum. The boys were all shouting like savages.

I turned quickly and left. I was always a sensitive kid.

This was sixth grade.

Elizabeth

There was a girl, twelve when I fell, thirteen when she left. I was terrified each time I called and her mother picked up, so I'd hang up the phone and call back.

"Is Elizabeth there?"

"This is Elizabeth." *Jackpot!*

"Oh, hi."

"Hi!"

Jared came up in the foyer one day before school. "Elizabeth told Marsha she'd open her mouth. You gonna go for it? Slip her the tongue, dude," he kind of demanded, chuckling and cold.

"I'll do it," I responded defensively.

"No, you won't," he said, antagonizing me.

"Shut up, I will."

"Okay when? We're going ice skating this weekend. You gonna invite her along?"

"Yeah, I'll invite her."

"Yeah right, I'll believe it when I see it."

She walked up, smiling at both of us, holding her books to her chest in the hallway.

"You gonna come ice skating with all of us this weekend?" he asked her.

"Yes, if my mom lets me go," she answered, smiling, and I smiled back. Jared smiled too, and then left.

I finally made the big move! On the bus to the ice rink, I mustered the courage and kissed her sweet lips. We held hands for the rest of the ride with her head on my shoulder.

"I kissed her," I told him, "and I slipped her the tongue!"

"What, you want a medal or your dick to pin it on?" He'd really become quite a jerk. I guess that we all have our wars. His father was a murderer after all.

The Note

"She wants you to write her a note," said Marsha, her friend. *But I can't write a note.* I thought, panicking.

"Uhh….tell her to write me one first, then I'll write her one back."

Jared walked up and chimed in, "Dave *won't* write a note, just like he won't make a move. He's *scared*."

"I *made* the move, dude!" I insisted, then looked at Marsha, "I'll write it later, in study hall." I always felt everyone laughing.

Jared jeered, "Took you long enough," he said, then laughed in a way I was used to. "Fine, maybe you'll write her one, maybe you won't. It's still gonna take you forever." He laughed some more. He was always laughing. My insides were puddled with tears.

"She wants it before gym so she can read it in the locker room," Marsha urged, standing there, holding her books to her chest, "so you had better hurry up." She walked away.

I went to Math and then Science, and ran into Marsha again.

"She's still waiting…," she said, almost demandingly.

"Uh, tell her I'll write it later. We're going to the movies tonight anyway."

"I'll tell her," she answered, then left.

The Movies

Despite all the terror, I loved her with all of my heart. I'd glance over in class, seeing her brown eyes and red, rosy cheeks, and the way that she smiled when our eyes caught each others'. I yearned for those afternoons in the first period after lunch, knowing I'd see her and that we'd exchange a few awkward words before and after the lessons about the constitution, history, and the laws of our country. The teacher was Mr. Persico.

Even now I can see her, the lights brightening the aisle floor to our left, Tom Cruise Top-Gunning in front. Her face to my right, her mouth and her teeth and her lips, lit by the screen as the movie cast shadows and light. I remember that night in the theater—holding her, kissing her, the way that she smelled and her taste—Skittles and popcorn and Coke. I wanted to live in her blood, to father her kids, to have her be with me forever. I was sure this would happen and we would be married someday.

In the spring, we went to the lake in the evenings, after dating each other all winter, finding secluded areas to lay in the grass. I kissed her, touched her, and felt her young body beneath me. I loved her that spring, and remember her face in the moonlight that shone through the trees, and the way that we whispered sweet words back and forth in the dark.

"I love you." I meant it and she felt the same.

We kissed for an hour, and then walked and held hands in the park. Her brown hair hung down past her shoulders; her eyes were wide and beautiful. She looked at me then looked away while we smiled and laughed.

"Jared keeps farting. It makes Beth really mad."

"Jared's disgusting," I replied, agreeing, "he's a dork. He was burping in her ear in the hallway the other day."

"Gross!" she responded, and both of us laughed as we walked through the trees, past a tennis court, and down to the lake where the moon reflected off the water.

"*You're* a dork," she said.

"I know you are but what am I?" I shot back, grinning and going along.

"No, like, I'm serious. You are like a serious dork," she said. I let go of her hand. "And why don't you get some new shoes? I can smell those from here. Like what in the hell is wrong with you?" It felt strange, as if suddenly I'd committed something grave.

"I don't know, what's wrong with you?" I thought she was kidding around but then realized she wasn't.

"With me? Nothing's wrong with me, my god!" Then she stormed off alone and went home. I didn't know what I had done.

I ran into Marsha on Monday. "She's mad that you'll kiss her but won't write her notes."

"I'll write her one later. I promise this time."

"She says you're all talk."

"He is." Jared had walked up behind us.

"But we made out for over an hour!" I insisted.

Jared chimed in like he always did. "Look, man. All of these girls are the same. You write them some notes. Ask them out. Hold their hand. It's easy."

"It totally is. Why are you scared?" Marsha asked.

"I'm not scared!"

"Yeah, you are." It felt like all Jared did was laugh.

But suddenly things became different, as I'd set myself up to get hurt.

"I forgot to do homework, I guess this must mean I'm not smart," I said jokingly and self-deprecatingly to Elizabeth one evening as we were walking along near my house.

"Yeah, I guess you're right. What's wrong with you?" She was also just kidding, going along with the joke, a joke that I had started.

"I don't know," I replied, playing a role in what seemed like a game, kidding around as kids did.

"Yeah, I don't know either. Jesus. You're like seriously stupid. You're a *moron*." And then all of a sudden it wasn't a joke. All of a sudden she meant what she said. And then all of a sudden her words became true as I turned into things that she made me.

And then she abused me with more than just words, threw me around on the grass at the park. Wrestled and pinned me. At first, it was fun— joking around with my girl—but then she got cruel and sadistic, meaner with each passing moment. She was tiny but I was much smaller. I couldn't fight back, or I didn't know how. She grass-stained my pants, scraped up my elbows and knees, flipped me up over her back and then threw my back down. This happened in front of some others, all who stood watching. "Elizabeth's beating up Dave again," one of them said to another, matter of factly.

"You're just a dumb moron. *What. The. Hell. Is. Wrong. With. You???*"

She squeezed my skull in a headlock, smashed her forearm across my cheekbone harder with each twisted word. I cinched myself close, tried to defend, but she slammed me back down to the grass. "Whoa..." said some other kid, awed in amazement.

"What's wrong with you?"

She demanded I answer. "I'm an idiot. I'm sorry. I hate myself."

"I know you do.," She got crueler with each passing second. "Now say you're sorry." She got more evil.

"I'm sorry, I'm *sorry*, I'm *SORRY!*"

Then she became even meaner, demanding, "SAY IT LIKE YOU MEAN IT!"

I pleaded. "I'M SORRY! I'M SORRY! I'M SORRY!"

Something perverted was breeding itself deep within. It all seemed so normal, like this was the only sane thing, like for lifetimes and lifetimes I'd only known this—desperate shivering fear at the foot of a girl. She might have donned leather in one of those lives, whip in hand, making me beg like a dog, pissed on me and fed me her shit.

These scenes repeated, over and over. I turned masochistic, got off on abuse. *Asked* for it. Begged in my dreams.

And then, all of a sudden, in a swift-assured kick to the pit of my soul, it was over. Jared moved in at a party I wasn't invited to. "We're broken up," is all that she said on the phone.

I stood outside class and I saw her on Monday. The lockers were orange and lined the hallways where she walked past me and went into class, looking as pretty as always; and she saw me too but the magic was gone, not even a smile or a nod. I tried not to cry and a girl walked up and she told me she heard and I did; right in the hallway I cried like the child that I was.

I'll always remember the nights that we went to the park. I'll always remember the movies. I wished I had known what to say in the note that she wanted to read before gym, but Jared knew better than me. She was now his and I didn't know how I could live without her in my life.

And now there were all these *new* feelings that I had to feel, like the anger evolved into heartbreak and then twisted inward; and now all I had was depression, punching my insides instead of the walls. It hurt and it hurt and it hurt.

She'll always be my Winnie Cooper.

Skating

I remember the night that it clicked. I went to Hawthorne instead of a dance, the parking lot of one of the schools they shut down in '81; and there in mid-air, flying off one of the ramps, it just sort of happened, this deep sort of subculture love was now part of my soul.

They spoke their own language, and soon I was part of their world. The tricks that I learned felt like unfolding memories pulled from some life long ago—judos and frigids—wall-rides and methods—ollies and nose picks and grinds; and the girls that they liked and liked them, and who followed them out at night to parking lots to hang in the shadows of yellow street lamps felt like the ones I should know, hot in their own little ways— black shirts and Converse and pigtails and polka dot socks. It was all the same growing-up dream, just shaded in different colors from that which was deemed typically adolescent; sports teams, good grades, dances and bonfires, then college and marriage and kids and a mortgage then death.

"Skater fag now, huh Dave?" One of my friends said to me by the bus before school.

"Flaming homo," I said while I looked in his eyes and kept walking to class. I only wore skate shirts and Vans. I was starting to get who I was. The thrill of the stoke will teach things to the soul that the ones without stoke never learn; and so they make fun, call them dip-shits or faggots or queer or whatever, all the while knowing they *can't*. They can't be them- selves, could never skate vert. Deep down they want to be something besides who they are so they beat others senseless.

I heard Naked Raygun and things deep inside me turned punk, and I heard The Descendents and music was suddenly new, like hearing Bob Dylan or Hendrix before they were stars; an entire adolescent universe, a sort of coming-of-age eternity we found ourselves drifting around inside of that all of us knew mattered more than most anything could. There were ghosts in the future but this was all innocent love, the last time we got to be kids, and the purest expression of angst that we ever could know. Drugs weren't part of the scene.

It had its own sound—urethane wheels over blacktop and grinding on curbs, tails tapping sidewalks and the whooshing sound of the wood on the ramps. It was different from skating before when I got my first board. We rolled by each other—nothing but jargon in fragments.

Beauty of a method, Clark.
Thanks, Earl.
That curb sure is slick.
Waxy and quick.
Slap it like Barbee.
I'll slappy like Natas. He's slicker.
I've dialed in wallrides and whittled them down to a science.
Bullshit you have. Bust out a frontside.
Touché!

I felt like I really belonged for the very first time. The skaters were dorks and that's why, and different from most of the punks. The skaters learned tricks while the punkers were off huffing glue. The skaters had balls. Some of the punks had guitars. Some of the skaters were punks but the groups were distinct. But the punk rock was part of it all. It seeped its way into the blood.

We went to The Turf in Milwaukee, the last of the great concrete parks. I skated the keyhole and clover. I dialed in the vert fundamentals—rock and rolls, grinds, and small backside airs, then pop tarts and rock and roll fakies, and I nailed the drop-in the first time I tried. There were garage doors they opened to let the park breathe in the sweltering summertime months. The music was loud and it echoed around—punk rock and metal and rap and the Cure.

I thought that I'd live to ride vert, learn big airs and then move to California and hang with the pros in the movies we watched in Chicago.

The girls would show up and then sit on the lawn or the roof while we skated the ramp. The ramp was in Wheaton and Wheaton was different—Wheaton College, Wheaton Bible Church, Wheaton North, Wheaton Warrenville South, Wheaton girls. The fall was the best time to skate and we all wore our sweatshirts. The evenings in autumn were living and breathing and fun.

"He ollied and slid the whole thing," Tom said to George about some kid named Steve from Geneva.

"Fucking bullshit he did." George was pro-caliber good, and was slowly becoming my friend.

"I fucking swear. He slid the whole fucking thing," refuted Tom, "Kahill witnessed it."

"Whatever," George said jealously, knowing he'd have to himself if he wanted to hang with the pros out in Cali. The rail was nine stairs. His father had left. A thing like a skateboard is different to kids without money.

Some of my friends in eighth grade were already on drugs. They seemed like a waste of existence to those that could skate.

Skating Changed

One night it changed. I thought he was messing around, a teenager joking on an adolescent evening, but the skaters rode up one by one and all started to scream.

I skated to where he was lying, thinking that this was a joke, but as I got closer my wheels started going through blood and I knew it was bad. He was shaking on blood-spattered pavement, with blood shooting out of his face and his nose and his head, puddling out and expanding so that *everyone's* wheels went through blood as they moved toward the spot where he lay. His eyes were rolled back in his head, white as ghosts, and his legs twitched around on the ground. I looked for a second, felt sick to my guts, and then ran away, almost in tears. I pictured his brains shooting out through his ears and his eyes popping out of his skull. In the blink of an eye, the entire scene shifted toward death as I thought he was done.

It was still fun but was never the same; it was suddenly disturbingly and horrifically frightening. I'd seen his insides, the whites of his eyes, and convulsions that night on the ground. Skating was life but now skating could also mean death. We were all kids. What had happened required adults—the paramedics, the ambulance, the cop cars, and the parents from one of the neighboring yards who had called 911.

He came back a couple of weeks later. There were stitches inside of his nose. He had smashed his face into his board when he went for a frigid. He didn't remember a thing.

There was another event a couple of months later. We were skating at Main Street School one night in eighth grade, grinding and doing ollies and flatland tricks on the basketball court. It was a crisp autumn evening, lit by an orange streetlamp. The leaves were all starting to fall and blow across the court and we were all wearing sweatshirts, the best kind of weather for skating. All of a sudden, some other kids showed up—mean ones from some other school. At first, I felt tough, ready to stand up and fight. I wasn't the least bit afraid. I puffed up my chest, preparing, but the kids I was with cowered, sat down on the bench, and became submissive.

"Why you boys be bitches?" one of them asked, grabbing my friend's board, pushing him down to the pavement and then throwing it at his head. He lay on the ground as the streetlamp cast shadows, not moving, then got up and walked away, head down and shoulders hunched. One of them flicked off my hat. "Why you got your hat busted, boy?" he demanded, suggesting that I was in a gang. One had a mullet and chain, presumably for beating skaters, and the brim of his hat was turned up and said *INJUN* in airbrushed art. He stood in the darkness, away from the light. We all sat there, shivering and terrified and not saying anything. They finally let us go. Skating was never the same.

And suddenly, there was this fear, like I could be hurt if I tried to be too much of me.

Adolescence and Early Drug Use

The Castle on the Hill—The Kids at Your School—Chewing Gum—The Subject of Fear—Dropping—Stoned—Andrew—Life as a Stoner—LSD—Acid Rumors—Peer Pressure—In Order to Understand—A Household—Our Little Group—The Coalition—Grateful Dead—Rotten Log—Bad Trip—Lunch Money—Tussin and Scotch Guard

The Castle on the Hill

Every school has drugs. They're part and parcel of this thing that's America, always have been; and forever they'll live in the darker, malignant fabric of this beautiful planet named Earth, in this beautiful U. S. of A., and even in the prettiest school in the prettiest town with the prettiest girls and the handsomest boys, there were all sorts of drugs to be done. There were pieces of paper you put on your tongue, cheap Mexican brick weed, and the occasional pill which wasn't nearly as prevalent. It wasn't like *everyone* did them, there were plenty of 'good' kids around, but lots of kids did, and almost everyone drank.

Skating faded and then one day the magic was gone, and now I was fifteen, and then sixteen, in a castle on top of a hill, at a high school named Glenbard West. It had oak trees and ivy and a Liberty Bell replica, a real John Hughes kind of feel in suburban Chicago. There was a lake behind the football field and the team had won state in '82 under the direction of a coach named Covert. There were cheerleaders cheering, pep rallies, and football games in the fall which I cared very little for. I tried to keep skating but skating had faded away as the last remaining bastion of innocence. I joined the cross-country team under pressure to get into a sport.

The kids loved to party; chugging beer, cheap vodka, Purple Passion, and wine coolers before homecoming dances and proms. They rented Greyhounds for after, had the driver pull over, and pulled kegs out of the bushes alongside the Prairie Path. Then, the bus driver drove to the city, to a place that would let the kids drink, Gino's East or one of the restaurants in Greektown; and this was what normal kids did, boozy busses complete with blowjobs in the bathroom for the luckiest guys on the cruise. I thought that our adventures as rich kids on LSD, which happened a couple of years later were a lot more interesting, but whatever. Most of the apparently popular ones haven't done too much all that interesting anyway since, houses and babies—the typical daydream. Still, I had fun and was often a big enough part of the "in crowd" to be included in such activities, having dates for the dances and going to various parties.

The Kids at Your School

The kids at your school see the person they think that you are, and you want them to think you're the role you're convincing them of, but everyone's making shit up; it's all a big farce, and you don't have a clue of what's actually happening beneath the facades of the things you believe to be real. No one knows shit but they think that they do, and then they get mean toward the others with different thoughts, different ways, and different homes they return to—all with different messages sent from different parents, all who had parents themselves. It's all *vibration*, but no one's aware this is so. The entire world *seems*. It's always just seeming. There's nothing but seeming that's going on everywhere always. There's the way that things seem and the way that they are, and the truth lurks around in a shadow somewhere, if such a thing even exists, and everyone's lost, playing out fantasy roles—of heroes and villains, cops and robbers, cowboys and Indians, sinners and saints. So, why was that cheerleader mean to that girl in class? What happened inside of the walls she went home to at night? And what did the one she was mean to decide about life? Why did the jock, that bigger and stronger machine of a budding young man, viciously punch the weak child in the hallway that day? Was there something to gain in that disturbing vibrational exchange? In that violent clash, that trauma-event, what *really* unfolded that day? What sorts of things did he hear from his father at home? From his earliest moments alive, what were the things he was made to believe were the truth? And why was this blood their expression? The other was weaker, ineffective, and kind, and just trying to get through the day. He encountered a violent beast who had beasts of his own.

And so all of us walked through the halls, and some of us started on drugs. The drugs took us places that most children shouldn't explore but were places we went anyway—under pressures from moms and from dads, from messages sent from our heavens and hells, from the others who'd taken drugs first and convinced us we should. There's not really much rhyme or reason; all of it just sort of *happened*.

Chewing Gum

I laughed at fucking everything. I laughed so hard one day in choir that I had to stumble out into the hallway and almost pissed in my pants it was so fucking funny. The teacher, Mr. Whitecotton, who we all called Dick because that was his name and because he was one when the Christmas concert drew near, was yelling at this kid Scott for chewing gum. Meanwhile, the entire time, this *other* kid Gavin who stood *next* to Scott had put an entire Laffy Taffy into his mouth and was chewing it, unbeknownst to Dick, who was angry with Scott. There was a purple line of drool oozing out of Gavin's mouth and Scott didn't have any gum. He was just standing there singing, but Dick thought he did and believed in his heart that he was the gum-chewing culprit, and had slapped his baton on the music stand like he always did when he was pissed and was yelling at Scott, proving himself to be really quite stupid for not seeing any of this for what it actually was. I saw the whole thing from the row in front of them where I sang first tenor, and the complete and utter ridiculousness of it, the absurdity had set me off and I laughed until Dick, seeing that I was unable to contain it, sent me into the hall, which I was on my way out to anyway on account of being afraid I was going to wet myself.

This happened before all the drugs. I always thought things were so funny, and it was always the observation of the sheer ridiculousness of the human conundrum that set me off on these tangents of laughter. This book I've been working on has a tendency to highlight the dark, the macabre, the odd, and the peculiar and violent, but there was always a hilarity, an absurdity I couldn't help seeing in everything. And there were brilliant, smart kids telling jokes and exposing the world for what it was, and I saw the things that they saw. Perhaps I saw more, and there was some sort of destiny for me and my friends intertwined with the knowing that the world was fueled by nothing more than great, big, fat, freaking lies. Most of us saw that the teachers were out of touch, save the occasional one who knew what was *actually* happening, and still, being friends with a couple of those teachers now, I can see that they didn't, and couldn't ever know what was actually going on inside the lives of the students at large. Generation gaps speak volumes about that which remains eternally un-understandable to those who are born in times distinct from one another. And what could anyone have said? Were the variables they could have inserted into any of the equations we were trying to solve ones that would have resulted in any of us coming to any definitive conclusion about how any of this could have gone differently? We were late 20th-century children of God, not children of coaches or parents or teachers. The good kids, the ones embracing traditional pathways toward death, were obviously more prone to listening to those above them. But the adults they entrusted themselves to, and who had plenty to offer to their ordinariness and the traditions they embraced, would have had little to offer me and my friends, many who had tried as desperately as possible to be normal and to fit into the molds they had cut out for us–to win sports competitions and achieve things in academics and on student council or to make honor roles each quarter or to win at anything at all. I remember practicing gymnastics all summer long after my sophomore year and only being more and more scared of the rings and the high bar, the only events I was good at, having gained very little competence in relation to the apparatus, if any, and feeling very defeated and like I had failed.

Then, these kaleidoscopes happened and there was a world. And the world was exciting with colors and sights and songs. It was totally different from any other world in the universe. And we were inside of it, making things happen, dancing around, and spinning and laughing the most perfect laughter that ever could be because we had realized that it all was a joke, not that there *were* jokes, but that it, *all of it*, was a never-ending parade of ridiculousness. And even though so many of the trips we took with the acid had so many unsettling components and instances, they were profound learning instruments downloaded onto our budding adolescent minds that demonstrated lessons about the nature of the cosmos and the basic tenets of reality. The great paradox in all of this is that it is mostly unsuspecting children who ingest such a powerful substance, one that only a seasoned adult has any business dancing with.

The Subject of Fear

There was also the fear. I was scared—of people and places and things. Scared of the jocks. Scared of the girls. Scared of kids down the street. There was a boy who was younger than me, short with an underbite, and strong. He wrestled, I think, and I made up a story inside of my head about how he had wanted to hurt me. I remember a dance and him eyeing me from across the gym. My friends didn't know and it wasn't a thing I'd discuss. There was nowhere to go with it all, so it squished up inside me and twisted around in my cells. It went to my brain. It leaked from my eyes. If he'd seen them then he would have known, so I had to avoid him and hide in the shadows away from the lights and the music and dancing. Nobody knew. I didn't have words, and I still sometimes flash back and see him that night in the gym and I feel it all over. I thought he would kill me and I was alone. There weren't any words. There weren't any friends. Each of the kids was their own type of alien being when I came to this place.

Dropping

"I'm thinking about dropping," George said to me at my locker as kids shuffled by.

"Dropping what?" I asked.

"Acid, you idiot." He often made fun, was a good enough friend, and had also stopped skating around the same time I had. I didn't know acid existed, like actually for real, and that taking LSD was a legitimate option for a fifteen or sixteen-year-old. It was honestly the furthest thing from my mind, not something I had ever remotely considered, and then all of a sudden, here it was, and I was intrigued. How could I not be? Who *wouldn't* be, at least just a little?

On top of this high school scene, which now involved the possibility of ingesting serious drugs, I started having dark thoughts and paranoia, of being chased down and beaten and bludgeoned by various kids who I passed in the hall, and had thoughts of my teeth being scratched against chalkboards. I'm not sure where all this was from.

Stoned

I still had the anger. It was all the same tantrum—things like spilled milk or Mario falling in fire; rules I disagreed with and thoughts of injustice would trigger it all. Anytime life wasn't fair I'd go into "the fit," scream at the sky and curse God for the horror He made. My teeth clenched together, my eyes bulged and popped, and I squeezed my fists into cold bricks and then punched holes in walls.

All of it started with anger. It was first on the list of the things that I 'needed' to live; not the most pleasant addiction, but when the brain shoots its poisonous concoctions, the body adjusts and gets used to the way that it feels when they blast through the blood. It was also a form of control. When things didn't go the very particular way I was used to, I'd scream my most visceral screams and the family would cave. I twisted it into a science of sorts and it kept things relatively predictable albeit traumatizing for all parties involved, those parties being the ones who were unfortunate enough to be stuck inside the same house as me. It was also something I had little to no control over, paradoxically. There was no conscious decision that went *Okay, if I terrify them enough, then they'll cave to my every demand*, but there was, at some point, the realization that I did in fact have control when I acted out in the ways that all of those in my immediate experience had become far too acquainted with. These intricate mechanisms of survival exist unbeknownst to us and dictate the way our existences go until we wake up, *if* we wake up, and realize that they're running the show.

There were also the sugary snacks—Now and Laters, Gobstoppers, Alexander the Grapes, whatever I could get my hands on at the pharmacy, and I spent my allowance on candy before I found drugs. There was also the blanket and Garfield doll (my safety), not to mention the abuse—from the various neighbors, supposed "friends," and Elizabeth. My brain had been mixing elixirs for over a decade, as if I'd been born to experience non-traditional states of awareness. So, what happened the first night it hit me, like *really* hit me, was just a continuation of what had been set into motion for many years prior, occurring like some sort of fix, as if I was *remembering*.

We were smoking a bowl in the back, behind his house by a fire pit. His parents had gone out of town. There was me, a kid James, and another kid, John, who I knew from Hawthorne. It was John's house. I had smoked weed before, a handful of times, and felt its effects here and there, but what happened that night in the fall spun a different tune.

We took several hits, finished the bowl, went into the house, and sat down, myself on the floor and John and James on a couple of couches. The T.V. was on and I stared at the screen. Cigarette smoke wafted through. Then, very suddenly, I floated up out of my body like some sort of sage. My legs jumped around underneath me, like foreign appendages belonging to some other animal, but I'd focus on them and they'd rest back in place, as if they'd been caught misbehaving. If I moved my eyes out toward the rest of the room, over at John or to a picture on the wall, then they'd be moving again, as if they were playing a trick. And everything else started moving along with my legs. The whole room was spinning around. It was such a new *feeling*.

John was on the other side of the room, laying down and staring at the television. The room shifted colors; shadows danced, and everything became unquestionably hilarious with an absurdity I had never experienced; beautiful, deep, and profound. I had faint hallucinations while voices from the television got tweaked and distorted, speaking my name: *More news at eleven, Dave. Dave sure is stoned, isn't he? Dave is aaaaaaallllllright. Aren't you, Dave? Dave? Are you there, Dave? What have you done with Dave, Dave?*

"What?" I asked, and John started laughing.

"I didn't say anything, *Dave*," he said back, as if he had heard the same voices that called out my name.

"Wow," is all that I said, looking around at the room, as if staring outward from inside a prism.

"Oh shit, man. You're like a first-timer? Like this is the first time, like the *real* first time, isn't it? Your cherry's been popped, bro. HA!" He continued, "it only gets better from here." He was older. We had skated for years before drugs.

The room spun around but I didn't get sick from the spins like I did from the booze. It felt like a wide-awake dream and my cheeks ached like overworked muscles from laughing so hard. I saw planets and stars— Jupiter, Neptune, and Mars, floating around in my head, and then looked at the moon through the window, which didn't seem far out of reach. I started to rise from my body and fell to my face, resting my head in a pillow, hysterically and uncontrollably laughing as hard as I could.

A galaxy birthed in my brain. I saw into the sixties and opium dens, and knew Hendrix and Jim and Garcia. I suddenly knew what the stoners at school were doing, what the kids who'd quit skating were up to when they abandoned the parking lot scene back at Hawthorne. It was as if they'd been patiently waiting for me to indulge in the magic with them, just like the folks in recovery I'd meet soon enough, but with a long and harrowing journey in between now and re-birth. It seemed meant to be that I walk through this gateway. *Ohhhhhhh…* I thought to myself.

"Dude, I'm fucked up…" The words oozed, moving across the room and catching James's attention through the cigarette smoke and television noise; then I laughed more, uncontrollably, and sunk more through the pillow and into the floor.

"Don't piss your pants now, Dave," he said as he laughed, and as he mentioned it, I thought that maybe I had!

"Dude, after a while you get used to it, so you'd better enjoy it for now," John chimed in, also laughing, "and don't piss your pants either, *Dave.*" I left on my bike, riding south toward my house. The trees hung out over the sidewalk, drooping, seeming to have their own lives, and to breathe in the crisp autumn air in the same way I was. The sidewalk was pushing the bike like a magical carpet. I smiled, loving the feel of the wind on my face and the breeze running through my fingertips and teeth, like my body was new and the night was alive.

Dave...Dave.....Dave! A voice from the shadows rang out. The moon was full, I was wearing a sweatshirt, and a cool breeze was blowing my hair as I moved toward my house. I stopped, looked back from where I had just ridden and into other directions, thinking it might have been Cheez, a friend who lived up the street; but no one was there. I stood, straddling my bike on the sidewalk, then laughed some more, collapsing over my handlebars and then peeking mischievously upward toward the moon from under the hood of my sweatshirt. The houses stared blankly, also alive like the moon and the wind and the leaves. They seemed to be laughing along.

I got to my house, knowing my parents were up. Alcohol stunk and I hadn't been drinking. Weed was entirely new. I wasn't worried.

"How was your night?" Mom asked.

"Good."

"What did you do?

"Hung out at John's."

"Oh…" she said, and went back to watching the news.

I felt like I needed to re-learn talking, like the words didn't match what was happening inside of my head. If I'd been drinking, I'd have to watch what I said, but with this it was more about figuring out what I thought, *then* speaking, then seeing if what I had said had made sense.

I went to my room and lay in my bed in the dark. I put on my head-phones.

This is the end
Beautiful friend

Everything melted away, as if this was the cure for the tantrums that haunted my youth. I toyed with myself in the dark, thinking of girls from my classes, and drifted to sleep.

Andrew

I ran into Andrew the following Monday at school. We weren't friends yet, but had started talking; he was trying to sell me acid from the sheet he'd bought from some other kid a few days earlier. He was on his own trip, dirty and reckless, covered in acne with fever blisters on his lips; his hair was grown out, reddish-brown, and he wore thick black-framed glasses that clashed with his pale complexion. He had sagging overalls that covered a ragged, white t-shirt, a smart, gifted child caught in a phase of rebellion. We started to bond in the ways that kids do.

I saw him in front of the botanical garden at the bottom of a wooden stairway.

"Dude, I got fucking stoned on Saturday!" I was dancing up and down, delighted.

"Yeah?" He drooled out his words with a warm, smirky smile. "Hahaha…and…?" He'd recently been to Jamaica with his sister. She was older and scared me to bits. He'd met some Rastafarian dudes who'd popped his cherry with weed. *"Welcome to Ganja Land"* he said that they said when they saw that he'd passed through the gate.

"Shit was awesome, dude! I couldn't stop laughing! We were over at John's and it hit me and I was like *woah*, and that was just the beginning!"

"Yeah?" He looked a bit like Raggedy Andy.

"Fuck yeah, dude! It's like I went into space or some shit."

He stood there, grinning. "Yeah, man. The first time it hit me, I decided I'm smoking forever."

"Yep," I said, agreeing.

"I mean, why wouldn't you?"

"Totally, dude!" I exclaimed. "I gotta go to fucking class."

"Fuck class," he laughed a bit. "I'm supposed to get this good shit called Christmas Tree from Jamaica, I'll let you know when I do."

"Cool, dude." I walked off to class. It was sunny and brisk. The birds swirled around in the sky as the marching band practiced in the distance. Kids ran the track. A whistle sounded, signaling the end of the drill that the soccer team was running. Something felt new.

Life as a Stoner

It took just a couple of months from that night in the fall. I'd get a bag on a Friday and then ceremonially remove the stems and seeds, settling into my desk for the ritual, picking the dirt weed apart. From the first time it hit me that night on the floor I was hooked, and then came the culture which was there all along, "under the bleachers," so to speak—tie-dye and Grateful Dead shirts, incense and bell-bottom pants, corduroys and beads. Hippie girls—totally hot but in different ways (I was still such a dork with them all). It helped me to sleep, alchemically mixing my thoughts and emotions. It was like I had found a new world.

There were kids smoking weed in the lot, or over at this dropout kid's house who lived near the school, and driving around smoking bowls—one kid, the one who was technically driving, smoking, while another one steered the car. There was "jonesing," which meant you had run out of weed and had started to *need*. Old dead people started making sense through their music. Blacklights lit everything up, turning life purple, fluorescent, and glowy while we sank into sofas and sat.

I found a new crowd. Jeremiah got a truck, faded and red, and we drove around smoking all night. I'd get home, fall into bed and go drifting away every night. There were others inside of their own little worlds as well, glancing outward from inside kaleidoscope eyes.

All of this happened so fast in the midst of what was already such an awkward adolescent experience, complete with hormonal changes, incessant masturbation, and the pressure to go to college; which was all of a sudden my mother's obsession. Now there was this new variable, this curveball that came out of nowhere, this path that seemed like a destiny of sorts, inescapable and unavoidable like it *had* to happen.

The honeymoon didn't last long, and what had initially started as something novel suddenly became a seething necessity, and when a child becomes obsessed there is little that anyone can do to dissuade him or her. In the early stages, soon after the night a few months before, I'd go to a party and kids would be passing joints around, listening to Hendrix, The Doors, The Dead, and whoever; and the kids who smoked pot were all part of the same group of popular kids, mostly, a bit of a sub-group but most of the kids at our school got along. Everyone partied. I didn't have cravings for weed right away. I'd get high and collapse on the floor at a party, laughing hysterically as always. It wasn't serious. I kept up my grades, showed up to class, and was still relatively normal inside, so I thought, except that I wasn't. I never was normal. It was almost as though I was born to go fucking insane. There are certainly ways to be responsible for one's use of drugs, and not every child becomes hooked. Lots of the kids would take acid once, which there is nothing intrinsically wrong with. There is nothing about morality in all of this, although many who use end up doing despicable things.

Kids will do drugs and have sex, drive too fast, tempt fate, cheat death, etc. It's just how it goes, part of growing up, but then suddenly all of the drugs we did mattered. And this is where things became blurry, and the timelines got mixed up and spun because this was all the beginning of what amounted to an incredible journey that led me away from a path that those who were raising me desperately wanted me to embrace—that of the normal American boy. I'm not sure the moment it happened, but before I realized it, pot was a part of my life, something I needed to function at night and on weekends, but not something I realized I was becoming addicted to as the affliction set in. Again, it just sort of happened.

All of a sudden you're hooked. All of a sudden it matters, running out, and so you start rationing, keeping an eye on your stash, preemptively calling a tambourine man in the jingle-jangle morning. You don't want to share. You calculate how much you'll need to get through the week, and panic when the guy with the beeper doesn't call back. You wait by the phone because you don't want your mother to answer. Your parents are different, *enemies*, and sneaking becomes sort of normal. So was there a literal moment I could have pushed pause, turned around, and gone back? What if an adult, a real adult who knew about real life and about what we were really doing, one who sought not to punish but only to teach us the actual rules, came along and effectively warned us.

'Look kids, I know what you're doing with the weed and the acid and the bike rides at night. You gotta be careful. There's a way to make it all work. Don't lose sight of your grades. Go out of your way to hide it from your parents, just doing that shows that you're responsible enough to maintain everything else. And for God's sake, do not ever drive. Also, beware of the Dead if you end up at one of their shows, those guys aren't as cool as they seem.'

It was an obsession just like skating had been, but without the inherent ambition. With skating, every new trick was a challenge, and the culture was much more evolved; built on progression and courage, and skill. Drug culture was quite the opposite, as there's little that's earned with drug use; built on degression, on spiraling downward to places you're not supposed to go. There was something akin to a quest for enlightenment with acid, but we didn't have guides, and so it was really something that amounted to a very serious and extremely dangerous form of tomfoolery, and soon came The Dead and the shows they put on for the kids.

LSD

"David, what they don't understand over there, those boys drinking beer, is that what we're doing, it's like *intellectual*. Like, this stuff is for grown-ups and they are all children, except we're *all* children, I guess, but we're much more grown-up." Jasmin was waxing; she never shut up; even when dosed on the acid her gums would be flapping. Jeremiah rolled his eyes while I listened. "I mean they're getting sloppy over there," she pointed to the other room, "and we're over here, like, visiting dimensions, dancing out jingles and jangles. I mean, this entire world is like just some big, dumb fucking illusion we're all caught inside of." She stopped and then stared into space. We looked to where she looked and then all started laughing. Something was moving; a wall was collapsing. The room filled itself with contortions of colors and fractals. I started to drool and pointed out into the air.

"Woah, it's like not there but it's totally there but it's not."

"I know!" Jasmin exclaimed. "Nothing is there, but here we all are!"

"Where's here?" I asked.

"Here's where we are," Jeremiah replied, taking a hit of his weed. And here we all were, a ship of fools staring blankly toward space, a bunch of kids staring at walls. Some freaks on the floor of a bedroom.

I remember my dad, years earlier, upon hearing me refer to "acid-drops," a skate trick I did off the porch, correcting me one day. "Hey, David, we're not going to call them acid drops anymore, how about we just call them drops?"

"Why?" I asked innocently.

"Because acid is a VERY dangerous drug," my mother chimed in, informing me sternly from the other room. "It makes you see monsters, makes you think buildings are falling on top of you. You should NEVER take LSD! Ever." And at that moment, being more concerned with skate-boarding than anything else, I figured that not dropping acid was probably a good idea, and also not probable for me to ever do anyway. I also knew that I wasn't changing the name of the trick but whatever. I had very little interest in drugs at the time the other kids started, but high school got real, very suddenly, and so now here I was a couple of years later, on a floor in a room at a party staring at the same collapsing wall my mother warned me about a few years earlier, as she was encouraging me to stop

*skateboarding in the same breath. She wanted so badly for me to be good
at something else, soccer or whatever, gymnastics, something traditional.*

A kid named Jason, blond hair and blue eyes, walked in wearing a
letterman jacket and drinking a beer, looked at us all on the floor, rolled
his eyes, and left.

"Looks like Jack *TRIPPERS* in the house," he announced to the jocks
in the other room, then sipped an MGD. They had their party and we had
our trip.

"Stupid fucking jock," Andrew said.

"We used to be friends," I replied.

"He's a pussy," he pronounced, cackling, his eyes shimmering like
deep wells of disturbing memory.

"What?" I responded.

"Him, he's just a fucking pussy."

"Pussy," I repeated and laughed.

"Pussy," he echoed, laughing some more, and then all of us laughed,
not like the laughing from weed, something entirely different, wracking
and convulsive, almost sinister—until we forgot what we were and then
came back to the floor. We'd *gone somewhere*, taken a trip, so to speak.

"Well, there goes Lucy again," Jasmin continued. We all felt our
blood and nerves working.

"Lucy?" I asked.

"In the sky with diamonds, David..."

"Lucy in the sky with di-i-a-monds." I sang it and knew what it
meant, and then knew the Beatles as well. I saw colors that didn't have
names and knew songs by the Dead. There were so many things in these
instances that made so much sense. But there wasn't a language. There
weren't any words, but this was accompanied with a kind of remembering, *a returning to.* We went outside, a beautiful evening around Hallow-
een. I pointed up at a tree in the yard as its leaves drifted down through
the night. I saw that it had its own life–a spirit and soul and a purpose
and path–sitting right there in the yard. "Man, it's a tree, but totally like a
different thing from what a tree as we know it is, but is still just a totally
badass tree, man."

"Yeah, man," Andrew continued, "It exudes so much tree-ness,"
laughing and pointing.

"Man, that shit's like the king of the suburbs right there," Jeremiah
asserted.

"The King of Glen Ellyn."

"Don't you mean queen, Jeremiah?" Jasmin interjected while Josephine rolled her eyes.

"Whatever," Jeremiah replied, rolling a joint as the night meandered on.

Acid Rumors

A girl named Melanie had given me, somewhat randomly, my first hit at Hawthorne one evening in the summer between my sophomore and junior year; sometimes the kids would still hang around there. It was plain white "blotter" acid, which was a generic name given to hits that didn't have markings. Later on, as my LSD use increased, there were hits that had pictures of sperm cells, blue and pink, some with red lips, and some with gold stars. One of the best hits that I ever took had a picture of Jesus Christ, The Savior Himself on it, suggesting that you would see God when you took it.

It sat in my wallet for months, wrapped in a pink piece of cellophane. I took it out often, resting it on the desk in my room, careful not to touch it and get any of the acid onto my finger, and then subsequently into my bloodstream. Sometimes I moved it with tweezers, like a teenage mad scientist, insisting on discovering its secrets using all means except for ingestion.

There were stories regarding its potential to make you insane—urban legends, one of a kid who took it and had since been sitting in a mental institution believing he was nothing more than an orange, often screaming at and ordering the staff *"Don't peel me or I'll die!"* as they changed his diapers, or so went the legend. There were tales of "bad trips" or "bummers," where kids went insane, spiraling downward into eternally dark, disturbing, and Dantean realms of consciousness that haunted them decades later with flashbacks that never stopped happening and recurred at regular intervals throughout adulthood. There were stories of kids who believed they could fly and then leaped from the tops of tall buildings, falling to their deaths and creating folklore that no one could prove nor disprove. There was Manson, murder, disembowelment, and sacrificed babies viciously aborted in twisted, ceremonial rituals. There was Helter and Skelter, the Grateful Dead, and the rumors of older kids who vanished forever after seeing the band play one time, becoming part of a psychedelic family circus of sorts.

These were the things that transpired through the minds of the children who contemplated taking this drug. There was always the enigmatic and relevant question as to whether or not you would die or go insane, but there was no evidence from anyone *I* knew that this would *actually* happen. And all of this was juxtaposed with a deep, fiendish curiosity and call to adventure that very few heeded, and that set one apart from the typical adolescent daydreams that most kids were living. We wanted to feel the unreal.

Peer Pressure

Jasmin and Josephine were the first to drop, several months prior, as sophomores. They were best friends, each complimenting the others' opposite qualities; Josephine was dark and reserved with a propensity for drama and all things macabre. Jasmin, her friend and antithesis, was the comic relief; ditzy and talking a lot, typically from a place of knowing it all. Both were good-hearted and kind.

"David, I sooooo wanna trip with you! It's—like—the most amazing thing ever," Jasmin said to me one morning, enthusiastic and twirling her curly, blonde hair.

"I'm afraid I'll freak out and have a bad trip," I responded, concerned. I was still such a child.

"That stuff's all rumors. It would be *impossible* for that to happen. No one freaks out," she responded reassuringly, standing in front of her locker. "It's like the coolest thing *EVER!*" Kids fluttered by in the hallways as Josephine walked up and whispered *"David, you'll really like it. Trust me."* We weren't really friends as of yet, but I trusted her; she was dimensional, not a textbook pretty girl like most that I knew; she was real and had ghosts of her own.

"Stop being such a fucking wuss," Andrew said, more to the point. We'd also somehow become friends as the year had evolved.

"Dude, it's not gonna happen. Bad trips are rumors. I seriously doubt it could happen.," another friend, Christopher, insisted, arriving at my house in his Jeep, enthusiastic about what happened the night before. He, apart from Josephine and Jasmin, was one of the first, and couldn't contain his enthusiasm. He was smart, with a brain that would make you feel safe; like his intellect convinced me of something the other kids couldn't. He wasn't a druggie and didn't smoke weed. He got good grades and sang in the choir. We'd been friends since sixth grade. He knew things that the other kids didn't.

"We were sitting there and nothing was happening. I figured they were duds, but then all of a sudden George gets up and starts walking across the room and leaves this trail behind him! It was fucked up, man. Then he pulled on his tie-dye and the colors flew off it and into the room! I got surrounded by color, like I could *feel* it." He was convincing. "Then we rode bikes, all over town, waaaay down the Prairie Path, and hung out in the woods all night. And dude! We all got the same visuals, those orange fences you see at construction sites! They were everywhere! It was like we were all connected or something, like to something greater that was in charge of the whole fucking thing. Fucking crazy, bro!"

"Woah, dude. So what's it like seeing things that aren't there?"

"It's fucking cool, dude, but not how you think it would be. It's impossible to explain. You gotta try it. Trust me." His piercing blue eyes were convincing.

I thought of the hit in my wallet. "So you didn't freak out?" I curiously asked.

"Dude, it would be impossible for that to happen…you gotta do it." So John had now dropped, and Josephine and Jasmin, and I became more and more curious. This is how peer pressure works. It wasn't like I had to, no one was twisting my arm. I genuinely wanted to try. I was ultimately responding to myself more than anyone else.

In Order to Understand

In order to understand what happens in high schools and crack dens and treatment facilities, or in any of the other places people, very often children—get drugs, eat drugs, smoke drugs, shoot drugs, or do whatever with drugs, you must first understand homes. You must understand families. You must know about daddies and daddies' daddies and daddies' daddies' daddies. Just a kid from the burbs, I was set up for success in the most traditional and privileged, white-bred American way. Beyond the parking lot, one of the places of congregation towered a castle, solid and brick, with ivy-covered towers watching on to assure the townspeople that every student who walked through its halls was destined for the greatness that only a castle could provide the opportunity to earn.

There were others, my friends, all of whom had the same supposed opportunities, and who also came from families themselves. Their homes were different from mine. Different moms. Different dads. Different brands of cereal, toothpaste, and milk. Different favorite shows and flavors of ice cream. Different restaurants they ate at and levels of income. I can't say that I even wanted them. They were more like assignments, appointees; just the ones who had similar jokes, observations, and opinions about things. Like everything else, they just sort of happened.

A Household

Imagine a household—a mother and father, a brother, and sister. All of them really are children in various ways. Even the head of the household, the *man*, is a boy with a bunch of projections, most of them stemming from some sort of unattended wound, wounds that probably exist unbeknownst to *any* of the members of said family. He is, in so many ways, a mosaic of varying traumas and fractures of self. His father was just kind of mean but he pushed through it all and left home. He marries a woman who is also split up into parts; and the necessary compartmentalization of each of them which she deemed, subconsciously, as necessary for survival, gets mixed up with those which he thinks that he's hidden. Communication ensues, between each of each other's parts and their corresponding counterparts. Part-counterpart, part-counterpart—and on and on—and so on and so forth. There are aspects of each other's true selves as well in the love that they have for one another, perhaps shared in the jokes that they tell and the moves they like, etc.,, and so it becomes a mixture of shadows and light dancing and swirling around, all mixed up. Neither has had any therapy or even one honest conversation ever about their state of internal affairs, much less how said affairs are affecting their external experiences. They're just sort of going along; projections are slippery occurrences. And then they have children! They love them so much, their own flesh and blood. And one day, years later, as these children are growing he says *something*. He doesn't mean for the words he uses to be the type that hurt; they just sort of slip when he's watching a game or remembering something his boss said that he's making mean something. But one of his children develops a fracture as well, a similar wound to the others they all have incurred as the result of being a part of this particular ancestral lineage, but also a wound that's distinct because this child is a new expression of what it means to be a part of *this* family. So then this recently wounded one projects onto his or her sibling a wound they don't realize they've incurred. Then the mother, the most well-meaning, well-mannered mother, projects all her stuff toward it *ALL*, the entire family system, which includes everything she grew up with! And so now, suddenly, there is all kinds of stuff, swirling around in the fabric of this supposedly happy family.

Then one of the kids blows it up.

Our Little Group

My dad was in Nam. I was sick as a child. My wounds are a war and the hospital bed. This makes my minutes a danger.

My father dropped dead at age forty. My wound is a stark abandonment. This makes my hours as lonely as ever could be.

My father is having affairs on account of my mother's narcissism. My wound is one that comes from nobody ever listening because they're too busy obsessing over themselves. This makes my life one that I seek to destroy all in sight.

My wound is my sister. She's pretty and popular. This makes my life a continual striving toward something that never will be.

My mother's controlling and can't handle complex emotions. My wound is suffocation. This makes my days filled with clawing and needing freedom.

Jeremiah's dad fought in Nam, and Jasmin's father passed away when she was thirteen; rotted from cancer. There was also Jeremiah's aforementioned affliction—the tubes and the tests and the months of school he was forced to miss so as to encounter more doctors and nurses than any child should ever have to. Josephine sat in the shadows of a younger and prettier sibling, really just wanting to draw and write poems all day while her mom pounded wine. Andrew was mad as a hatter, possessed it seemed at times, and I was a good enough kid, angry and scared about life who had found the "wrong crowd," the wrong crowd being our little group. Each of us fought our own wars, but no one discussed what they were; nor were we even aware of the things that we carried. We just *were*—angry, sad, rebellious, hateful, etc.—fulfilling our jobs as wasteland teens. And then came the acid. So there's this angry and lonely young kid who finds others, just as angry and all just as fucked up in their heads, and then all of them start taking drugs, like *really* taking lots of this *very* powerful substance, a drug so intense that it made people stark raving mad, struck terror in the heart of the establishment decades prior, and was adopted by the C.I.A. for various mind-control experiments, one of which being to drive Castro insane by secretly dosing him with massive amounts as he slept! Or so went the rumor. They say Kennedy took it as well, as a gift from Monroe, and that he knew its powerful secrets, which he was eventually killed for. It also meant prison for those who got caught as some other kid from the scene found out a couple of years later. These small bits of paper held power beyond measure, and we were just kids, plopping them onto our tongues and then taking adventures on bikes, thinking that all would be fine, but then chaos ensued when these children, all with their varying traumas of varying degrees, ended up inside their own version of the electric Kool-Aid acid test. It was deadly, to say the least, but part of being caught up inside of a deadly experiment, one that could mean incarceration for life or hurling oneself off a cliff, is not realizing it. This was also what made it so fun.

On the outside, at least for a while, you wouldn't have known, as I, looking back, didn't know what my insides looked like and was mostly just joking and smiling, still making everyone laugh and wanting the teacher's approval. I hadn't put the pieces of the puzzle regarding my own woundedness together as I eventually would decades later. Andrew was much more overt in his hatred of things, "The punks are just a different flavor of pussy; they're really the same as the jocks. Fuck every last one of them bitches. Everyone's full of their own type of shit caught up in some sort of popularity contest," he said one day as we smoked a bowl out in front of the school, which was suddenly just sort of normal.

Each of us went at night after school to these places we had to call home, to the families we were born into. And what is a family other than that which we know, that which we are intimate with, and that which dictates the fabric of these little universes we find ourselves toddling into, emerging as little beings as those instances arise that soon make up the backdrop of our memory palettes? So what did my family know? They knew terror and pain. They knew all my punches and tears. They waited, like soldiers in war who knew that eventually, much sooner than later, a grenade would be thrown and that people would die. This was the life that I gave them in reciprocation for the one they gave me: the terror of boogie men coming to life. I forced their poor souls into the same dark nooks that my mother was forced into herself. *I became him*, was the blood of my grandfather—the sweat on the factory floor where he worked, his pain, and his cancer and cheap disregard for all that was sacred. His cigarettes.

His bottles of scotch. His kicks. I was his family, born seemingly only to perpetuate.

And we, the children and grandchildren of those who have faded to ghosts, end up in tribes that are both distinct from the ones we are born into and also and often eerily similar in ways that we're never aware of. This is where things often go horribly wrong.

It's the agreements of the subconscious minds between those in peer groups, the lack of understanding of what those agreements entail and express, and the discrepancies between what is *actually* being said between one another and the things that are *factually* said that get us into trouble.

Wanna head out tonight? Maybe crash my parents' car?

Sounds like a fucking plan to me. My mother never understood a thing about me anyway. Come pick me up.

Awesome. Interestingly, I never figured out how to stand up to mine because, well, she won't listen to the sounds of my soul, so I'm finding it very difficult to say no to your 'good' idea.

Fuck yeah. I say that we're friends, and we are, but you're also, how do I say it, a utility.....

And I know this. Deep down I know that I'm shit.

So am I. So is the world.

Let's destroy it and ourselves in the process.

Onward!

The Coalition

Andrew was smarter than almost everyone. He talked about books and philosophy and music. We formed a coalition and Jeremiah joined. It was mostly *against*. Against what, we didn't know or weren't sure, but we were against it. It even felt like sometimes we were subverting the punks. They seemed formulaic and caught up in their own sort of popularity contest. They had rules. We wanted to break even theirs, to shatter everything, to burn the town down to the ground.

We hid under the optimistic eyes of the masses who marched through the hallways. We exposed them, even if they were blind to it. We hated them with all our guts. There was something that needed to die and we killed it. Sometimes this meant suspending the otherwise healthy and conscious morality we were raised with. It meant that we'd lie. It meant we would steal. Sometimes it meant that some other stoner kid, a good enough soul from the parking lot, would end up doing a few years in federal prison three months after he fled Glen Ellyn to find himself and to catch Jerry on as many good nights as possible, which were rare by that point.

Andrew pretended sometimes that he didn't care at all about anything. I think that maybe he even tried to convince himself that he was capable of murder, robbing banks, and of being an actual outlaw in the great old-Western tradition—a modern-day Jesse James. But James was evil, an old-school racist confederate in the most loyal sense. He stole from whoever and gave to no one. Andrew was kind. Jeremiah was good. I had a place in my insides, below all the anger, that glowed like happy tears shed from angels in wondrous delight. I knew this. I saw all of our wings. I knew we were good, not to suggest that everyone who was part of the scene was, but our little group, our little pack within the pack, was gentle and loving and smart. Mostly.

It's not seeing things that aren't there that makes it so peculiar, it's the state of your being that *makes* you see things that aren't there, and even though they aren't there you are sure that they are, except that you're not.

So what was the acid? A monster in every shadow? A punchline you finally got that made madness make sense, and then threw in some extras—bells, whistles, things that go bump in the night and might haunt you forever? Voices from deep, hidden parts and from faraway lands?

"What are you doing this for?" one asked me one time, some goblin or being, an alien force. I didn't know what I should say. *"I don't know..."* is all that dripped out. *"Well, you'd better figure it out because things are about to get weird..."*

Grateful Dead

We walked along Michigan, approached the edge of the lot down at Soldier's. It was entirely full by the time we arrived. We'd taken the 9:26.

"The thing about drugs and the Dead," John said to me on the walk, "is that the rumors about them are true." I'd heard this, from a friend Eric whose brother was into the band—*"My brother went to a Dead Show. You walk down the aisle at Rosemont; they're like 'shrooms, acid'... everyone's doing drugs..."* All of us thought he was lying.

"Are they? I thought that shit was overblown. Eric was always talking shit about what his brother said."

"You'll probably be offered acid within five minutes," he continued as we approached. Within the next couple of hours, a naivete that the castle, the sports teams, the teachers, and all of the parents had sought desperately, albeit unconsciously, to preserve would forever fade into the background of a previous existence.

"No way," I responded.

He slurped a bit, "Yup." He always slurped when he talked. His hair was grown out and there were a couple of dirty dreadlocks forming in his thick brown hair, which was littered with hair wraps and beads. "You'll see. They're everywhere. Everyone does tons of drugs." I wasn't too sure how to take it. We made our way into the scene.

"I need a mir-a-cle...." A beautiful girl, nineteen or twenty, standing on the pavement and waving her hips in the sun, seductively sang as she looked in my eyes—almost as if she was guarding an entrance. It was summertime-hot, sticky, with a light breeze from off of the lake, and stunk of patchouli and weed. There were drums and balloons, and everyone seemed to be living in some other world. People sold crystals and shirts, patchwork goods from Guatemala, and all sorts of trinkets and other rare stuff.

Doses...

This kid from our school had a van, grayish and silver and blue-colored, a real behemoth and relic, where older kids chilled and relaxed—cokes and beers, devil sticks and hacky sacks. Mountain Dews in a cooler. John took off his shoes and slowly adjusted himself to the new surroundings, then sat in a lawn chair, trying to snag a bit of shade under another's umbrella. I stood there awkwardly, fidgeting around a bit.

"Whaddup Dave!" one of them said cordially; an older kid from the hallways named Dan, a year or two older than me.

"Hey man!" I responded, stoked he remembered my name. I settled in, sat down, and relaxed.

"Welcome, my friend. Life won't be the same," he assured me.

"Thanks, man," I said as he shook my hand.

"First show, Dave?" a kid, Tony, asked.

"Yeah, man," I responded, wanting somewhat desperately to fit in.

"You might wanna turn around now, bro. There's no turning back once you walk through the stadium gates." He was joking around, but with an almost sinister seriousness, and I didn't quite get what he meant. I laughed, hoping that I'd be accepted. This was a clique and there was a hierarchy, something a part of me always had sought an escape from. *The previous years, as a freshman and sophomore, I had friends. There were four of us in total and we were all equal. We had poker night on Fridays and on Saturdays we watched Saturday Night Live together after watching movies or doing whatever type of innocent fun we could think of—launching water balloons with a launcher I got, having bottle rocket wars with each other at another kid's house who lived by Lake Ellyn, and driving around when we first got our licenses. We went to a cottage in Wisconsin that the parents of one of us had and went water skiing and knee-boarding, the four of us sleeping upstairs in the twin beds they had. This was the last of it all. I was still small. I was really afraid but I didn't know this was the case. Everyone in high school was big. I started to separate from them. There was an artist inside me and they were all jocks. I thought that the hippies I met would be different, but they existed inside of a hierarchy.*

"We gotta get doses," John declared, looking around, and just as soon as he made the suggestion, a short, dirty hippie appeared.

"I got lips." He spoke clearly and quietly, looking over his shoulder in both directions.

"Is it good?" John asked while I hung back, figuring he'd get the deal done.

"It's *real* good," he assured him. We bought two or three for five dollars a piece. I put one on my tongue and cinched one inside of cigarette cellophane.

The kids sat around near the van, discussing the upcoming show. "Gonna see a sweet Scarlet-Fire tonight, I bet," someone postulated.

"Nah man, not tonight; they played it in Vegas; might get a Dark Star, though."

"No way," another chimed in, "they'll save that for Deer Creek; won't bust out the Dark Star in Chicago. Prolly be a bluesy night, on account of the windy city," he said as he sipped on a beer.

"You never know, man. The boys do what they feel," John argued back, "China Cat maybe?"

"Nah man, Vegas. Again. Heard the shows there were *sick*! Next year I'm hitting the whole tour."

"Jerry's been looking like shit," a girl named Marsha said. She was hot with big tits that poked gloriously out from her tie-dye. I was a virgin with maddening adolescent desires to deal with.

"He's good, man," Dan replied. "They got a few more good years in them." He sipped on his beer, soaked in the sun, and packed another bowl. He was excited. Everyone was.

A few minutes passed and then, all of a sudden, I felt like I'd walked into Woodstock, or down to Haight and Ashbury then over the Golden Gate Bridge. There were oceans and tides with the sun shining down, and it all came alive as the circus around me began. The scene in the parking lot shifted, from something ordinary albeit eccentric, to something seemingly reserved for time-traveling mystics and sages. I puffed on a bowl and the acid went deeper—into the core of the Earth and the salt of the lot; then I realized *what* the band was—traveling pranksters from some other time, outlaws of sorts; and I was a kid, all of us really were kids, even the ones who were older were still growing up, and now sitting around in a parking lot tripping on lips. We decided to take a long walk.

There were so many people who flooded the parking lot rows—roaming, wandering aimlessly, tripping on acid and looking around, up at the sky, down at their shoes, into the minds of the others who also were lost—runaways, beggars, thieves, freaks, and kids who would end up in jail before the sun set. Cops and DEA strolled undercover, looking to lock people up. Toothless old men with bushy, gray beards hid in the secret nooks in between cars. It was hard to tell what was real, what was unreal, and what danced between these two worlds, as if the unseen became seen and all that was real was suddenly very *questionable*. It felt like I walked through a door and down into a hole—to the insides of faraway places and forbidden lands, where mad hatters served up their brew.

Doses...

The Dead makes this happen, I thought to myself, totally fascinated. I'd forgotten I'd come to hear music. People were drumming in circles, twirling and shaking and moving around to the rhythms of Earth and the Sun. It felt like the spirits were watching the whole thing unfold, as if they'd been consulted and knew exactly what to do. There were girls in flowery dresses that flowed to the ground. There were rattles and bells; sounds seemed to fly from the sky.

A little child got my attention: *"What are you doing, Mister?"* he said through the fog, grasping the dress of his mother.

"Cassidy, he's on a trip...." she said to the boy, and then looked in my eyes as I stood there, motionless. A wisp of hot air filled me up and went into my skull.

"Whoa..." The word drifted out as if spoken from some other place, toward John who was lost in a world just a few feet away. I continued, *"it's like one of them......Hindus from the airport..."* He laughed. Both of us laughed then forgot where we were and came back.

His words drifted lazily back, *"Woah...it totally is..."*

"Yeah. Woah..."

The bald-headed Hari was beating a drum, wailing away at the sky lost in some sort of trance. He was healthy and thin, and ancient sounds flew through the wind as he wailed to his God, his voice in a sweet, cackly yodel, singing falsetto, the veins in his neck popping out.

> *"Hare Krishna*
> *Hare Krishna*
> *Hare Krishna*
> *Hare Krishna..."*

"Dude..." There were swarms of avatars and angels in the sky overhead, dancing and singing along as a wandering wind found itself brushed up against my cheek. There were voices from faraway lands, savagely whispering dark lullabies. And amidst all the mystics and tour-trampled souls, there was something I had to *endure.* Acid is work. It takes everyday life and it twists it. It takes music and brings it to life but this comes at a cost. It highlights the profound implications of all that we do in each individual subtlety of our existences, and it takes us on trips that we never completely return from.

The vibrations flew into my heart.

I saw an American flag. It waved in the wind off a Volkswagen bus.

The sun was a ball in the sky shining down on the lot, and it glittered its light through a faraway crystal that dazzled my wakening eyes.

Doses

Grilled cheese.....

Help—slip me a birthday ticket, would you brother....
Super dank, kind veggie burritos!

I need a miracle!!!!!!

Jerry ain't got too much left in him.....
Phuck Phish.

Kind trade for a ticket?

Stinky green buds...

We finished the walk—it felt like it lasted a lifetime—and climbed into the van, sat on the floor; my head swirled around in a daze. We finally walked in, through a colorful medley of sights and sounds, beautiful girls in dresses that blew in the wind, and the rattling of bells that had merged with the songs of the Earth in the summertime heat. The stage was lit up in the front, peaceful and calm. There were two sets of drums, and tapestries draped all around.

"You're gonna see when they start, man. They're the greatest band in the whole fucking world." I didn't *get* it, but then they came out, tuned up, started, and I did.

Wandering souls found themselves as the music came on. The stadium echoed and sang with the sounds of it all. The singer had wavy gray hair, and stood like an overweight angel of virtue and vice.

There were turtles and bears. Skeletons danced on a screen. "What the fuck is going on?" The music was out of this world, like delicate thunder, savagely gentle, whispering beautiful memories from where I'll return—with galloping angels inside of the notes, screaming and crying and whispering silvery sounds. Beach balls fell out of the sky. The instruments talked back and forth with each other, picking up each others' whims and finishing each others' sentences.

"It's the Dead, dude. They're doing the thing that they do!" Dan shouted back through a puff of smoke, dancing like a wild, cackling clown.

"But what the fuck are they doing!?"

"I don't know!" The drums were like cannons; my head swirled around in a daze. He laughed, waved his hands in the air and kept dancing. The guitar player man was an avatar unto himself. The air bent itself in the wind around his fat body and wavy gray hair.

His voice felt like that of an angel who giggled and purred.

Fireworks blasted in front of the moon. "I'm very impressed," another kid, Matt, said affirmatively. His skin was clammy and worn from *his* hours on acid. Lots of us took it that day. We stared at the sky from the stadium seats, said goodbye to the band, then started to move toward the exit.

Everything now would be different.

So it seems as if the Dead were as significant in all of this as the acid itself, the soundtrack to all the ensuing mayhem. A group that had managed, very successfully, to get a significant majority of those who ended up at their shows to follow them to the ends of the earth. There was a girl from the neighboring town who I knew who had put another girl I knew, her friend, into the very awkward position of notifying her parents that she had decided, at some point in between walking onto the parking lot and the band's final notes, that she was not coming home and that they would not have any way of getting in touch with the daughter they loved and who they'd raised as best as they could. "She'll call from a pay phone," my friend told them, being loyal to her friend, and that was it. Their daughter was gone, and so there were her parents, about the age I am now, who had to contend with the fact that their daughter had basically vanished—herself having shown up to see this *band* she had heard so much about, then dropping some doses and becoming subsequently brainwashed by this group of supposedly peace-loving hippies.

She ended up strung out on crack just a couple of years later. The later years of the Dead were dirty and sick, a reflection of society and culture's slow and steady devolution.

But the music. The fucking music. It was not something I was prepared for. It's not something you can explain. I surely understand how many, having less of a preference for jam bands, or who have not ingested the appropriate concoctions before or during the show, might find it all to be nothing more than the noodling whims of a handful of drugged-out hippies—the fattest of all of them being propped up out front with a guitar. I get this assessment, but this was not what went on inside of my blooming and blossoming, still highly impressionable, adolescent brain. For me, it was thunder from Heaven and raindrops from stars. It filled up my insides with secret melodies, coated in cashmere and dancing to ancient, forbidden rhythms from faraway lands, banging and booming and loud, a cacophony of cannon fire. Each time I saw them, at least with the appropriate *dosage*, there were memories of Heaven or of some land I'll someday return to. I think everyone went to this place. It gave us a peek. It hummed at the soul. It had its own separate collective unconscious—its own memory bank and its own stored-up thoughts and emotions. It was its own great big, magical and musical world.

But it started to crawl through my brain like a worm, a lovely psychedelic serpent that seductively whispered into my ear that it was safe to buy acid on the lot and to keep it in a cellophane inside my hip sack. *I mean, really, do you think that the cops would pick **you** out of all of the riff-raff?*

Rotten Log

"The fences."

    "Yeah man, the fences."

    "And Andy on his bike."

    "Dude, that shit was funny as fuck."

    "Yeah, dude."

    "That thing that happens happened again."

    "That shit was fucked up."

    "No shit."

    "The visuals were intense."

    "It was more in my body."

    "You took different shit."

    "The blue sperm were badass."

    "I had the pink."

We sat on a log, watching the water and varying things it reflected. The sun breached itself through the trees—a hot, sticky, day in the fall as the birds fluttered through. I smashed the dust into the screen, pounded the bowl into the log. I'd spent all the money I made mowing lawns. My shoulders were slumped. I was kind of burned out from it all. "It's cashed, dude."

"Bummer," Andrew said, "I'd rather you smoked it all. It's pointless for us to be half-baked."

"Agreed." I nodded.

"Yeah, man." Andrew continued, waxing. "What if you died on acid? Like, where would you go? Seems like there'd be nowhere, like you're already dead or something when you're dosed, or at least in some other place. What would happen? Me and AJ were talking the other day, dosed out so fucking hard, and started wondering. It's like you're there, but not, like you're dead already or something. So then what if you died? Like, got hit by a car or something when you're chasing some rainbow or something? Where in the fuck would you go?"

"Man, I got no fucking clue," I replied. "I'm not really sure where you'd go. I mean, where do you go when you die anyway? Is all this just, like, over, dude?"

"I know, man. It's like the acid takes you somewhere already, so I got no fucking clue what would happen if you died tripping."

"Fuck. No shit, dude." I changed the subject. "The Dead fucking rule, dude."

"They're a fucking brain-washing operation, true professionals," he replied arguably.

"Dude, they're fucking amazing. That shit was like nothing I ever seen."

"But Dave, you were tripping. You *think* it was good."

"Dude. No. It was good. The shit is like magic and I know that a part of you knows it. I'm touring next year. Fuck all this shit in Glen Ellyn."

"Have it your way, but there's something about all that shit that ain't right. It's just another popularity contest, but with acid and nitrous and tie-dyes."

"Nah, man. Jerry's like God up there."

"He's just a fat fucking hippie."

"Dude, shut up."

"You can think whatever you want, but all those guys following them are such fucking assholes, collecting bootlegs like some kind of cool kids club. Shit's so fucking exclusionary, total crock of shit. Everyone's following trends everywhere."

"But the music, man. The music is, like, from somewhere else. It bounces around in your brain, like they made it especially for tripping. Like that's what it's *for*, man."

"Meh." He may have invented that expression.

"Plus, dude. You love Nirvana. That shit's a trend and a half."

"Kurt's different, man. I wanna drive out to Seattle. Meet up with him; shoot up some smack. That might be the coolest way to go, like you're there, then you're not, like you just fall asleep and your death becomes part of the dream. I don't wanna live too long anyway, maybe thirty or so."

"Dude, fuck that. I'm gonna live for fucking ever."

"I wanna die before I get old."

"Hope I die before I get old..." I sang.

I've heard it said that acid isn't addictive, that psychedelics in general are not, that you go through a phase, and that the phase eventually wears off and you move on. This is partially true. But we were addicted; our little group was hooked. It took us to places we had to return to, artificial Shangri La's so to speak. Drugs were our blankets, our cures for the spiritual maladies we didn't realize had consumed us. They gave us the feelings we thought made us safe, ensconced us in all that was familiar, and in all that we thought that we needed. They took many forms and then became who we were, things that were *us*; part of our marrow and bones.

It happened so fast, as if a corner of my clothing had been entangled in the spindling mechanism of a massive washing machine; which then pulled me into the cloudy suds and turbulence of the water. I was already starting to drown.

With weed, life was good. Without, not so much. With acid, much better, but also a dangerous game; and all of this suddenly *happened*. It's like one day, as a freshman and sophomore, a couple of beers was the most I would do—the typical experiment, and then came the weed out of nowhere that night in the fall; and so acid, *Lysergic Acid Diethylamide* to be exact, then, was simply a logical step in an unknown direction. And then came the Dead, who mixed it all up in a pot with the thousands of others, all who were living their own separate, mixed-up illusions—babes lost in various toylands and missing a leader, but the one who could fly them to safety had never been there. And the kids found the band, or the band had found the kids, and the music played tricks in their brains like a maddened pied piper, so they jumped into vans and then traveled all over the world. The music was so fucking good. And Jerry was larger than life. And it all seemed so right at the time.

By the time you're sucked in, it's too late. The dark path determines your lot, and it is only an act of providence that will save you.

The day dripped along, went down with the sun and slipped its way through the afternoon, then made its way into the evening. We walked down the trail, our feet patting the cool, black mud. Branches whipped at our ankles as the trail wound through woods; the pond sat off to the right. The log, still old and dead, was where we had spent the whole day. Things had gone pale. The drugs weren't the same as before.

Bad Trip

The first time it got bad, it turned into a "bummer;" I learned that there wasn't escape. There weren't scary monsters like I heard there would be—it was more of an unsoothable psychological condition that never ended, a meltingness that never stopped melting, a fire in the synapses that wouldn't go out. The absolute worst thing that could happen in certain respects was the bad trip or bummer. There was a kid who saw Jesus somewhere near the parking lot of Wheaton College, and who never took it again, and another, *a he who is now a she*, who would bang his head into windows and walls every time that the acid got real. And, each time he did it, he thought it'd be different, but he lost his shit every time. And as I said, the he that he *was* is now a she, so it must have brought up some deep shit that he just couldn't handle, made him stare straight in the mirror and see what he believed to be *actually* there, which was in his case, perhaps, a budding adolescent girl stuck inside of the body of a budding adolescent boy. She's some sort of actress and activist now. Thank **God** for the acid. Life's just a fucking illusion.

There was something deep and dark and dangerous about acid, mysterious and haunting, some sort of powerful spell, all with this small piece of paper, less than a half-inch across, with a cartoon stamped on top. Each piece of paper had different things to be seen, with associated hallucinatory voices and themes. Sometimes it made us see fences. Everyone saw the same kind; plastic and orange, surrounding Lake Ellyn Park. Some shit was all in the head, twisting the brain into fractals. The walls might not cave but you might hear the colors, and voices might whisper dark nothings that scared you about stepping into whatever it was that the next moment had in store.

We rode our bikes all over town, under the trees that lined the streets, past friends' houses, and along the Prairie Path at night where the branches loomed over the trail, moonlight shining in the distance. Sometimes we'd be out in public and see someone's mom, or a kid whose shit was together in ways that ours wasn't. These were the scariest parts, seeing authority figures or parents. The town was so pretty, the people so perfect.

Sometimes we'd set off for a lemon, on the understanding that the lemon would increase the level of hallucinations, but we'd often forget what we were doing in the middle of the quest and end up lost on some bench, not knowing anything at all, wondering what we'd become.

"I'm confused about time and space…" James once said, to which I responded, "I think that we've all gone insane."

"Lucy in the Sky with Diamonds," James sang the response. It had become a joke of sorts, some sort of reference point to make things feel less insane in the midst of the peak of the trip. The peak was when things would go blank, the universe morphed, and all sorts of strange things would happen, often suggesting, for me, that I could not in fact handle reality. All of the fears were still there. The monster still lurked down below.

Lunch Money

I got ten bucks on Fridays from Mom and saved up my money from lunch, two dollars a day, then combined it all at the end of the week, twenty bucks total, to buy weed from this kid down the street. My stomach got achy and hurt, but I saved up the cash, starving myself to get high.

"What's that smell?" Mom started lurking and creeping around in the shadows.

"Nothing," I replied, defensively.

"Nothing? *That's not nothing.*" She nagged, seeming mean, but her child was suddenly gone. You'd be mean too.

What's a parent to do when their little person, the one who they nurtured and loved in his innocent years, is becoming their *own* type of person, and the person who they are becoming is fundamentally threatening to them, in some deep sort of way, which they aren't even really aware of? All that they know is that they are *bothered* or perhaps even repulsed by who their child is becoming, and are unaware of the deeper psychological mechanisms at work within *themselves*, be they projection, denial, or some other form of perceptual reality-twisting we are all prone to fall victim to as the result of living inside of this human conundrum. And now they have little to say to the neighbors regarding who their offspring are becoming, which is perhaps who they're *meant* to be, and who they're trying so hard to become, which is that who they truly are. But, anyone who dares to discover who it is that they *really* and *actually* are is bound to threaten establishments, the nuclear family being the primary one.

What if their children, as part of what is supposed to be a normal process of maturation, one which is honestly awkward for everyone, develop preferences or at least curiosities involving the ingestion of very dangerous substances, or have inclinations toward peers who would introduce them *to* them? After all, there has always been that "bad kid," whose parents were never around and who fended to make meaning out of life when latchkey-ing and its associated thrust-on-responsibilities were all that they knew. So they started with weed, which made their latchkey lives more bearable, or presented something to them that seemed to make things make more sense, mainly *the high*. And then your child meets this one, in his or her class or in the hallway, and they like each other even if the relationship has a dynamic that isn't the healthiest, and they bond in the way that kids do. So now what? Does the parent, if he or she even knows about the existence of this other, less-well-off child and his or her influence, forbid the relationship? Is that even possible? Are we children of parents or children of God? So where's the fine line? And what can parents do anyway? Could *you* stop a runaway train?

At some point I started on beer, like the booze was a cure for the strange person I had become. College was soon and the midwestern heat was electric those nights that last summer.

Tussin and Scotchgard

By this point, toward the end of high school and the following summer, we were all doing all sorts of drugs—wicky sticks (joints dipped in embalming fluid), cocaine, and occasionally heroin, almost anything, but mostly just acid and pot. James had *ideas*, and held up a can one evening in his garage: "Hey man, didn't some kid from Wheaton *die* from this shit a few years ago?" he asked ponderingly, then continued, "He did! I remember Dave Smalley was all bummed out at gymnastics practice after it happened." He was smiling. His blond hair was long in the back, spiked on top.

"Yeah, dude. I remember that. Some punk-rock kid," I replied.

"Man, we gotta try some of this. I heard you just spray it into the cap and inhale. Might get *FUCKED UP!*"

"Yeah, dude, but he died," I replied, "I mean maybe it's not the best idea, bro. I mean, like seriously, *Scotchgard?*"

"Dave, that's what makes the idea *good*, don't you see? We want to be huffing on shit that makes other kids die; it means the shit works. Plus, it's not illegal. We can walk into Ace, get a couple of cans, and go party; and what is the likelihood that *two* kids from the western suburbs die from the same shit, much less three?"

"Yeah," I eventually agreed.

So now, all of a sudden, we were smoking wicky and huffing Scotchgard along with the rest of the drugs; and then the kids started on tussin, sneaking through Walgreens and Osco, snatching a bottle or two, mixing up Slurpees and puking all over a sidewalk, or in someone's bedroom or car. I couldn't get into the tussin. It was nasty. This was when things became weird. No one could stop with the tussin or tripping or weed, and now huffing came onto the scene. The kids were now suddenly different, possessed, and marching to different drums that were far too obscure, like living inside of the songs by Nirvana and all headed toward the same place—wastelands of children destroying their lives.

Andrew walked up at a party, sickly-looking but with some demented newfound enthusiasm reeking its way through. "We went to a show in Wheaton last week, some crazy, weird-ass punk rock shit, man. You paid them three dollars and everyone got their own bottle. All of the kids were on tussin. The music was totally weird. It felt like a vampire gathering."

"That's fucking weird, dude," I responded.

"No man, shit was next level. The world is collapsing. I wanna destroy the whole town. I'm doing two bottles next time." There was something about it that reeked of decay, as if this type of shit could make kids eat the flesh of their classmates. The ones who drank tussin insisted it made them un-dead. They'd show up wherever we were, looking like monsters as if they'd been sipping on blood. The vibes weren't right. It felt evil and scary and wrong.

"We're gonna kill time. It's all just a fucking illusion," Andrew said.

Colorado

Arrival

There were mountains that rose in the west. My roommate had come from a trailer in some random town in the mountains. I pulled out a bong and then watched him get hooked, to the pot and then acid, then to all sorts of other new drugs—ecstasy and cocaine, then weirder shit like GHB and ketamine, a washing machine of his own, all in the blink of an eye—over the course of the next several years in Fort Collins.

James was here too. He'd come from Glen Ellyn, along with the tussin and all of the bad ideas he had for partying, but by now I was drinking and wasn't as worried. Booze was the cure to the strange things the acid was doing. I'd started the end of the previous summer, scoring with Elizabeth the night before leaving for college.

"Pull out if you're gonna cum," she instructed me, with more compassion than I had ever seen from her before I went in, "and don't worry if it happens too fast. It's like that for most guys at first."

I had sex with a fat, ugly girl the first night I arrived. We drank a handle of Rikaloff amongst several of us in a dorm, passing the bottle around with a two-liter Mountain Dew chaser, and I was left stranded, half-dead beneath a Master of Puppets poster. "I'll take care of him," she had apparently said to the rest of the kids as they left. I remember the black widow, a tattoo that she had on her tit, and then puking the moment we finished. *Welcome to college,* I thought in a daze. She lay there, portly and Rubenesque, eyeing me in victory and smoking a Camel. I remember her hair being red, the acne, and that she wasn't the prettiest version of plump, and that I had fucked up. I'm glad that she wasn't my first.

The dorm was a twelve-story tower. All the boys grew out their hair. A lot of the hippies were assholes, a short kid named John in particular who'd wrestled in high school and who insisted that Phish were the cure to the musical woes that had beset our generation. "Dude, what in the fuck is this shit that you're listening to?" he said about Nirvana one day. We were driving to Boulder, myself and another kid Dave and another kid Ted. Ted was a hippie and Dave was a rock and roll guy. "And why does this bat smell like shit?" He found it so funny, the suggestion being that the Dave who was driving was sticking the bat up his ass in order to pleasure himself.

"I played baseball in high school," was Dave's only response, John's humor seemingly lost on him. But Ted laughed with John; and so now the hippies, at least the two I found myself inside the car with, were really just jocks in disguise. John had a mullet and wore tie-dye. Ted wore a poncho. Neither of them were very nice.

We saw hawks on the drive, and an eagle, golden and perfect, ascending itself in the hot August air. The city of Boulder was beautifully perched up against the Flat Irons, which were bigger and meaner mountains that the ones that sat outside of Fort Collins. At the time, Fort Collins was a bit of a second-rate version, still the wild west and unknown. The Boulder kids raised up their noses, some kids from Glen Ellyn had been accepted there, the ones who'd received A's and B's.

The Night in the Dorms

Matt ripped off chunks from the sheet. All of us took what he gave us—myself, James, and a cowboy from Texas, and another all-American type, *Steven*, I think was his name. James talked them into it, which was, in his mind, his *contribution*, a mark on the earth he was proud he could make, deflowering farm boys with LSD.

Jeremiah was in Iowa, would soon be a flunkout, and Andrew would travel all over, sleeping on floors, invading houses and dorms, and otherwise acting a nuisance, spitting blood in the face of the world. He arrived here one night, he and the other kid, Matt, who was handing out acid. He had bugs in his skin, scabies or some type of mite, and jumped up and down on a bed with a bottle of vodka as a terrifying moonlight shined in, his eyes dark like icy, black pond water, as if envisioning murder. The music was loud and the room had a sinister feel as the walls started melting. *'Why did you take so much acid?'* was all I could think. There were all sorts of shadows. I'd come here for mountains and streams.

"I wanna hear Creeping Death," a skeevy girl with scraggly hair and acid-washed jeans, named Monica said; she'd taken some too, so we played it as loud as we could, a psychedelic tribute to Metallica. Things changed that night. It was just a few weeks into the school year and I'd found the wrong crowd. Another kid Mike had some too, a big chunk that Matt ripped him off, and he dropped out the following Monday. *So let it be written, so let it be done...*

Then, Andrew blasted Nirvana, and there was this moment in the midst of the screaming mayhem when I looked straight into his eyes, seeing the emerging darkness in mine reflecting back, and heard Kurt screaming:

And there was a moment of black magic right then, some sort of mystical unfolding that happened and a descent into hedonism that only providence would save me from.

There were different people, going camping, exploring the mountains, and getting away from the dorms. I was told making friends would be easy, but these were the wrong types of people.

Post-Rosemont

We partied all night after Rosemont, rocking the Holiday Inn with the rest of the Deadheads, back from Colorado for Spring break. Craig, another one of Hawthorne's fallen angels, stole a bottle. I had to drive.

I'd gotten us lost, and Jeremiah, the one who knew everything always, was passed out in the back seat, dead to the world and useless, so I figured it out by myself. I pieced together a way to get back from the Horizon using some sort of directional logic I pulled from a hidden compartment my brain somehow accessed. I don't think I've ever thought harder than I did that night.

We pulled into a gas station and Matt, who always brought trouble, started wrestling with Andrew (who was also trouble by this point) in the parking lot, which quickly caught the attention of local police who turned on their sirens and lights and surrounded the car. The cop reached in, aggressively turning the engine off, opened the door, and lifted me out of the seat.

"GET THE FUCK OUT OF THE CAR!" he shouted and shook me a bit. I cooperated. Another one searched the car and found the bottle. He pulled it out, held it up under the streetlamp. The liquor splashed clear in the moonlight.

"What in the *FUCK* is this?" he asked sternly, toying with each of us who was suddenly somber and sober. The Dead had stopped playing at midnight, an eternity had passed, and now here we were, under arrest in some town near the airport somewhere. The dawn wasn't too far ahead.

"I have no fucking idea," I politely and assertively responded, not really caring too much about anything—about the fact that there was probably acid in the car and that I could probably end up in prison because of this.

The police had thought Andrew and Matt were *actually* fighting, not play fighting, and this was what sparked the alarm, so one of them made small talk with us as the other officer handled the situation with the two of them. "So how was the show?" They were smiling, holding their belt buckles, fondling handcuffs. We looked at each other and tried not to laugh.

"Last night was better," I answered honestly, Scarlet Begonias still ringing around in my brain.

"So you goin' tomorrow?" he continued, in a thick Chicago accent.

"Depends," I told him. I wanted my bed.

We were fucked up but something about the trip we were on made them like us and give us a pass. There was mind control shit with the acid. With the perfect amount, you could capture a soul, almost as if you possessed some sort of beam, not like a laser, but something that grabbed hold of another's mind and made him or her do things—a Wonder Woman's lasso-type of a phenomenon. This was what acid could be. They were caught up in their dreamworlds; we were all sure of ourselves. As odd as it sounds, we were making them let us all go.

Or at least I imagine that this was the case.

"OKAY, who's driving this fucking thing?" Another of the police came back, questioning all of us.

"I am, officer," I said as I looked into his eyes.

"Take this bottle here over to that dumpster and throw it away and go home. We ain't got the fucking energy to take you all in tonight, which we could definitely do. Do you understand me?"

"Yes, sir," I responded respectfully, taking the bottle and throwing it into the dumpster.

The sun was rising as I finally pulled into Glen Ellyn. I looked to my right at a red light on St. Charles Road and stared straight into the eyes of Jeremiah's dad who had *somehow* managed to end up in his car on his way to work in the lane right beside me at seven o'clock in the morning! I pointed and laughed as he pulled his car into the middle of the intersection on Main Street, blocking my left-hand turn. "Open the fucking trunk!" he screamed in my face in a Vietnam-furious rage, so I popped the trunk as he proceeded to pull Jeremiah from the back seat, furiously shake him, and threaten to beat him senseless in the middle of the intersection. "Where in the fuck have you been all night!?" Craig intervened, sparing Jeremiah a well-deserved beating as he had promised to be home for dinner the previous night but had gone to the Dead show instead. He got in his car and continued his morning commute.

The Dead were the ones who had sort of made all of this happen. Children who didn't get let off as easily were released from prison twenty-five years later.

So it goes.

The Big Bang

"Did you know that you're stardust?" Cheez asked us both.

"What do you mean?" I asked, quizzically as Andrew looked into the distance. We were lost in the woods, somewhere near Perry's Pond but having wandered away from the entrance, sitting on a log, tripping on acid, and passing a bottle of whiskey around.

"Like, dude, we're all dust from stars. Like four billion years ago, the Big Bang erupted and blasted all of this shit into existence. It created the stars, which eventually coalesced into galaxies, and around all the stars there are planets, some like Earth. It's been estimated that there could be somewhere around FOUR MILLION planets like Earth just in our galaxy alone, which is a goddamn hundred fucking thousand light-years across! You know how fucking big that shit is?"

"How fucking big?" I inquired.

"Well dude, check this shit. Light travels at one hundred and eighty-six thousand miles *PER SECOND!*"

"Woah..."

"Yeah, no shit, totally woah! And a light year is the distance light travels *in a year*, which is one hundred and eighty-six thousand miles per second times sixty seconds in a minute, times sixty minutes in an hour times twenty-four hours in a day times three hundred sixty-five days in a year. It's like six trillion miles for one freaking lightyear! And the Milky Way is a hundred thousand of those across, dude."

"Jesus fucking Christ..."

"No motherfucking shit! And get this. There are one hundred billion fucking galaxies in the universe! Wrap your head around that shit!"

"Woah..." Cheeze was smart, smart like Andrew, Jeremiah, and I. He came along toward the end of high school and started to bond with the rest of us.

"Woah is goddamn right, motherfucker! I mean we're like angel dust and shit. I mean dust from Angels or God or something, just fluttering specs, drifting around on this *ball*. I mean, what in the actual fuck? It keeps going and going and going, like forever. And time is a construct. It's totally made up. All of this life is just bullshit anyway, so you may as well take as much acid as you possibly can. It's like all this shit is nothing more than a movie. We're really just actors. All of it's like total bullshit, ya know? May as well party." I was astonished.

"How in the fuck did you learn all this shit?"

"A Brief History of Time by Steven Hawking, and a bunch of other shit, science journals and magazines."

"But where did you get it?"

"The fucking library, dude. Don't you read?"

"Not really."

"Well you should."

"We're gonna call this trip 'Cheez describes the universe,'" Andrew said, joking and finally chiming in.

I laughed, "Yeah man, like he's a secret fucking genius or some shit."

"Huh huh, yeah, like the last person you'd expect to read a fucking book," Andrew said, both of us laughing our asses off. We'd wandered away from the trail. There were some lights from houses off in the distance we could faintly see, creating subtle glows of orange and yellow. The leaves were dried and blowing around in the wind, and there were icy patches underneath the brush. The ground was squishy.

"Fuck both of you guys," Cheez said, his feelings hurt.

"Sorry dude," I said, apologizing and feeling bad.

"Sorry Cheez," Andrew filed suit.

"Whatever," he answered.

"Fuck you, then," Andrew antagonized.

"Fuck everything," said Cheez.

"Pass me the fucking bottle," I said to them both, grabbing it from Andrew and swigging off the handle.

"Dude, you know that there is quicksand in forty-seven out of fifty states?" I asked both of them. "We could be standing in it right now."

"Where in the fuck did you hear this?" Asked Andrew, annoyed.

"Fucking Discovery Channel, dude, and the encyclopedia. Think about it. It's like some sort of equation, like the water overly *replaces* the sand that it *displaces* and you fucking sink to your death."

"See you *DO* fucking read!" Cheez said, happy.

It was suddenly well after midnight and the three of us sat there, our bones sort of frozen, our jaws not quite working. The night had gone frigid with low steam rising up off the pond, and off in the distance, way out in the dark, there was something that seemed to be telling me I had to go. I remember the shadows of twigs on the ground, and the way that the few remaining leaves clung stubbornly to the branches above us, and how each of us had become sort of ragged and worn out from all of the drugs we had done in the last handful of years—each of us lost in our own special way. Each of us fading to nothing.

I ended up stealing the bottle and running away, not toward the light from the houses that sat in the distance, but into the dark, through the woods, leaving them stranded without it. I got lost, chasing something, and stumbled out somewhere in someone's backyard, still lost, eventually making it home before morning arrived.

Lilah

There was hope. A girl came along with a Lisa Loeb look, pointy-framed glasses and all; with a cute little figure and outfits of darker pastels—dark pastel orange and dark pastel green, petite, with cute little braids in her hair; a real look of her own. She drove a stick, a little white compact car with a flower sticker on the back windshield.

"DAVE!" she was always so happy to see me. Her voice was high and her eyes magnified themselves through the thick lenses of her glasses. She was a couple of years older, with an odd type of sophistication, like she had seen things that I hadn't. I spent hours in her room, staring into her eyes and holding her close to my heart. She was slender and quiet and fragile. We went to some punk shows together and stood in the back.

"Dave, there seems to be some perfect type of magic when we're together, don't you think?"

"Yes, yes there is!" I agreed, and started planning the tape I was going to make her.

"I mean, it might be true love, don't you think?" She was my chance to escape from the booze and the drugs, but somewhere and somehow I turned her off and she retreated.

I followed her all over campus, positioning myself in the exact places where I knew I'd see her, not exactly *stalking* per se, just kind of hanging where I knew she would be eventually, which sometimes meant casually skateboarding around in the same spot on campus for an hour and then popping out from behind a bush.

"Uh, hey Dave," she would say, less enthusiastic than before.

"I was just skating around," I would say, shaking a bit, "and look, I ran into you!" But my lip would be trembling. *What did I do?* I would think. *She said that she thought we were magic.*

She decided I wasn't her type and then Andrew came back, got drunk in my room and the cops showed up. I got kicked out of the tower by some sort of disciplinary committee, on account of her dumping me, me having no one to hang with, and then Andrew showing up unannounced and ruining the night.

So I'd sit in the dorm, the new dorm, and watch Lisa Loeb on TV, imagining that she was Lilah and that Lilah still cared. And I thought about killing myself. I'm not sure why I was born crazy, or why all these women insisted on breaking my heart. I needed to find a new girl and then all would be fine.

Sunshine

The following year, she, a new one named Sunshine, sat cross-legged on a cushion across from me, brushed her lips lightly over my open palm, handed me a crystal, and looked deep in my eyes. Then she sat still for a second. "Don't take this the wrong way, but I think I love you, Little One," she said. Her voice was soft and musical, and told different tales that were deeper than mine. She was *experienced*.

There was a pause, and a rush of excitement inside. "I love you, too!" I proclaimed back, then gushingly continued, "my god, I feel like this cosmic connection to you, from the first time I saw you."

"When I called you Popcorn?" She responded in rhythm.

"Yes! From that time in the street! I knew it right then."

"I thought you were him! That was weird. I mean, you're right, we *do* have a kind of connection."

"It feels like **true** love to me," I exclaimed, going a little too far.

"Easy now, Little One," she responded, a bit condescendingly, twisting the flame down a bit.

I was certain that she was an angel, standing inside of a light shaft that shone down from Heaven. She had dreadlocks and perfect blue eyes that were wise and profound, the wells of deep remembrances. Freckles peppered her skin. I snuggled myself near her feet and then drifted to sleep, hearing each breath that she breathed, my heart pounding wild like rain.

The Dead played McNichols that Fall and I went to her place after one of the shows. There was a guy in her room, some dreaded hippie who reeked of patchouli. "Hey brother. I'm Bill." He reached out his hand and I shook it. *Who is this Bill?* I thought to myself. There was all of this status with *tour*, and this was a tour guy. I surmised he was more of a man than I was, and that she was a woman and I was a boy. "Care for a toke, brother?" he asked, and passed me a chillum. I smiled and reached for the pipe.

"Sure, man."

"I know Bill from Shoreline," Sunshine said as they looked at each other, "he's a righteous brother."

"You got a good one here, *Dave*. Don't ever do her no wrong, *okay*." He sat cross-legged, wearing a poncho that covered his knees.

"I know she is, man," I said agreeably. We sat in a circle with him in between Sunshine and I.

"Man that Uncle John's was sick, eh?" he said, sparking conversation, "the da-da-da-da-da-da da part at the end, man, they just kept going and going and going.."

"Yeah, man," I agreed, smiling awkwardly as he continued, touching her knee. "Sunshine, you remember that Terrapin at Shoreline?"

"How could I forget? I thought that I might lose my mind at that show."

"But I saved you, *didn't I?*" he said as he looked into her eyes.

"Stop," she demanded, smiling, then looked in my direction. "So Dave, Bill's hanging around for a while. I'm trying to get him a job at my work."

"Cool," is all that I said, while wondering very uncomfortably if she'd fucked him, and so here was a *new* type of feeling, kind of like anger but different, mixed in with love, odd and unfamiliar, but scary and deep, a new type of feeling in charge of the way things would go.

She was as soft as my childhood blanket. Her wild wet eyes made me foolish and blind, and fluttered gazes that shot through my innocence.

The smell of her, patchouli and incense and sage, her sweet breath and soft, pouting lips. Her breasts. Her mouth like a flower, her movement; the wind. I couldn't escape from her grasp. Her words were the sweetest I'd known and dripped from her lips like ancient, soft melodies I'd forgotten and had now returned. I lay near the foot of her bed. What she was doing was nothing that I understood, some dark type of magic disguised as the kindest of lights.

She made me a patch for my corduroy pants, stuck a bead in my hair, and wrapped a swath of it in red and green embroidery thread. I thought she was God.

We walked and we talked. She came by my place after classes and pulled down her jeans. The seasons were changing, switching from summer to fall, and my lonely dark nights in the basement were ceasing to be, replaced with the light of a pretty young girl who had finally seen who I was. Someone had finally realized I was a catch!

"In the spring, for your birthday, if we're still together, I'm getting you a Pisces tattoo," she told me one crisp afternoon a few weeks after our initial encounter.

"We will be; I know it. I can *feel* it." I quickly replied, smiling and sitting across from her Indian-Style, our knees touching, the sun shining. *What does she mean?* I thought to myself.

"Little One, the only thing constant is change," she said with passive condescension. But I *knew* that we'd go on forever. The feelings inside me were perfect and pure. I glistened and glimmered and drifted and floated; my problems had come to an end. I'd live for the love that she gave me and we'd last forever.

Miranda

Sunshine hadn't been treating me well and I couldn't tell why. I mean, I followed her *everywhere*—to her job and her classes, and all over campus and then back to her house in the evenings, and around the kitchen as she cooked and then into her bed, only to wake by her side—most definitely making a point of letting her know the full extent to which I *seriously* needed her, saying things like *"you're the only one in the entire universe who understands me,"* with the deepest conviction. It had been such a magical three or four weeks but she wanted a Friday night break.

"I need to be with my sisters," I think was what she said, so I went to a party instead at this place called The Swamp.

It was there that I spotted Miranda after drinking a handful of beers, a girl I recognized from campus. She had a nice smile and huge tits with a jagged scar on her leg, and was beautiful with blonde hair, highlighted purple. Her eyes were brown. "Hey!" she said the moment I saw her, and started smiling and laughing.

"Hey!" I said back and we made a bit of small talk before promptly deciding to leave together. I didn't give Sunshine a thought. She had, after all, been snubbing me for most of the week and was now on a date with the sisters. Plus, there was Bill.

We got to her dorm and then fucked for a couple of seconds. I got embarrassed and left.

A Few Days Later

"So, um, Little One. I don't really know how else to say this but I first want to say that the only thing constant is change. Like, it's really all we have and I want you to know that I still want for us to be friends, *good* friends, but I can't be in a relationship with you anymore, because well, it's just not where I'm at and I think life is complicated, and vast, and so I just think that for us to be friends, *good* friends, would be best. I mean, we can't be intimate anymore because I don't think that that would be healthy, but your friendship really matters to me."

I started to sweat. A candle flickered. Things quickly turned, from steam-sweaty summers to the iciest frigid of night. A dark, dreary frost settled into my blood; my heart turned to black and then shattered. I started to cry as she hugged me, a collision of mercy and tears.

The next day and most everyday afterward, I'd knock on the door of her house, pretending to have lost something, a notebook or pen or whatever, and she'd answer the door and eye me with pity. It was cold, wintertime in Colorado—January—and snow blanketed the front yards while crows perched themselves in ominous rows on telephone wires. I was nineteen.

"Oh hey…"

"So I think I left my sweatshirt over here. Have you seen it?" I was shaky and nervous and trembling, heartbroken.

"It's not here."

"Are you sure?"

"Positive. I've been cleaning today. I would have seen it," she insisted, flatly.

And I'd stand there, fidgeting around, and she'd invite me in hesitantly. Her roommates were there, drumming a bit or cooking or smoking, and they'd see me just like she did and we'd all eventually start talking, and then Sunshine would go to her room and close the door almost completely and I'd knock, then sort of invite myself in, and we'd talk a bit but nothing was ever the same. She still burned her candles and sage. There were still the same relics. Her bed, just a futon mattress, was still set in the corner, smelling the way that *she* smelled. I still heard her roommates outside her room, laughing and watching T.V. She still smoked cigarettes inside with the window open, flicking the ashes out into the yard.

There was nowhere to turn. I plotted to take my own life.

Pills

I started on pills at some point soon after, Benzodiazepines mostly, loving the dreary relaxation, like my old blanket was warming my cells from the inside and oozing quiet lullabies into my bloodstream. They were just sort of *warm*.

A loose configuration, blue and yellow Valium, along with Vicodin and Flexeril, sat on the nightstand, not in a bottle or bag, some sitting up on their sides and rolling around and onto the floor. I loved how they settled my insides. I'd get home from the bars or a party, take one or two and drift off.

It was cold and started raining that spring and it felt like it never would end—a cruel Colorado monsoon. There were two hippie girls who I knew from the dorms who I'd sometimes run into on campus.

"I don't think this shit's ever gonna stop," one of them said, huddled beneath the massive awning of the Clark building as droplets dripped down and all the kids shuffled around wearing rain jackets with hoods.

"Fucking tell me about it. So fucking sick of this goddamn rain."

"What the fuck else are you sick of, SuperDave?" the other one asked.

"Sick of this entire goddamn life."

"That's the attitude."

We laughed. One of them, a girl from Connecticut, had wavy brown hair, littered with beads she was dreading. The other was pretty and blonde, from Chicago. I guess they were sort of my friends.

Kim

A girl came along after Sunshine, with brown hair, freckles and overalls like Raggedy Anne, a couple of dreadlocks on top. We broke up because of my feelings, the bad ones I carried around, and I'd pick up some beer, thinking that things would go well and that I'd party the heartbreak away, then I'd run into her at the bar, find the nearest wall and put my hand through it. One night I grabbed some dull scissors and slashed up my arm. It didn't go deep but I still have the scar. Alcohol by this point had become the biggest of all the crutches.

416

We lived in a house on the east side of town, myself and three others. The first year was fine. I had a new girl and I got along well with my roommates, good enough, at least. One was named Creed. Creed was a pain in the ass. He was always arguing and starting fights with people at the wrong places and times. It was always the stupidest shit—where to stop for a bite on a road trip or the type of chain lubricant to use on a mountain bike. He'd get heated and then storm away. He was into maroon—maroon sheets and shirts, shorts, and mountain bike accessories. His feel was just kind of *maroon* if that makes any sense. If Maroon was a person, the person it was would be Creed. He listened to Led Zeppelin IV and The Cars on repeat.

I lived there with him, this other guy Aaron, who was more like a brother than a friend, and Rico, my roommate from back in the dorms.

"I think Creed's a virgin," I said to them both in the kitchen one day.

"Most definitely. Kelly keeps trying to bang him but she says he's scared," Aaron added, referring to his girlfriend's roommate.

Rico chuckled cynically like he always did, then took his dog for a walk. We had all come of age in Fort Collins. The years had gone by, one melting into the next and we'd kind of grown up.

We lived in this beautiful neighborhood, lined with beautiful trees, with beautiful people walking dogs and parties always happening in the various backyards. All of the houses and blocks were connected with a vast series of alleys that traversed the east side of Fort Collins; they were fun to stumble through drunk coming home from the bars after drinking all night. It was magic back then in the nineties.

People would hang out on porches, smoking bowls, relaxing and listening to the Dead. The summers would span on forever; the temperature up in the hundreds, dry and smoldering like a sauna. I had the most amazing skateboard that I rode all over town for years.

And then college ended. I didn't have plans. I was lost and confused and now suddenly paying my rent, with a janky-ass, liberal arts degree and I'm just realizing now that my major had always been partying. The dishwasher from the Mish, a cute girl named Bree, started showing up to shifts on heroin and I started getting a little bit from her here and there, and I realized there was a dark side, it lived on the north side of town, and another scene made itself known. This was the end of my college career. I'd been slutting myself for a while, had given up on love after another one, a blonde named Martha had tortured me like all the rest, turned me against Aaron then saw to it that knuckles got bloody. When I opened my heart I would end up with fists against bricks.

I guess all I wanted was love.

Mishawaka

A parrot flew through the bar, and there was a peacock that eventually got run over on the highway. Behind the stage in a purple cabin, we huffed on a tank of stolen nitrous oxide before work. Bugler, one of the other cooks sat hunched over, passed out on a couch. His lips were blue.

"Is he dead?" someone asked. It was ten o'clock in the morning.

I had burgers to cook, and wings and cheesesteaks, along with a cacophony of other short-order items, all day long, from morning 'till night. The nachos, the fucking super nachos, a popular microwaved delicacy, were a particular brand of pain in my ass throughout all of the shifts that I worked. Last I checked, a guy I started with on the same day named Harris was still there, managing the place in the totally vested way that he always did.

Good short-order cooks are astonishingly hard to find.

"It's the butter that makes the burger," he'd say, and I knew what he meant. It was; the subtle pairing of various greases created short-order comestible masterpieces. There's a lot I remember about Mishawaka—named after a town in Indiana which was named after a Shawnee princess—the burgers, the heat, the grease, the booze, and the drugs. There's more I remember little to nothing about.

It was hot, over a hundred degrees in the scorching summer months, and the owner, whose name was Joe, would come through the kitchen shirtless, gut hanging out over the waistline of his pink OP shorts.

"Cook me a burger. Please. Fries, extra crispy." I liked him; he was honest and angry like me. "What we need around here," he'd say in his more jovial moments, "are some hot bitches who like to suck cock to just hang around on the patio out back and service us whenever we're up to it like in the old days." He sort of smiled as if he was sort of joking.

"You'd still have to wait in line for sloppy seconds or thirds, fatman," Dan said, taunting him, "the last time one of these supposed hot bitches sucked your cock, it was 1977, and I highly doubt she was anything to write home about." Everyone laughed.

"Who needs any of them fucking whores anyway?" Carlos, a man with a swarthy, black beard who later hung himself, interjected. He was hilarious, brilliant and mad and a man I looked up to.

"Carlos over here gave up a while ago; he's a realist," Dan said, puffing a red.

"At least I sleep soundly at night," Carlos responded. His soul had matured to a level of torturedness that mine would eventually reach. I wanted to be just like him.

"Who needs them fucking whores, anyway, " I added.

"SuperDave's right over here," he said, laughing, and puffed on a red of his own.

Dan tested Joe like the son of Sam tested New York; one time pulling a fry from the fryer with tongs, smiling an evil smile to the rest of the cooks, and then dropping it into the crack of his ass as he stood there unsuspectingly, shirtless and hairy and tanned. I can still hear the scream, just like a girl, as the scorching hot fry nestled itself in the crack of his ass and he squirmed to remove it, squealing as the Oakley Razors flew from his head and landed in the bar outside the kitchen.

It was a beautiful scene, one of Earth's prettiest places, situated up Poudre Canyon, twenty-five miles from town in a different world, distinct from the Fort and without any college town feel. They were mountain folk here, drinking and driving the canyon, shooting guns, and watching for black bears in summer. "Aim for the throat," the gold miner said as he lent me his gun for the day in the case of an attack on the kitchen. "They're everywhere this time of year and we have to be careful. Don't fuck around. Them black bears are friendly enough but they'll still fuck you up."

Mountains rose from each side of the river. Kayakers paddled Mish Falls which drifted past behind the stage. The bighorns would come down the hill in the summer, which was dotted with cottonwoods, varieties of willows, box elders, alders, and elm trees, along with Northern Colorado wildflowers and various evergreens. The hawks would descend themselves in wide circles down toward the river, then quickly ascend back upward and into the clouds.

I vomited blood after eating some mushrooms one night, drinking myself half to death on tequila, and working some twenty-odd days in a row. I was twenty-three, had graduated, and life had become something different from what it had been in all of the years leading up to this. I had no plans for what was to come. This booze had become commonplace, a friend to rely on but a bully of sorts who ordered its sidekick around. Everyone else drank tequila so I drank it too. Everyone else did cocaine, so I did it too. Everyone made fun of Joe so I made fun as well. I was always just going along, but I also needed the drugs just like everyone did.

(When you're going along, you forget your true self, if ever it even was there; and if no one, in those formative years, teaches you that this is the most important thing, to know and to be your true self, then the drugs and the booze will replace this life lesson, and then all of the sudden there's this big empty pit in the heart of your soul; but that's not entirely true because the real you, the actual you you were born to become, is still screaming from deep down inside, below all the booze in some saddened dimension howling "Be me, I'm all that you are!" Nothing makes sense in the worlds of the prodigal sons. Drugs make no sense just like war makes no sense, but lies make senility seem like the greatest of options inside their sick worlds, and so you choose battles, casting peace out the door for endless suffering eternities.)

I got off my shifts and the music would play—Grisman, Kottke, String Cheese (unfortunately), Wooten, Fleck, Dark Star Orchestra, among so many others those summers. It now seems forgotten, a rustic old cabin on the bank of a river where beautiful music surrounded the souls who arrived for those magical nights.

A girl named Sarah, a sweet teenage girl with dirty blonde hair who helped out in the kitchen, flipped her car off the road at five in the morning, landing herself in the river upside-down without air, sustaining permanent brain damage, a casualty of the party that ensued in the Poudre.

I got angry here too. The tickets came in and I wouldn't be able to deal, and I'd throw things all over—wing baskets, tongs, the spatula, whatever was there in front of me. There was this peculiar juxtaposition between the healing energy and beauty of the Poudre and the deadly debauchery that ensued in this mystical place, a beautiful yin, and a mindfucking yang.

And one day, after what felt like a lifetime up there in the Poudre, and after college was over and nothing was left, I packed my shit and left Colorado, bound for Chicago.

Victoria

"Dude, it's fucking *DUMP-ING*," I extolled to Jerry.

"Yeah, bro, gonna ride pow in the morning. Fucking sick!"

The champagne dumped down all night long, with fluffy white flakes like great fluttering moths layering themselves on the mountains above. The moon disappeared and the sun wasn't there in the morning, save a faint distant ball that tried to poke its way through the frozen mist.

We lined up outside the gondola at six; the mountain would open at eight. People had coffee and bagels, and made minor adjustments to helmets and bindings and gloves, zippers and boots. Steam rose from cups. Everyone's breath made a cloud. We finally got on the gondola.

"She's got a big ass but that pussy is tight," Aaron said, matter-of-factly.

"I didn't fuck her; won't go there," I interjected, "she sucks a good dick though."

Rick chimed in, "It's like that big fucking ass squishes the walls of her pussy in tighter or something." He motioned his hands, outward to in, as if testing a basketball's firmness; made a farting sound. We all three had gotten her naked; Vic, she called herself.

"I love the way she says *horny*, all English and shit, like some sort of call girl from London, classy but not."

"What, on account that she sucked your cock in a trailer park last night? You're all class, Dave," Aaron said, giving me shit. I laughed.

"Dude, we're pigs," Aaron continued.

"Yeah…" I agreed, "that ass is *sorta* good now, but wait a few years, after she pops a kid out."

"Totally, it's not *sustainable*. It's why you marry the B-cup and medium ass. Twenty-four's one thing but forty-two's a whole other story." Rick was sure; he'd dated older women. I wiped snot on my mitten, hacked, and spit out the window. It fell through the sky to the snow.

We got off, sat and fastened our boots to our boards, and went riding through fields of fresh powder, drifting through white-blanket-space. Fluffy white flakes coated the tree tops and the blanketed meadows spanned on for miles.

I floated up out of my body and into the clouds, and then through a doorway and into a magical land; a wide-open thicket of snow-frosted

Aspens and Pines. The snow would go into the lungs—freezing cold breaths, but perfect and warm in my gear, sweater and jacket and mittens and wool socks and boots. Helmet on top, goggles sealed over the eyes. Cheeks rosy red. Lips chapped and dry. It was silent and still with the billions of flakes, inside the pillow-soft world.

Our mittens brushed up on the trees as we rode down the hill. The snow brushed our cheeks like the soft touch of angels.

"Dude, I scored face shots all the way down! That shit was sick!" I screamed ecstatically.

"Return of the fucking Jedi, Man!" Aaron yelled back, also ecstatic.

"Totally! Just like a fucking speeder-bike ride!" Jerry agreed.

We hugged at the bottom. Our cheeks hurt from smiling.

Days After Powder

On the days after powder, the mountain got groomed and made corduroy grooves in the snow. I nestled my chin to my chest, pointed the front of my board, and screamed down the hill like a space shuttle exiting orbit. The sun shone its gold-yellow light through the blue of the sky. I floated up out of my head and turned bright like a star. The speed was so fast I felt drunk.

I'd go down and then back up the hill. The frozen, black bench of the chair on the Morningside lift, the one without bars for protection, sixty feet up from the frozen, white ground down below, moved with the gusts of the Earth back and forth in the wind. There were so many days just like this, a hundred or more in a year.

I played all day long like a kid, then went to the kitchen at night.

Coral Grill

"Keep your fucking skis off my board, kid." It was sunny, a beautiful blue-bird-type day a couple days after a dump. Karney yelled at an eight-year-old kid whose father was apologetic and tried to lighten the mood, "We're sorry, it's his first time on a *real* mountain. We're visiting from the midwest."

"Well tell your fucking kid to watch my new board." He was never too much less than a straight-up, fucking asshole all the time, a dude from Chicago like me. His parents were rich and had bought him a house. He loved Widespread Panic and reggae. I bumped into him, along with the berated family, on the mountain before we had work at the job that I scored the first day that I got here, after promptly leaving Chicago after just a few weeks.

He'd invite me to smoke in the walk-in and then he'd talk shit. "Fuckin' Dale, dude thinks he's *Rasta*. Dude, the Rastas I know would eat him alive." A ponytail poked out of the back of his hat. He continued his rant. "Fuckin' so sick of his shit; fucker always shows up late, never wants to shuck and tries to pretend he doesn't see the order come in. He's a bitch, straight up."

"He's alright," was all I said back. It was true, Dale was not a bad guy, and everyone knew about Karney; it was also true that Dale wasn't exactly the hardest worker either, but what did you expect in a ski-town kitchen? I took a few puffs, closed the walk-in door as I left, and checked on the sauces, then walked over to the dishwashing station.

"Whaddup, Dale?" He was scrubbing a pot with steel wool as steam rose up out of the dishwashing machine.

"Dave! Jah get I and I down the mountain to get irie-I!" He pronounced from his station, packing a chillum and sharing his herb just like Mike, blowing the smoke into steam of the dishwashing machine to conceal its odor. He was from Illinois also, had gone "Rasta," adopted an accent of sorts. "I and I share the irie-I." He washed dishes and hated the owner, whose name was Phil. He thought Phil, a fifty-year-old coke fiend from Philly represented Babylon, and that Babylon would fall, and that his part in Babylon falling was to don a false accent, listen to reggae and curse behind Phil's back. *"I and I washing the dishes, just like my fadda' before,"* he sang, making it sound like Bob Marley. He was cool enough.

Dale was angry like Karney. One evening, wanting to kick Karney's ass, he waited outside by the dumpster, cold breaths breathing furious anger out of his nostrils and mouth. His hair was pulled back, tight and tied off, keeping it out of his eyes to ensure he could fight. Karney had semi-intentionally splashed him with juice from an oyster while shucking, or otherwise done something of a provoking nature. Dale was *Irie-I* up to a point, but beyond that point was a rage-filled, violent, and dangerous individual.

Karney had wanted the griller position, which was mine, so he took his angst out on Dale, the person below him on dishes. But Dale got up, stood up, challenging Mike to a fight near the dumpster, who promptly backed down when he realized Dale was serious. "I can't fight, anyway. Don't want to get in trouble or go to jail or some shit."

"Karney's a bitch." It's all Dale said, then kept on singing his reggae. The kitchen returned back to normal.

But the work scene here was *mellow*, unlike the vibe of The Mish. It was large and spread out with a six person team. Pots and pans hung from the ceiling, music played loudly through a system. I had the grill, burners sat off to my left. To my right was a fat guy named Rob; he was hammered on vodka all day.

"Smooth and easy; that's our motto here at the Coral Grill," he said every night before the rush began and the tickets came in.

"Smooth and easy," I responded. And this was my new cooking life, day in and out, to the mountain and then to grill, four men to cook fifty plates. No more nachos or microwave ovens, no more fryers or salsa or beans from a number ten can, no more ketchup or french fries or wings. No more chaos or rage. Something went drifting away.

"Order in!" A waitress named Jeannie with a bubbly ass and bubblier personality put in her ticket, blonde as blonde could be.

"I wanna hit that," I whispered to Karney.

"Hmmph, we all do," Karney agreed, rubbing his beard, smiling, nodding. He wasn't *always* a dick.

New Years on Blow

"Fuck him. This isn't goddamn Burger King. You get it our way or go fuck yourself."

"That's the spirit," Rob replied, obediently re-plating the steak in spite of his hatred for the customer's complaint.

We scored an eight ball to ring in the new millennium, hadn't started snorting it yet and were looking forward to getting close to being finished so we could start having what amounted to a very typical New Year's Eve experience following a long shift in a kitchen. It was mostly just pot, "safety meetings" they were called, but on New Years we planned on cocaine, did it up right. I threw the steak back on the grill.

By the end of the night, we were smoking—mixing in baking soda, rubbing it onto some foil, turning the coke into crack, "foilies" they were called, which exploded our heads as we huffed in the fumes through a pen-casing.

"I got it," Phil insisted, "you'll waste it if *you* hold the lighter. Let me do it." He was a master of foilies. He smeared it and cooked it just right, then went on a bit of a rant after we took a few huffs.

"I mean, here's the thing, man. A restaurant like this, up in the mountains, serving fish, bringing that shit over the pass in an already landlocked state like Colorado. That shit's gonna cost way too much motherfucking money to be even remotely sustainable. And people don't know. The average dipshit diner don't know shit about what good food tastes like, so you make it look pretty, dazzle them a little, throw on some parsley or a lemon or some other shit, dress it up right." He paused, pointed the Bic at the foil and sucked up the smoke, splitting the foilie with me.

"Woah." My head felt like it had exploded and shattered to pieces.

"Yeah, *woah*." It's really all that there was to say. Our eyes shot out of our heads. Phil clawed his beard. Our jaws started moving around. We sat there a minute and took it all in. He continued, offering the solution to the owner's problems with fish-waste and other such things.

"So we should at least make our own stocks, no more of that shit that you order from Sysco. That shit's fucking garbage. We could take all the bones, cook 'em down and cook our *own* stocks—chicken, seafood, even veggie—and then make soups and sell them all over town. He's throwing money away like a sucker up here."

"Totally, man. We gotta talk to him about it. First thing, next week. We gotta get through the fucking holidays first, but that's a fucking solid idea, bro. We could start our own biz–Coral Grill soups and stocks—make money and shit."

"Totally, man. Get him to let us use the brand and sell the shit all over town. Everyone gets a cut."

"Fuck yeah!"

"Yeah, Dave. We can do this."

"We totally can. There's no reason why we can't."

But it was just talk. The coke would wear off and that feeling, that god-awful feeling as if you had woken in Hell crept in toward the end of the night. We were grinding our teeth and our good ideas faded away. There was work the next day. The snow was falling, another powder day but I wouldn't make it to the mountain. There were more and more days like this happening, ones where I wanted to ski but was way too hungover.

Sometimes I drank Goldschlager, then woke up and shit out reminders of what I had done, smelling the cinnamon fumes wafting up from the bowl, a shit-stained, golden-lined cloud of sorts, dusted with flakes in the water.

Riding The Canyon

I stayed off the drink for a while, just smoking a bit after work and then driving home to a place in the country where I lived with a hippie named Jerry, a guy who I knew from Fort Collins. We rode every day and my board became part of my legs. I got better and better and better and felt like a pro.

We ducked a rope and then cruised out of bounds, "poaching" fresh tracks in between aspens and pines, over snow-covered logs, and off to a secret location; a spot called the Golf Course, a wide open meadow that hid on a north-facing slope, overlooking a canyon. We flew off the rocks at full speed, soaring up out into space and then splashing down into pillowy blankets of powder. The clouds would close in as the sun tried to poke its way through.

Drinking Alone in the Cabin

The drinking came back, from a place that was dear but forgotten. I started to drink at the bar after work; a bottle of Bud, crisp and delicious and cold from the fridge, specklets of ice in the bubbles. Soon I was picking up cans, twelve at a time, and driving my way to the country to finish them off.

Things would get gold as I finished the second, then the third then the fourth then the fifth, up to the twelfth and beyond. I listened to Dylan then dressed myself up in my gear and sat out on the porch. The evenings were silent and still, with stars in the sky and coyotes howling off in the distance through the cold rustle of the wind as the snowflakes fell out of the clouds. The neighbor would sometimes shoot guns and the shots would ring out. The alcohol warmed up my cells and my blood as I breathed in the crisp, frozen air. I put on my goggles, pretending that I was a spaceman on some distant planet—a castaway. I went in and I sat by the fire, letting the music transport me, then raided the cabinet for Nikolai's whiskey. "I did not giffe vu bermizion to drink mein whiskey." He said to me beratingly in his thick Austrian accent the next day.

"Sorry, dude. I'll replace it," which I did, but then drank it again. Then made another promise, but then did it again, and again after that.

"Now I vill hide it," is all that he said, which he did. I couldn't find it after that.

But I'd wake up, dust myself off and get going.

The Crash

There was a crash. *My* crash happened after a *previous* crash.

It was cloudy and gray, a day with "flat light," where the contours of the mountain couldn't be made out and the landscape was murky and drab. The girl was no older than six and had sort of *appeared*, very suddenly, right in front of me. She was focused and I was a freight train. Her goggles had flown off her head. Her poles had been ripped from her hands. She was crying as hard as a child ever could, with deep heavy tears dripping off of her trembling chin.

"Wiggle your arms!" I commanded to which she obliged as the others appeared.

"Boy, I saw you come screaming down that mountain at what musta been eighty miles an hour! I'm about fixin' to kick your skinny ass!" I think they were Texans, that this was her father, and that she had others who loved her and were coming to get me.

But I had a moment with her in the snow where I told her how sorry I was, and I took her small hand and she told me that she was okay. It was quiet. I reached down and felt a regret like I never had felt and I looked at them all and expressed it profoundly.

I am certain that she could have died. I think maybe angels were watching.

"I'm hitting the park," I said to my friends, and I rode off to do some 360's.

Then I was stuck on my back in the snow. It was cloudy and bleak with flurries fluttering around in the wind. My brain banged my skull, my lungs screamed for air, and my collarbone felt like a sledgehammer smashed it to bits. The pain from one part had its own type of scream, to which each of the other ones answered, brilliantly, as part of some agonizing orchestrated symphony. I thought I had punctured my lungs. It was like I was deep underwater.

"He's repeating himself," someone said as I sort of came to—frowning at the sky, whimpering.

I remember a light in my eyes and the *scanning* machine. There were also some x-rays, then some sort of brace, and then pills. I turned twenty-five the next day.

I hope that the girl was okay. God, in all of His infinite wisdom, had seen to it that I was justly punished for the atrocious act involving the near-death of the helpless child I'd recklessly slammed into. I can't think of a more perfect hand being dealt to a person so truly deserving of the suffering inflicted upon him...

The Doctor

I got the 411 that there was a doctor in town who gave out the *real* medication, a new type of pill, some time-released morphine I heard about through the grapevine of various injured people who fell out as the season wore on. People called them "oxycons," I think, and there was a doc who prescribed them; and I figured that as long as I was hurt, I may as well try to book an appointment with this doctor I'd heard about as I wouldn't be riding or working for quite some time.

It was easy. He examined me, assured me the injury was nothing too severe, and then, with the friendliest of smiles, said "So, I'm imagining they have you on a six-hour pill, yes?"

He was so nice about it and I remember clearly answering him and saying something to the effect of *"Why yes, doctor, you are right! It is only a six-hour pill they have given me!"* I was smiling inside but trying not to show it as I did not want him to pick up on my budding excitement.

"Well then, how about a twelve-hour pill? You see, this way you won't have to remember to take them."

Teacher

It smelled like childhood—markers and construction paper, red rubber utility balls, crayons, and glue sticks. The kid's name was Joe. I guess he was some sort of problem, but he was smart, not with books and math and whatever other public school bullshit, but with motors and machinery—things that *mattered*; and when he stepped up to the plate during kickball, he blasted it out of the park. "I can't!" he insisted, regarding the usual mess of assignments he was handed on the part of Mrs. Mink, who was just sort of mean to them all.

"No, dude, you totally can. So we look over here on the right. You see the nine on top of the two? What's nine minus two?"

"Six!" he exclaimed. He might have been trying to be wrong.

"That's right! That's nine minus *three*, so now tell me what nine minus two is."

"Oh...uh seven?"

"Exactly. Nine minus two equals seven. Say it, 'nine minus two equals seven.'"

"Nine minus two equals seven."

"Again. Nine minus two equals seven."

"Nine minus two equals seven."

"Got it?"

"Got it."

"Good. Correct. High five." He slapped my open palm.

"So we look over here on the left and we take away two from the six and so what do we get?"

"Three!"

"You're right! That's *five* take away two, but what about six take away two?

"Oh! Four!"

"Exactly. So then what's our answer?"

"Forty-seven?"

"That's exactly right. Do you want red or green?"

"Green," he said reluctantly.

"And you tried to tell me you couldn't." He shifted around at his desk and sat up.

"So now try the same thing with this one and then I'll show you how to borrow," I said to him, then went on to the next one they'd assigned me, namely the rejects.

He plastered the star to his folder, went to his cubby, and headed out to recess, ten minutes behind the others.

"Looks like you've carved out a nice little niche for yourself," observed Mrs. Mink.

"We're so happy to have you aboard. You really connect with the kids." This wasn't a thing I was used to, namely anything positive, purposeful, or encouraging.

"It feels kind of normal," I responded somewhat quizzically.

"Perhaps you've found your new path. We're always in need of good teachers." She continued, "Do you have something else that you do? I know this position is volunteer. I sure wish they paid you guys more."

"I'm a cook down at Jay's."

"Ooh, I bet that's an interesting job!"

"Never a dull moment." I went in to work after school.

The Bistro

"This fucking cocksucker wanted sauce-on-side. Run this shit underwater and throw it back on the grill." Miguel was short and as tough as a brick.

"Fuck him," I responded rebelliously.

"Yeah, fuck him, but we gotta suck his dick cuz he's paying our nut. Here, get this shit out of my face," he replied.

"Order up!" I hollered, replating the steak and setting it in the window.

The uppity owner stormed through the kitchen, barking orders and otherwise making our jobs more stressful than they already were. "You know what, I just had an idea. Take a little bit of that hoisin and mix it in with the duck sauce. That way the sour will have something sweet to balance it out."

"Okay," I sort of stared, disgusted and busy as could be. "I fucking hate that cocksucker," Miguel, the chef, whispered to me, keeping his voice low enough to *probably* not be heard. "He never knows what the fuck he's talking about. His fucking bitch wife probably told him the sauce was off. She doesn't know shit either."

"Yeah man," I said agreeably, "they can both suck my fucking cock." I had too much shit going on at my station to worry about it too long.

"You know how they make this shit?" Rick, the guy on my right, asked, sort of baiting me and working sauté. He covered foie gras in chocolate sauce and served it on top of a waffle as a special dessert for the evening, stealing what nibbles he could, dipping baguette in the grease and soaking up scraps of the deliciously sinful culinary delicacy.

"How?" I asked, humoring him as eyes lit themselves from within.

"They shove a fucking tube down the baby duck's throat, force-feed them grain til they puke."

"It's actually a goose, Rick," Miguel corrected.

"Dude," I leaned in.

"Whatever, man. Fuck you anyway, Miguel. Goose, duck, some sort of helpless creature. So yeah dude, they feed it and feed it and feed it until its fucking liver ruptures, turns to the size of a football or some shit." He continued, speaking sadistically, "It's all hanging off its side until it can't walk, like some kind of intentionally-induced cirrhosis."

"Dude! Picture it crawling all lopsided and shit" I added, laughing but still working hard.

"Yeah, dude, but then they nail their feet to the floor so they can't move at all, so it gets even *fattier*. It's like the purest and sickest of fats you can eat. And *that*, my friend, is what we're serving tonight. I fucking love this shit." He pulled a piece from the pan and popped the whole thing in his mouth. There was a grim satisfaction in the way he described the cruel torture.

"Jesus, now I want some," I said ponderingly, snatching a piece from the pan.

"Yeah dude; It's fucking good. The French are fucking evil. They sat around for centuries figuring this shit out. After a while," he continued, "they start to beg for the tube, like whores begging for cock or some shit," he changed the subject mid-sentence, "you still fucking that old chick you met at the bar the other night?"

"If there's nobody better," I replied, classlessly.

"Atta boy."

"Order up! Get this shit out of my window!" I demanded, tearing the ticket and throwing it down near the plate, moving on to the next.

"Dude, that chick is fucking hot," I stated, leering lasciviously in the direction of one of the waitresses.

"Take a fucking number dude and good luck," Rick waxed philosophically, wiping his hands on his fat, bulging, belly, "I mean, who is she other than the girl who guys wanna bang? It's like her only job on this earth is to be some chick who line cooks wanna fuck."

"She does her job very effectively," I replied, putting another steak on a plate. "Jesus, you're telling me," he said, laughing in agreement. She was eight feet in front of us, waiting on one of her entrees, possibly just out of earshot, possibly not.

"Order up, *Alyson*. Dave made it special for *you*."

"Rick, you fucking fatass, why do you always do that?" I barked.

"Do what?" He threw his hands up and wiped Mountain Dew from his goatee, which was dotted with little polyps of grease from the foie gras.

"Dude, I could bang that shit if the mood was right, so stop making *all* of us look bad."

"Dude, she knows you fucked Ruby anyway, so there's no way that she's fucking you if she knows you're fucking her." I got mad, a part of me knew he was right.

"*Fucked*, Rick. I *fucked* her. Fucked her a month ago. That doesn't mean we're currently *fucking*."

"That's not how Alyson sees it. That shit is *quality*, the finest in all of Fort Collins and she knows it. Girls with the quality pussy only fuck dudes who fuck girls with the quality pussy, and I guarantee you she's heard of your philanderings, how in the fuck could she not? I know that you know that I'm right." He continued, smiling, shuffling a pan. "Plus, Ruby likes to brag. She mentions you fucked her every chance she gets. But to her, you see, you're *fucking*. So she tells the wait staff you're *fucking*, not that you *fucked*. And women keep track of this shit. They know all and see all. And to them, at least in this joint, you're the line cook who's fucking the manager who might get them fired if they move in on you."

"Still, bro. Dare to dream," I said hopefully.

Miguel chimed in, "the two of you need to shut the fuck up and get this food out of my window, but Rick's fatass is right, Dave, you'll never tap that ass."

"Fuck both of you. Order up!"

As the night wound down, I reached for the bottle, Christian Brothers brandy, and poured myself shots in a ramekin, then we shut down and scoured the kitchen—sweep, mop, wrap, scrub, empty the fryer of grease, ice all the fish in the fridge, drink all the drinks that we could, pouring box wine over ice, sometimes mixing in beers, then we'd head out the side of the kitchen and into the alley, pack up some bowls and wind down. "We fucking busted that shit out tonight," Miguel acknowledged us all. It was true, we worked like a fine-tuned machine. We all headed out to the bar.

Camel Toe at the Trailhead

One of the waiters, Shane, tapped my shoulder, grinning and pointing a bit to our left. "Don't look too fast but we got some serious C.T. at ten o'clock."

I looked a little too fast, then exclaimed "Woah!"

"I said don't look!" he demanded.

"Fuck, sorry dude," I was laughing, "but for fucking real would you look at that shit!"

"Indeed. I could drive my jeep up into that one."

"Jesus, Mary and motherfucker Joseph; that shit is majestic," I said, beholding the sight.

"Admit it, you secretly long."

"I long, I long," I agreed, laughing and more or less staring at the poor, unsuspecting woman who stood, chalking a pool cue and waiting her turn, swaying a bit to the music.

Cindy, a waitress at Jay's walked up, orange neon reflecting off her tanned, brown skin and big breasts, holding a shot and a beer. "What are we looking at over here?" she asked, curiously, "what's so funny?"

"Epic camel toe action at ten o'clock," I said as I shifted my eyes subtly in the woman's direction.

"Holy shit!"

"Don't look!" Shane retorted.

"Sorry," she laughed and spilled a bit of her drink and stumbled, "but, I mean, I never in my entire life…."

"I know!" I agreed and then joked, "could you imagine *fucking* that shit?" I asked, mainly of Shane.

"I can and I have," answered Shane definitively.

"I knew it," I jabbered, "suckling the teet the whole time, weren't you, Shane?"

"You don't suckle a teet, SuperDave, you suck it," she said, squeezing her left one, then continued, "You boys are filthy."

"As filthy as a fox….or something…I guess…"

"You realize that makes no sense, don't you, SuperDave. You've been blinded!"

"By the light!" I added, hysterically.

The girl walked by and we laughed and she looked; then we laughed some more then took a shot.

"She's gotta get off on that," giggled Cindy, "I'm going outside for a smoke. Care to join?"

"Sure, hook a brother up."

So much was so fucking funny. There was always the laughter and jokes. There was music that blasted the brain cells and made people dance. There were nights when the town was electric, with speckles of ice in the bottles of Pabst, and golden, tanned-skin girls who were easy and fun, and the town was its own, interconnected organism of service employees, mountaineers, kayakers, skiers, and rock and roll people and hippies, with everyone more or less friends. If you didn't know someone then someone else did and I finally felt like I belonged. I was twenty-eight and the hottest shit that I could imagine, having finally *arrived*. And I figured that I'd be a teacher, and that this life of being the life of the party, would seamlessly fade into the background and somehow magically cease.

The Cooler

But there are parts of it all I'm ashamed to admit even happened, mostly little things like the way that I showed off my switchblade, or the leather jacket I wore, or the time that I picked a fight with the club owner who pounded me bloody before the cops showed up to stop it. One time I drank so much whiskey that I needed to rest on my shift the following day. I never drank whiskey; it fucked up my world every time. I sat on a five-gallon bucket—'baby killers' we called them—in the cooler, head on my knees, and the owner walked in and took pity on me and then told me that I should go home, and I knew he could fire me right then and there but he didn't, and so I also then knew that he wasn't the asshole I thought that he was. Then I felt bad and realized I still had a conscience, that it hadn't been washed down the drain with the whoring or pills. He dealt with this stuff all day long: nothing but kids in their twenties, drinking and smoking and screwing and showing up late. I just looked at him, agreed, and left. Then I went to the bar for a 'hair of the dog,' but that turned to one more and one more after that, then another, and I got just as drunk, but on shit that I normally drank so I managed the shift on the following day; then I went out again and got drunk after work, again, and the night after that and the night after that. I said stupid shit. I did stupid things. I played stupid games. I won stupid prizes. I rolled around town on my skateboard, looking for other cold zombies to fuck. It was all rotten fruit. The whole fucking town was just corpses and ghosts.

All of this is devastatingly embarrassing to admit even happened, and that's about *all* that it is when I look back recalling the glory days, I guess you could call them. Was there anything glorious at all? Would you consider hoping you didn't catch an STD and then not catching one, glorious? Is not getting arrested when you're breaking the law an accomplishment worthy of celebration?

Was the time that the two girls took turns sucking me off in the front of my truck really something to brag about? Yes.

That one's a definite yes.

The Demons

There are demons adrift in the bars. They whisper the prettiest words in the ears of the patrons. They capture good souls and entrap them, then they make them do things that infect them with sickness and death. They torture them in the early afternoons when they've finally woken from the spells they've been placed under, and they scream evil thoughts in their ears, stoking regret, one of their poisons of choice.

Look at the fool you've become! Who is this girl or this boy who you've
woken beside? Look what you said! And then look at what they did!
Look at the big fucking mess all of this has become! I know they looked
pretty as pie when you led them away after cocaine and shots. Now
here, try a needle. Push the shit right in the blood. It sure doesn't hurt.
Pretty soon, boy, you'll be dreaming about the syringe!

They hiss and they whisper grim tidings as dark as the night, and they thrive off horrific mistakes—killing joy, perverting love, murdering dreams, disguising themselves as the things that they think that we want: licks on the neck, wet pussy, and throbbing cock, or a bump of cocaine which you're sure will be all that you need as the bar closes down. They twist our biology into sick, suffering lust. They make hunger a gluttonous rampage, sex pornographic and vile, and twist the need to earn and survive into deadly, malevolent greed. Rest becomes sloth. Upset; wrath. Comparison; envy. The spirits make all these things happen, or maybe it's us. Perhaps it is all up to us to transcend the places we're stuck.

How might the angels reply?

Sure, blame it on 'spirits.' I mean, yes, there are these darker ener-
gies. We're aware of them, believe us, and yes, there are people who
often are 'made' to do things that they never imagined they would in
their earlier years. And some are in fact possessed from the start, and
seemingly don't have a choice which still works out for more than you
humans can know with the blinders you wear. All of this is true, but it's
also true that you have choices. That's why you signed up for this ride
in the first place. All that being said, our finest communications are
made to the soul with his or her face in the bar, when they know in no
uncertain terms that none of their charades is bound to end well without
something big. And sometimes they listen and sometimes they kill or
they die, but we do our job every time we're afforded the luxury of doing

so. We'll help you but you have to ask. Some say you might have to beg.
The Big Guy up there who we work for likes begging just fine. It's one
of the most honest ways you can show Him you care. Beg humans, beg!
Throw your sick souls at His feet!

I digress.

"You got any Vikes?" By this time booze didn't work by itself, so I'd hit up Ruby as I knew that she had a supply. I needed the booze but had started to crave other things—Vicodin, Percocet, Lorcet, Lortab— anything morphine-derived, whatever would give me the *feeling*, and the uppity thoughts that made life exciting and fresh.

More Teaching

I'd called the number on the flier at the Pizza Casbah and then met the AmeriCorps woman, then been assigned to the school, which was right down the street from the house I'd been living at with Rico and Chuck and his dog. The dog always shit in the house.

"Dude, you gonna clean up the dog shit?"

"You woke up first."

"That's not the point."

"Isn't it? I guess it's on you if you wanna sit there staring at a pile of shit all day."

He'd slept until five; had been up snorting coke until nine. His dog took a shit around three. The stench woke me up and I'd gone to the Trail-head where they sat at the bar, telling jokes:

Bartender, give me a drink.

SuperDave! What's cookin'? You feeling okay? You were in rare form last night.

I'm good, bro. The roommate's dog took a shit on the floor.

How's the teaching gig going?

Dude teaching's the fucking best. I love these fucking kids.

Yeah, I bet you do, SuperDave.

Dude, no fucking with the children.

What's better than fucking a nine-year-old Taiwanese boy?

Dude.

Don't act like you don't wanna know.

Okay, what?

Nothing.

Bro, that's fucked up.

Yeah, but it's funny as fuck.

True.

What do you tell a woman with two black eyes?

Tell me.

Nothing, you dun' told her twice.

Dude.

I know.

Everyone laughed and we all had a shot. By this point, I only drank shots and day-drank often on Sundays, my only day off.

"Now *there's* the point, dude, the *last* fucking thing I wanna do is stare at a pile of goddamn dog shit."

"Right, but you did."

"No, I went to the bar."

"Without cleaning it up."

"Exactly."

"You ever consider that you might have a drinking problem?"

"Every fucking day. What do you tell a woman with two black eyes?"

"Nothin' you dun' told her twice. You went to the Trailhead, didn't you?"

"How did you know?"

"That one's been going around. That bartender's funny as fuck."

"I think he might be a molester."

"Eight-year-olds, dude."

"That's the funniest scene out of that whole fucking movie."

"I can't believe you *just* saw the Big fucking Lebowski."

"I know, dude. You gonna clean up the dog shit?"

"After a bong hit."

"Alright, fine."

"You know you didn't *have* to move in here with me, man. You coulda stayed up there in Steamboat."

"Bro, I know, but it's a dead-end town in a lot of ways."

I went back to school the next day. The kids were all happy to see me.

Ruby

There were other adventures in cooking—getting head in the dry storage room that sat under stairs—a girl named Ruby, AKA Red, the red-headed manager girl. She stormed through the restaurant on busier nights, her feathered hair wafting and bouncing in ceiling fan breezes. She was easy. Easy was safe.

Someone had bought an old church and then used it for raves. I climbed up a gutter and dropped through an old stained-glass window (her ex-boyfriend was manning the door and would not let me in). I took ecstasy, felt her up in a pew in the back of the church, and then, later that night, walked out the door holding hands with her; I stared at his face and then spit while maintaining eye contact, a move that I learned from Bukowski. He stared at me like I was evil. I stared at him back. She kissed my neck, and looked in his eyes while she did. We went back to my house and fucked until dawn.

The Lamp

"A man could lose his identity fucking around too much." ~Charles Bukowski

There was another, a girl named Marissa; Marissa was friendly with Ruby. She had gorgeous full breasts, pouty lips, and wide womanly hips with beautiful brown eyes that matched her shoulder-length hair.

"I think I love you, little rockstar," she said, lying there, blowing smoke rings up toward a ceiling fan.

"You don't," I assured her flatly, looking around for the bottle of wine I'd been drinking, then thinking she might have some pills. "Got any Pharmies?"

"For a cute boy like you, I just might." She opened a drawer, pulled out a vial of percocet, and poured a few into my palm.

"Jesus," I said, eyeing the bottle, "you shoulda hooked me up *before* we fucked, then I'd have lasted forever."

"I love fucking you; don't ever worry. Girls don't care about that shit the way boys do. Plus, you're like the cutest boy *ever* so you get a pass." She lit another cigarette. The smoke wafted out through the room.

"Don't ever fucking call me that," I demanded.

"Call you what?" She seemed confused I had taken offense.

"A cute boy. That's the gayest shit I ever heard. There were these Jewish broads I lived with a few years ago, and it was all 'cute boy this and cute boy that.' All they did was smoke cigarettes, get wasted, and bang dudes they brought home from Tony's."

"Are you saying you're some sort of man, rockstar? I bet you slept with them too."

"Once or twice."

"The greatest three seconds of their lives," she jeered, laughing and taking a drag.

"Fuck off." I sat at the edge of her bed, suddenly feeling ashamed.

"My *gawd*, I'm just *messing* with you!" She rolled her eyes. "You're *always* so fucking serious. And don't ever tell me to fuck off." She took another drag. "Why are you always so angry?"

"I just am," I responded coldly, fidgeting.

"You're like the unattainable, aren't you? I bet you've been hurt. That's why you're always such an asshole. Who was it? Who broke your heart, little rockstar? Was it that hippie? Christine from the bar told me you used to date this hippie girl a few years ago. River or Mountain or something?"

"How in the fuck did you hear about her?" I was suddenly irritated.

"I hear everything, rockstar. The walls in this town have ears and you know it."

"Jesus fuck. Nothing is sacred when everyone's talking and nobody's listening."

She rolled her eyes frustratingly. I looked around her room, some art supplies sat in the corner along with some paintings. Bobby pins, bras and cinched up, black pantyhose. Cigarette butts in a couple of ashtrays. An apron and all sorts of shit strewn all over the floor. It was breezy; the night had cooled down just enough. I was naked, searching around for my boxers amidst the folds of the sheets.

The Percocet started to work and then there was the *feeling*. That feeling I sniffed out from purses and pockets, and in this case the drawer of her nightstand. "I gotta go," I said matter-of-factly, imagining the longest possible way home on my skateboard. I wanted to skate through the streets, think about my life, and experience the heat of the Colorado summer. The alcohol faded, replaced by the *feels* from the pills.

"What! You're *leaving* me? You had so much to say at the bar like you always fucking do, then you get here, fuck me for three seconds, take my fucking pills and leave. Asshole."

"You don't fucking care, anyway," I said to her, matter-of-factly, and then her eyes twisted themselves into confused balls of terrifying fury.

"WHAT DO YOU MEAN I DON'T CARE!?" She screamed, then picked up the lamp from the nightstand and threw it across the room. "I LOVE YOU AND YOU'RE *LEAVING*!"

I started to exit as calmly as possible; once a woman is scorned, she will leave you to die in a gutter. "You gotta chill. Now you're breaking shit and making a mess, and you wonder why I gotta leave…"

By now she had started to cry.

"Look, I'm sorry. I'm not trying to be a prick here. I gotta get home. It's got nothing to do with you."

"For what?" she endured, drying her eyes. The moon cast its light on her teeth and brown hair. She put on her bra, one strap, then the other, and lay there almost naked and crying; her eyes were trying to catch mine but I was evasive. She put on her glasses.

"So I can sleep," I answered shortly.

"Sleep with me, rockstar."

"Nah, I gotta go."

A part of me wanted to stay.

It felt like a magical carpet. It was sticky and hot and the pills made me feel just right. I rode the long way home. The streets were wide and smooth, and wound through the various neighborhoods. I was up until dawn. The feeling was all that I needed.

The Needle

A girl named Maggie showed up to town with the pills.

"Dude, would you relax?" Miles assured me, "we're just fucking around a little bit."

"Dude, I'm relaxed. I'm just not sure about this shit."

"I mean, I'm happy to get the fucking Dilly off your hands."

"What in the fuck do you call it anyway?"

"Dilaudid, dude."

"How come I never heard of this shit?"

"It's only for seasoned pros."

"Why can't I just eat it?"

"You can shove it up your ass for all I care but it ain't gonna work to its fullest potential unless you slam it."

"Fuck it, give it to me," I said, nervously laughing, excited.

He ran the tip of his index finger over the inside of my elbow, finding the *median cubital*.

"Dude, you got the prettiest veins," he observed, chuckling and enamored.

"Don't you need a belt or some shit, a tourniquet?"

"Not with these puppies." Then he stuck in the tip and pulled back the plunger a pinch as the blood filled the barrel.

It didn't hurt. I wasn't worried about what I was doing or where it was going, or that an act of providence would eventually save me from death, which could likely have arisen as the result of these early experiments at the tip (there is some sort of reference to angels available here, but with devils dancing instead, and syringes. *How many demons can dance at the tip of the needle a junky slams into his arm?*).

It didn't go into the muscle, like an allergy shot or vaccine; it had to blast straight down the lane, into the blood. The sensation itself is impossible to describe, some call it Heaven—the ultimate bliss, euphoria, etc. and I'd be inclined to agree with each of these descriptions. More than anything, however, it just made things kind of *alright*—the most alright that ever could be, but still, just amazingly and perfectly *alright*; alright in the bones and the cells, alright in the eyes and the brain; alright in the way that I ordered a Sprite at the bar, and the bartender, a sweet girl named Kim, looked at me as if I had turned a new leaf and said, "*Alright*, Dave," handing me a Sprite with a look of pleasant surprise on her face.

I played pinball, ordered a slice, and made small talk, chatting up a younger girl to my right. "Where are you from?" I asked.

"Vail."

"Well, alright then..." I answered. "That mountain is epic. It goes on forever and ever."

"It does," she replied, agreeing with all that I said.

A band was playing, some solid punk rock from Chicago. I sipped on the Sprite through a straw, watching the people get drunk. It was *cool*. Miles walked up.

"See, what the fuck did I tell you?" He was shorter than me with tattoos, and was sipping a Coke. His red hair and freckles lit up under the neon *PIZZA* sign.

"Fuckin-a, man. I ain't never felt nothing like this," I said agreeably.

"Yeah, man. They only come around every few years so it's cool to indulge."

Psst

It's a strange type of thing, the earliest days with the rig; you can hide it at first because no one will notice at all. No one can tell when a junkie is just getting hooked. You get happy and calm, go dancing around through green fields in your mind and enjoy the sidewalk passing beneath your feet. For once life is fine. For once life is fair. For once things are good. For once there's no torture or pain or depression. There's nothing to fight and there's nothing to win. There's nothing to fear and there's no way to fail. You'll go skipping along for a while, ride the pale horse, rest in a perfect, warm tub; scratch up your arms and your hair and your knees and your neck. Scratch till you bleed. Scratch all the skin from your balls. The itch that you've had all your life has been finally soothed and everything's fragrant, pretty as punch. Everything's how it should be, like Heaven came down to Earth to the stool in the bar. *Nothing is wrong anymore.* You realize this when the pill, the one you crushed up and mixed in a spoon, hits the blood and goes straight to your brain. *'Where have you been all my life?'* you think to yourself.

They were some sort of morphine derivative, like Oxy but different, but mostly it all was the same if it gave you *the feeling*. The benzos were nice, but more traditionally medicinal, useful for anxiety and sleep and for coming down off of cocaine.

But this was the needle, a no-going-back kind of thing. A deal with the Devil himself.

Sour Patches

It was Wednesday. For fifty I got a pain patch, a sort of Flav-or-Ice pop for adults. A friend of a friend had a father with cancer who died. He left them behind with the rest of his things and she sold them to me on the sly. I tried to "use as directed," like this was some new sort of normal, walking around with a morphine-drip patch. But used as prescribed it was never enough so I cut off the corner and slurped out the liquid in drops. It was sour and tasted acidic, like something that came from a battery. It seeped its way out—onto my tongue and then dripped its way into my throat.

"You got one more left?" I asked the way that I always did, pleasant and polite, but scorching with need and on fire.

"Yeah, I got you, but this is the last one and it's a hundred. There's another guy who's offering one-fifty but you're one of my best customers so I'll ditch it for a hundred if you smoke me up."

"Sold," and the deal was done. She came over, dropped it off, along with a handful of percs, and I cut it open. The snow fell outside, cold and wet with big flakes lit by the streetlamp. It was late in the winter toward spring. I was toasty and lay on the couch, sort of awake and asleep in an opium dream.

I put on the Stones and heard Mick Jagger singing about morphine.

I didn't share patches. The supplier was dead and *I* got his drugs—thank god for cancer and death. If he hadn't died then his drugs would be his and not mine. He would have kept all of the patches, used them accordingly and as directed, and maybe his lack of suffering would have given him just enough will to live. But he rotted away and his body gave out, and he left me with sick, sour treats.

The Fentanyl nights were like presents, a once-a-month gift that I gave to myself. The supplies faded quickly and left behind something perverse, a twisted cruel need that could never be met and a craving for something obscure. For me to get more, someone I knew would need death to be close to their door, and then for a doctor to think that pain patches were necessary. Then, said patient would have to decide that they didn't like patches, that they caused nausea or constipation, and that living with pain would be better than the cruel side-effects; then they would have to discuss how they'd sell them for profit, to someone who knew how to get rid of drugs. Or maybe they'd use them and die, leaving a handful behind, and their son or daughter or friend would then find me in some random way, through a grapevine of twisted connections, sniffing around for the people who'd pay for this strange type of drug reserved for only the sickest of suffering patients. Then maybe they'd make a few hundred by contacting me. I knew all of this as I slurped the last one on a Wednesday.

Outside it was snowy and cold. My room was as warm as a womb. I woke up the next day and would never see patches again.

The place I came to as a kid was now ugly and dark. Something was lost, not to the mountains which take many people, but to vices that lurk in their shadows.

Bad Kids

"Are you sure you want to work here?" the principal had asked me at the interview.

"I think so," I told her.

"You'll see, *slowly* you earn their respect," she assured me, then hired me for a paraprofessional position, a glorified disciplinarian. My job was to add and subtract points from their point sheets, seemingly reducing the troubled youth to plusses and minuses. A polite "hello" earned them a point as they walked into the classroom, and a "fuck you," resulted in a deduction. After accumulating a certain number of points, a student could reach a new level, moving them one step closer to re-integration at the traditional school they'd been thrown out of, which they'd often sabotage as they got nearer and nearer to living supposedly normal lives again.

This was not an alternative school. It was one step below, categorized as "expulsion." The kids here were often in gangs or had been caught doing drugs, and in rare instances were sexual perpetrators. The staff more or less loved and respected them all. An entire book could be written about the experience here alone, but it was here that I heard about the graduate program I applied to and was accepted for, all of this happening while still slaving away in the restaurant world, assuming that it would be easy and that I'd get a job upon completing it, and that I'd leave my twenties behind me and take on life as a professional.

The Professor

"You have to ask yourself, *what's going on inside the mind of the learner?*"
He proposed this question to us quizzically, almost mystically, then continued. "We're shaping young minds. We're touching the future. There is no nobler and more important path than that of the teacher. It's the most important work on the planet. There's no argument here, and each of you needs to congratulate yourself for choosing this path."

I loved learning and learning *about* learning. The professor, a legend and guru of sorts, instructed the class from what seemed like a pulpit. I was transfixed and suddenly surrounded by *colleagues*. They were professionals. It felt like a job. I reported to class, on time and ready to learn with a notebook and binder. It was fall. I was a graduate student.

"The brain, the human brain, learns through best cooperation," he instructed us and then put us in groups, giving us problems to solve. "*Cooperative, brain-based learning* is the most powerful form of learning and cements the lessons into the minds of the learners. The best type of lesson a teacher can teach is a lesson a student remembers forever, and who thanks you for teaching them when you accidentally run into them years later. All of us are touching the future."

We talked about teaching. We called one another. We worked as a team.

Colleagues

"What in the hell is that?" I asked him.

"It's an airport," Joseph said to me, explaining the technology he had set down on the desk.

"An *airport?*"

"It's a portable router. It connects to a satellite. I'm a Mac guy," he said.

"Woah," I said back, very quickly realizing I was stepping into a new world.

We sat in the back of the classroom. Joseph put out pistachios. Another woman, Julia, joined us. We'd all seen the Dead just a few days before and realized this as the result of a team-building exercise we'd done first thing. "They shouldn't have opened with Scarlett," she said to us both.

"Agreed," I agreed, "I wish they'd warmed up and then busted it out for the second set, but, shit, that St. Steven was solid."

"Both of you over there are talking like Jerry's still around," Joseph interrupted, laughing, then looked over at us and sort of whispered, "by the way, do any of you know where to find the *candyman?*"

"I can hook you up," I whispered back.

"I'm liking this program already," Joslin said, chuckling. She was all about science and I was planning on teaching social studies. Joseph loved math. *"It just is,"* he would say and I was suddenly interested in a subject I had always disregarded.

The three of us started a tribe, and there were others we gravitated toward within the cohort, which I'd hurriedly applied for, barely making the cutoff.

The Dead shows were three weeks before, and the previous weekend was a punk fest called Stockage. I was wasted for all of it, drinking myself half to death in what I had told myself at the time was the last hurrah.

"My twenties are over," I'd been saying to everyone, convinced that all of this, *the last fifteen years*, would easily fade into the background. The program started, after all. It would be easy to stop, or I'd keep it to weekends at least, and I'd scored a couple of hundred Valiums to help me to get to sleep at a reasonable hour on the weeknights.

Student Teaching

"Man I'm telling you, I went through the same program ten years ago, and all of it seems like great stuff, but you see what happens when you start putting a bunch of kids into groups and having them teach one another." He'd gone to the Dead shows as well and was teaching me how to teach firsthand. "He paints it out all rosy, I get it, and trust me I tried that shit, but you gotta be careful as you start fighting *battles* you can't anticipate."

"Yeah man, but what about brain-based learning?" I retorted a bit, my bubble somewhat burst.

"Dude, I get it. I tried it. I applaud your idealism and you're welcome to try, but that shit never flew when I did. You gotta *manage* them all. That's the most important thing, *management*." Students walked by in the hallway, the first day of sixth grade for them—figuring out lockers and combinations and the sudden social ordering that had been thrust upon all of them. He got a bit quieter, then leaned in, "By the way, man, you know where to score any *green?*"

"I can hook you up," I told him as the first of the students entered his classroom and he gave me a fistbump. "I'll make sure that they give you an A," he said, sort of whispering, winking.

I loved student teaching. I woke up at five in the morning and a woman who lived down the street gave me rides to Longmont every day. She was on the same team as the teacher to whom I'd been assigned, and suddenly I was a teacher.

Except that I wasn't, because at some point, perhaps some exact instant, I'd developed an insatiable need, and this need had suddenly begun dictating how things would go for me—not only what I would do or not do but what I would think, how I would feel from moment to moment, and what I would say and to who. My entire existence had become a varying mixture of all of its permutations. It could make out the rattles of Vicodin pills in people's purses and pockets and loved getting sniffs of cocaine every chance that it got. It made me forget about sex to a certain extent. It became all that I was, and when it was satisfied, *the high*, its antithesis, emerged with its accompanying agenda, which was *seemingly* a list of appropriate courses of action, one of them, namely, to secure a teaching position that it, *the need*, had made impossible but which *the high* made seem probable.

The need then the high then the need then the high then the need then the high.

The need scored a bottle of ether and then buried my face in a rag. Then the high from the ether would help me forget about pills. The pills were the thing that I needed beyond all the others but the cocaine would help me forget about them. Then it wore off as the mornings arose and the sun shone on all of the chaos of what I'd become; a sick and demented cacophony of *various* needs, each of them screaming in competition with one another. But the need, in all of its evil, had led me to think that a job was the cure to it all, a classroom of impressionable young minds to influence for the rest of their days. It would give me the respite to deal with the brick wall I was screaming straight into. It was so perverse that it convinced me I needed one thing to take precedence over the *actual* thing required of me, which was to surrender the life-and death-game I was playing.

As soon as you get a job.

Selling Meat

I got another job, one in a long string of failures as life fell apart, doing sales of meat door to door. I scored the job in one of my desperate attempts to avoid total destruction. I gave sales a shot, assuming that it would be easy, that my charm would provide me a paycheck.

The job was to go in and sell them the "system," along with a grill, freezer, and cookware set, totaling hundreds of dollars a month and thousands over the course of the multi-year contracts we pitched to the front-range consumers. "You see, we're looking to match what they're already paying, and they get Whole Foods for the price of Albertsons. I mean, they'd have to be stupid not to enroll in our system," another pause, "Don't ya' think, Dave?" His sales mastery sold me right then, but now I needed to venture out to the plains, towns like Sterling and Fleming, swinging their system and going in for hard closes. "But it's not just meat. It's *natural* meats, vegetables, and other fine organic produce and products." He believed what he said. "It's a *system*, the system of the future." Part of *his* job was to make *me* see this, that the meat of the future was brought to your door by their food trucks.

"Now when you walk in, take off your shoes first thing. You're showing the client you're comfortable and establishing a position of dominance. Remember you're a consultant, *not* a salesman. *YOU* are the one in charge, and if you do a good enough pitch, they'll feel stupid for not buying in. Your job is to make them *think* that the two of you are making the decision together. Again, you're a *consultant*. This is the way of the future as far as food distribution goes. Grocery stores will be obsolete in a couple of years; just watch. And when we go public, Dave, we're giving you company stock." He paused and looked deep in my eyes. "Got it, Dave?" intentionally using my name.

"Got it," I responded, as sure as I could be, going along with his pitch and his training. His name was Kirby, a man for Jesus who believed in his system for food distribution and sales.

"Now read me your pitch."

I'd practiced the pitch on my own, dozens of times in front of the mirror at home, in between snorts or injections.

"Okay," I inhaled, feeling the *feeling* lead me along. "So let me show you the system you're currently buying into. You see you've got farmers, ranchers, and growers. Now the way this works is that they send their products to food distribution warehouses where it sits for days or even weeks, waiting to be sent off to grocers, who then mark up the price and sell it to you." He nodded along, pretending to look like a "mark" but then interrupted my attempt.

"Dave, I'm gonna stop you there. Let me ask you, do you believe in our system? I'm listening over here and I'm not sure you do. *You gotta believe it in order to sell.* And if you do, we'll pay you six figures. Ten sales a month and we give you six figures. I don't know how anyone lives on less, honestly."

So I was supposed to walk in, win over their hearts, and then sell them 'the system.' This would be doing them one of the greatest favors anyone had ever done for them and they'd thank me for saving them from the plight of the tyranny of grocery store lines.

Underneath I was falling apart. Beneath all my hatred for life was this dribbling need, for things more than money or sex, for right-minded thinking and feeling, delivered with little pink pills that disguised Hell for redemption.

I was lost. Driving around, trying to sell home-meat-delivery packages—up to Red Feather Lakes, through Poudre Canyon past the Mish, then south to Boulder, snorting the pink and green pills, thinking that I had enough, but then needing to hustle to Brighton to get some from Steve, a sketchy mustached man who I met working demolition the summer before—another job I failed at. *I couldn't even destroy things.* He had multiple refills to help with the pain in his back. He ruptured his discs and I got his pills for thirty or forty a pop. I needed to take more and more of them just to feel right. I'd failed at teaching. I decided to leave Colorado.

Back to Glen Ellyn

Morning Drink—At the Shrink—The West Side of Chicago—The Honeymoon—Japan Part Two—Teach Abroad and Get Paid—West Side Jail—Rehab (Getting the Meds, The Guys, Hilfiger Man, The Girl on the Smoke Deck, Chores, Girls, Frank, Getting Out)

Morning Drink

I wandered the stairways and rooms of the house, into the basement then all the way up to the bedroom I had as a child, wondering why I had left. I'd been gone for twelve years, a coming-of-age eternity, and everyone back here was different from people out West.

"Oh, what, you think *Kerry* would have been better?" one of them said to me accusingly in downtown Glen Ellyn one night. *Who in their right fucking mind?* I thought, riddled with judgments, thinking that this was a joke. *Nobody* voted for Bush.

They had houses and kids, husbands, and wives. A few of them of them snorted cocaine—Republicans on powder.

I got by on pills for a while, a couple of Xanax a day that I stole from the cabinet. They lasted a couple of weeks, but then there I was, very suddenly, with nothing to help with the *feelings* that I had brought back. I got kind of productive. I made it to the interview. I got hired. There were small bits of hope but the pills were suddenly gone and I all of a sudden had these feelings to deal with. That's what so much of this entire debacle came down to ultimately, the feelings I couldn't stand feeling. They were there as a kid and then there with the girls years later. They were always so much, and now here I was—in the basement at thirty, two weeks or so after a rash decision to leave Colorado, stuck, with nowhere to go.

It was dark with dusty beams of early morning sunlight poking their way through the basement window. The air wafted out from the freezer and I smelled an old smell—freezer-burnt pizza or ice cream; something stale.

I took a sick breath and a gulp, which was accompanied by a very clear thought regarding the fact that a deal with the Devil had been further forged, and an understanding that there would be no turning back once I drank in the morning.

I wiped my lips and fought a gag reflex, struggling to keep it down, then took another, opening up and letting it slide down my throat. It was 6:45 in the morning.

Several weeks went by. I needed to stop but was trapped. If I just had a little bit of something else that didn't take my energy the way the alcohol did, things would get better, I knew. I could barely get up off the couch or move up the stairs, grabbing the banister and pulling myself up, one step at a time, requiring all my energy and remembering how strong I once was: *mountains and rivers and Aspen glade fields, on my feet all day long in the kitchen, then drinking all night, chasing sex with loud music blasting.* Every day was the same; I'd wake up shaking, desperate, addicted, depressed, and insane, then go to buy my wine at Malloy's, get home and pour it over ice into a giant coffee mug and slam it, feeling the sugary taste flood my system. My cells danced a moment before they'd shut down and I'd wake them back up with more wine, doing this over and over until I passed out.

I drank the cheap shit from the cardboard display near the door—with prices scratched on with a Sharpie—and the bottles piled up in my closet. *Sixty. Seventy. Eighty.* There was a distinct clanking sound each time I threw a new one onto the pile, and they spilled their way into the room. Each time one landed I said I'd get better, that this was the last, but the pile got bigger and soon there were hundreds, spreading like cancer—a mountain of bottles that took on a life of its own. It was cloudy and gray as the winter wore on and freezing cold raindrops fell down before turning to ice and then finally snow.

I had bruises all over my arms and legs and was swollen and malnourished from drinking all day and night for months. I couldn't move, sometimes getting into a warm bath and pissing myself to avoid standing over a toilet, a useless pig-baby lying in a bathtub of water and urine, knowing I was powerless and insane, then standing and running the shower to rinse off the piss and filth to retain some semblance of humanity. I woke every morning to madness and lust for the drink, trying to force a bit down, but would vomit brown bile, churning out my insides and losing chunks of my body and soul to the poison. My eyeballs popped and sweat poured down my face, drenching me while I knelt with acid-flavored insides slipping out of my stomach and into the toilet, forming abominable, yellow-brown ribbons, then sank and went into the sewers. I could taste it and smell it getting caught in my throat, and it lasted all day and tasted like death because I wasn't really alive or human anymore.

I was a creature.

I lost track of time. It was December or January. The days were short and I often woke from binges, not knowing if it was day or night. The clock said 6:00 and sometimes I smelled dinner and knew it was evening, but sometimes I had to get up, sick and disgusted with myself, and investigate, so I could pretend I wasn't crazy when I ran into my parents.

It could have been six in the morning and I wouldn't have known—as if innocence had perverted itself into a peculiar distortion of what it was meant for. I wanted my parents to know that I hadn't lost track of the most obvious hours and that their son still understood some of the most basic understandings about life, like the difference between day and night, or when it was time to eat or sleep.

"You slept for a while," Mother said accusingly, afraid of who I had become, reminding her or her ancestry, her father and mother, and the disgusting way that she lived with the bruises he gave her. All of it came bubbling up as I crept through the house, a dozen years after I'd left.

At the Shrink

I arrived early, went to a Starbucks, and bought some pineapple and cantaloupe. It was a sunny day just after Christmas and a frigid, cold breeze blew through the plaza, freezing my bones as the sun hung low in the sky. Decay had set in. My insides shone out through to my aura.

I was pacing and shaking and couldn't eat because my mind was doing things that made my body hurt and not function, to which my mind responded by venturing further away.

I leaned against the counter, pale and frightened. The receptionist was cute and likable with brown hair and pointy-framed glasses. "I'm here to see Dr. Smith," I said, assuming that she had her judgments. There were others, everyone minding their business. No one made eye contact, intentionally, as if each was possessed by the same type of shame. Quiet music played and it was dimly lit with soft-colored, orange-brown wallpaper. There were magazines on a coffee table and I grabbed one and tried to flip through it but then put it down, fidgeting in the chair and chewing my nails to stubs. It felt as if bugs lived inside me.

"Just fill this out, he'll be right with you." She was nice. I thought about what she did in the evenings and who her friends were, and if she had a sense of humor about her job. Did she like bars? Did she go out to smoke and make small talk?

"I work in a shrink's office."

"With crazies!?" a guy resembling my former self might ask sarcastically.

"Not directly. I mostly just check them in."

"Sounds cool enough."

"It's a paycheck."

"We all gotta work, I suppose."

The person I *used to be* had become a strange and haunting presence in all my interactions. *Don't you know who I AM?*

That guy had vanished forever.

The doctor came to the door a few minutes later, smiled, shook my hand, and led me through a narrow hall back to his office. It was soft and serene; he was kind and inviting. I sat in a chair and sunk into the leather, relieved to be talking to someone.

"So, how can I help you today?" He asked, quite genuinely.

"I don't know, man. It's like ever since I left Colorado I can't sleep or eat. The anxiety is killing me. It's like nobody here understands, just a bunch of dumbass fucking Republicans," I unloaded, "and I'm living with my parents and they're terrible people, like all that they care about is their big fucking house and the neighbors and what they think. Everyone's so full of shit."

It seemed like he cared, was present and charming, and listened to every word. A cardboard Ambien brochure sat on his desk, perched upright. "I'm sorry to hear it's been such a rough adjustment. Moving is actually one of the most traumatic things a person can go through; did you know that?" He asked as he picked up his pad, grinning a bit, concerned.

"I didn't but I guess it makes sense," I answered, then continued, "the worst part is that I can't *sleep...*" He wore glasses, was probably forty-five, and reminded me of what *could* have been me had I made different choices, as if this unforeseen deterioration had somehow reminded me that things didn't have to turn out this way.

"We'll take care of that, at least get you started on something to get you some sleep, then maybe something for the longer term to stabilize your mood a bit," he answered, encouragingly. Chewing my nails, I looked at the brochure and then looked back at him, trying to not be obvious regarding what it was I wanted. I'd been drinking all morning. He had to have known, as it seeped out of the pores of my skin.

"Is there anything that's worked for you in the past?" he asked. I continued, as precisely as I could trying to not look obsessed, then tried to speak nonchalantly.

"I've been on Ambien a few times. It generally works." There was a moment of tenseness and then release as he grabbed his pen, but then set it down, along with his pad, and picked up the cardboard brochure, smiling again.

"So they've taken this medication, Zolpidem, the one that you mentioned has worked, and turned it into a time-released version." He pointed at the picture, "You see you've got this layer here, the outer one, to *get* you to sleep and then the inner one here to keep you from waking up in the night." He showed me the cross-section. It was pastel pink on the inside with a layer of light yellow inside of the pink one. It looked like a cake and I thought it was pretty, then I thought of the way it would crumble a bit, and then turn to powder and go up my nose. "I'll start you off on the ten-milligram dose and we'll go from there."

"Thanks, Doc," I said, 'happy.' He smiled again, then got up and walked me to the door and back down the hall and into the waiting room, shook my hand, and said goodbye. It seemed like he did this all day.

This was when things became weird—obscure if you will—and stranger than they already were. It was morning, and the pills were supposed to be taken at night, but that would mean waiting all day, and the days were spanning themselves into peculiar, drawn-out eternities.

I drove to the Walgreens, and walked to the back counter pharmacy, handing the slip to a woman with blonde hair and glasses. "That will be about twenty minutes," she said professionally.

"Great." I was polite, like always, but more so because of how pleased I was, suddenly. There were times back in Colorado when sleeping pills were all that I had, on the days when I couldn't score Valium or Vicodin and the only option left was the deep sleep I knew that they'd give me. But, that even stopped being 'deep' when my body adjusted and soon I was waking, just a few hours after taking them and needing more just to get back to sleep, then waking again in the morning, drowsy and doped up. Then, I'd fiend for caffeine, which would offset the pills, leaving me loopy and strange.

She came to the counter with a white paper bag and I heard the sweet victory rattle—Ambien on plastic. "Is there a bathroom?"

"Down to my right." She obliged, answering politely and gesturing toward a hallway.

There were blue pills inside that looked like the ones in the picture. I took out my driver's license and tried to crush one of them, but applied too much pressure and it flew off the toilet and onto the floor. I panicked; sweat shot from my forehead. I got onto my knees, crawling as panic ensued for a couple of seconds before it rolled into my sight.

I grabbed it and fondled around, then stood back up, trying to crush it again, finally smashing it under a crisp dollar bill, turning it all into fine yellow powder. Then I formed lines with my license and rolled up a dollar, snorting one, then the other.

I tasted the drip in my throat, sick and familiar, then went and got back in the truck, drifting down Roosevelt Road.

This decision is nothing I'll ever forgive. What if I'd slammed into kids?

What if, after a long day at the office, working to feed his beautiful family who he loved more than anything, a man came home to discover that part of it was now, suddenly and permanently, gone? And that I was the culprit? What if I'd murdered his son or his daughter or wife? What if my actions had altered his existence to such an extent that no single thing he ever said or did, no thought that he thought or feeling he felt, for the rest of his earthbound life, could ever exist outside of the thing that I did to him?

There could have been cops, after all. There could have been handcuffs and things that would make it much worse; a judge, someone's funeral, and then straight to a sentence I still could be serving. This could have been prison—concrete and steel, and bigger, stronger men plotting the things they would do and then doing them. Then maybe a personal Jesus. A Higher Power. A gang rape.

*Some of you surely have judgments. To more than a few this is vile, inexcusable, and far too perverse to even look me in the eyes should we encounter each other. Some of you hate every word, having been affected by deeds of this nature yourselves, and a part of me, a very substantial one, surely agrees that I should have been locked up forever. There's nothing I'll try to excuse about any of this. And sometimes living with what **could have been** is the hardest part of surviving this horrid ordeal. And I'll try to explain without skirting responsibility, that SOMETHING WAS 'MAKING' THIS HAPPEN. There was something in charge—the Devil himself, perhaps, or some otherwise mad and sadistic puppeteer? Something that crawled in when I was in one of my fits? The ghost of my long-perished grandfather? A goblin from one of the trips?*

*All this being said, however, and with all 'possession theories' aside, along with any attempt to discover the existence of anything external or 'otherworldly' that might in any way help me or anyone else to make sense of this madness, it must be stated, that I understand, unequivocally, that monsters should not be allowed to do monstrous deeds, and their deeds should never go unpunished, no matter what happened that set them upon their dark paths. **Each of us is ultimately responsible.***

There was a crash—a boulder I'd veered into in a ditch on the side of the road, and an airbag, then a long rest 'somewhere else.'

I woke up hours later. My face and ribs hurt. The grain of the paneled walls in the basement towered over me, screaming down. The shelves of books surrounding me stood in silent disgust at what I'd just done while a kind, loving heart still beat quietly inside my chest. Time stopped.

I knew what was happening.

There was nothing I knew that could stop it.

The West Side of Chicago

"You been down, man?"

"Down where?" I asked, getting clear about what he was asking.

"Bro, don't play stupid. To see the gym shoe kids, the kids swinging blows. Fulton or Maypole, off Cicero. Wherever."

I feigned interest for the rest of the call—a friend from Chicago I did pills with in Colorado—another minute or two. I didn't get specific. *But* **where** *on Fulton? What do I say? Do I have to get out of my car? Will they kill me?*

The suspense never left. All of the times I went down had the same sort of fear.

I still had a license.

I needed to take the Eisenhower.

I got in my truck. The windshield was spidered; the airbag was still hanging out from the crash. My mind was all torture and gore and I'd been drinking wine. I had a residual concussion with thoughts coinciding.

You certainly are a strange kind of fucked, don't you think?

You know that the door has been firmly shut behind you.

You are going to die....

I got to the exit and drove up the ramp, coming to a stop at the red light on Cicero. I looked left, then turned as I started to shake, moving northbound six or eight blocks, spotting the street on the right. I headed east into the neighborhood.

People were staring from porches. Ladies pushed grocery carts, not acknowledging or judging my visit. An old man was pulling a shopping cart up the street and into the wind toward a setting sun, insistent on getting it somewhere. It was chilly and gray, like most of the days after Christmas, and a few remaining leaves fell from the trees in the parkway and then drifted around, rustling. A prostitute crossed the street in front of me, slowed down a bit, made eye contact, and smiled.

Trash was littered around as kids crisscrossed the street, looking over their shoulders and shouting toward one another, breaking up the other-wise quiet scene, scoping things out and making signals with their hands, watching for police as customers drove down the street. My breathing sped up as I started to chew on my nails. There were two blocks to move down, then a right turn at Kenton, followed by a quick left and more driving eastbound under a bridge to Kostner. I got gassy and bloated, approaching "the tip," as it's called.

There were black kids in black canvas coats gathered around a store on the corner, wearing headphones and Timberland boots, eating chips and meandering around in the cold. They seemed to be all going places without really *leaving*—whispering, wishing, colluding, conniving; having a chance at it all, *the game* as they call it. I imagined them lying awake every night wondering, and plotting different courses for the next go around.

I wasn't afraid of the dealers, more of a cop coming around the corner, pulling me from the truck and asking questions. They were instantly something to fear. Andrew had stories.

*"They caught Tony down there, broke his arm on purpose with a fucking billy club then took him to jail. Tony gets to the front of the line and just wants to go sit in a fucking cell. There's all these other junkies— they were doing some sort of sweep that day—and some lady-cop asks him what's wrong with his arm and he tells her what happened and she makes him go to the back of the line. And he gets **back** to the front and she asks him again and he tells her he fell."*

"Jesus."

"Yeah, dude. CPD don't fuck around."

One of them looked toward me and nodded his head upward, asking what I wanted. "Blows," I mouthed from the car, but he didn't read lips. He got frustrated, rolled his eyes a bit, and grinned, walking up to the truck.

"Would you relax, man? You ain't no cop, right?" he asked, non-accusingly.

"Fuck no," I told him, assured.

"What-chu-want then, dawg, rocks or blows?"

"Blows."

"How many?"

"Two," I answered—still shaking, but now excitedly so.

"Alright, then. You ain't got nothin' to fear with us so long as you cool. It's them 5-0 you gotta watch out for, you hear me, G?"

"Yeah, I hear you," I answered, relaxing a bit.

He signaled, then someone was there, banging on my driver's side window. Another kid who had seemed to appear out of nowhere handed me two packets wrapped up in duct tape. I gave him a twenty and quickly drove away, over a dead cat in the road, making a right onto Kostner headed south toward Washington.

I pulled off to the side of the road and peeled the duct tape away. There was a piece of foil inside I unfolded, then I buried my nose in the dope. It tasted like battery acid, sick and sour. I gagged, but not like I did from the wine, and coughed a little and spit out the window.

It took a few seconds, and all of the fear went away. I got smooth, *real* smooth, like jazz from the '50s and '60s. I turned up the volume and bopped with the rhythm and bass, blending with traffic, the lights and the trails that it left, and the bustling activity of the Eisenhower Expressway. I took a deep breath, the first in a while.

The Honeymoon

Everything came back to life. I bathed and I slept and I put down the wine. I bought smokes, had one after another, and walked through the streets. *I've found the solution,* I said to myself.

The evening was crisp. It was late, after midnight, and all of the town was asleep. *It's like all that I needed was me.* The beginning is like this: you go skipping through fields in your mind, live inside daydreams, and turn into something that others wish they could become, like some sort of character very few will ever play. You might climb a tree. You might call a friend or go dancing, then stop at a late-night diner and chat up the staff.

"I can tell this is real hollandaise, not the powdered shit," you might say as you get used to having tastebuds again.

"I see you've put in your time in the kitchen," the waitress might answer.

"Eight years, non-stop."

"I knew I liked you."

It doesn't cost much to get started—cheaper than pills, better than sex, sweeter than wine—you assume this is how it will go.

Your friends might be happy to see you.

"Looks like you finally pulled your head from your ass," one of them says at the bar.

"I'm laying off shots from now on."

"Good idea. Have a beer and relax."

Things became *easy.* I stayed up late—walking the halls of the house, adjusting the knick-knacks, folding laundry. All of the things I'd forgotten came stumbling back.

Hey Dave, it's me, music. I've been missing you, man! Remember the way that I sound? Remember the things that you feel when I'm hanging around? This is some rich shit, man. Hang out for a while. Here, have a little Jerry!

Yes, I loved music!

Hey man, it's me, hunger. Yes, your appetite! Remember the tacos from back in the day? And the burritos you loved back in Colorado? Yeah, man! Let's go get some burritos. I've missed you, man. Good to see you again! Let's eat!

Food is delicious!

Hey Dave! Man, it's me, sex! Remember me?! Remember how much you LOVED me? Maybe with a little luck, we can hang out together again! It was always so easy for you to get me as soon as you called. Stay in touch, man. I've been missing you!

I'm gonna get laid! Soon!

Hey Dave, it's me, cold beer in a bottle! Man, you've been hitting that wine in the morning too hard! Lay off for a bit and hang at the bar with me. You used to love me before you went overboard. Sit down and relax!

So I did. I went to the bar, relaxed, felt normal and talked to the people around me. That crash had been some sort of calling for me to wake up! And now I would turn a new leaf! All I would need was a pinch, a nip here and there while I got my life back in order.

Psst.

*Hey Dave, it's me, **China**. Heroin, that's right.*

*You've finally found me! I knew that we'd meet, someday in some way. First of all, don't believe the rumors; people are always saying the meanest of things about me. It really hurts my feelings. Whatever you want to call me is fine—China, smack, junk, whatever; just don't call me tar. This is **Chicago**, after all, so don't mix me up with the shit from out West. Just know that I'm your friend now. And for God's sake, don't worry so much!*

Do you see how much you've been worrying!? For what!? Why would you worry so much? Can't you see that it's always been handled, every last bit of it??? And what did I cost you, twenty bucks? I mean, seriously, think about that! Twenty bucks for a couple of days. That's a steal! And maybe in another couple of days, it will be another twenty bucks. I'm cheap! But I won't treat you cheaply, I promise.

Trust me.

We're in this together now, just the two of us.....

(Just the two of us...you and I...)

The drink went away. The nights came alive. I drove to the city, scored a couple of bags, and went over to Jeremiah's, and we sat listening to records and looking at old pictures from back in the day.

"Shit, man. I remember that night." It was a picture of Josephine in Joslyn's room he had loaded onto his computer. "Where does the time go?" I asked, quizzically.

"Fuck if I know, man," he answered, somewhat stoically.

"Shit, man. What, we've known each other twenty-five years now? Time flies."

"It sure does."

"Fuckin'-a, man. I'm getting my shit together, finally. Had a rough go for a minute."

"You sure did."

"I think I gotta take that job."

"Maybe you should. Maybe not," I dunno, he said, fidgeting with one of his remote controls, not really looking at me.

"It's a big opportunity."

"That it is. That. It. Is," he answered, took a deep breath and stretched a bit as his hoodie cinched up. "I'm going outside for a smoke."

"Cool dude, I'm down. Lemme bum one."

"I've got a call to make. Have a beer. Relax. Here's the remote." I sat back, opened a beer, and whistled along to the music. He walked back in, sort of sighed. "So what, you're *whistling* now all of a sudden? You were nothing but frowns the other day,"

"Yeah, dude. I'm getting my shit together. Finally."

"I can see that."

I showed up a couple of nights later, excited to see him, smoking cigarettes, smiling, and whistling a tune in the wind, which had carried me swiftly through the city and onto his porch.

Jeremiah was quiet, half-heartedly saying hello. He went into his room and then threw a rag into my lap. It was filthy and smashed in a ball—a clodded-up, wadded-up mess that he'd kept for some reason. I picked it up, not knowing at first that the soiled object I was handling was in fact Andrew's blood-stained shirt.

Andrew had borrowed some reefer from Jeremiah a few years before, then traded it for blows. After successfully pulling off more than a couple of barters, he'd been kidnapped, pistol-whipped, and forced to drive at gunpoint across the city—from the west side to Jeremiah's in Logan Square, so that the dealers he'd been dealing with could rob Jeremiah of all of his weed.

"Dude, you can't be bringing dope over here anymore. Don't you remember what happened to Andrew?"

Hey, Dave. Don't worry, man. I would NEVER do anything like that to you. I mean, you know Andrew—always careless, getting into trouble, breaking the rules (at least a lot more than you). Don't listen to Jeremiah. Remember the way he would treat you when you were a kid? I love you, man. Shit, did I say it too soon? I ALWAYS do that. Well, I do.

It's true. And I'll never leave you.
Just the two of us…

I was feeling so good—as free as a fish in deep water—that some bloodied-up shirt could do little to hinder my flow.

"I'm gonna tell you one time. Knock it off. Andrew had the same shit; thought it was all chill. Thought he had it figured out. He didn't." He continued. "So you can hang here tonight—relax and drink beers—but I don't want you bringing any more of that shit over here from now on."

I didn't have too much to say.

DON'T LISTEN TO HIM!
I LOVED ANDREW TOO AND HE LEFT ME!

There were stacks of records and newspapers scattered around the filthy house where he lived on Western. "I hear you, man." I answered, sinking the tiniest bit in the cigarette smoke. But there were no intentions of stopping. The city was coming alive with my newfound happiness—a poppy field, wonder-filled cabaret. I was drifting along in green fields, dancing through freshly cut grass. The music rang tunes I remembered from lifetimes ago. I skipped through it all, delighted.

Japan: Part Two

The entire thing culminated in some sort of manhunt, almost as if I'd become my own very demented version of an international celebrity. Not that I was a fugitive, exactly, but a man on the loose nonetheless. My mother was dying from worry. My brother was out in Fort Collins, waiting to hear any news, and he'd told a few people, each who then told a few more, and suddenly it was a joke—the biggest in all of the Fort.

SuperDave's missing.

Missing from where?

Lost in Japan or some shit.

What the fuck happened?

Well you know he went over there to be a teacher. I guess he just sorta disappeared. Like no one had seen him for days so they unlocked his room and he was just totally gone.

Gone?

Totally fucking gone?

Where in the fuck did he go?

No one knows.

Why did he leave?

Fuck if I know?

Kidnapped?

Sure, by the Japanese mafia.

Maybe he banged one of their girlfriends.

I wouldn't put it past him.

Give me a shot.

To a successful return!

Perhaps they had all raised a glass.

There was an ad in the paper.

Teach Abroad and Get Paid

Months before, just after arriving in Chicago, I applied for a job, desperate to still be a teacher. I pounded some drinks on the train, then again at Ogilvie with the day traders at a bar, and walked to Lasalle for the interview. I'd been wasted for over a month.

I walked in, dressed in a shirt and tie, and gave the guy a bow. "Actually, Dave, we don't want to focus on Japanese stereotypes, but I appreciate your enthusiasm," the nice man said, adjusting the energy just a little bit. He was tall, much bigger than me, with a gentle spirit and thin brown hair parted to the side.

"Oh, my bad," I said, acquiescing.

"We'll cover the customs if we decide to move forward, but first I'd like to lay some of it out for you. Do you have any questions before I begin?"

"I mean, I have all sorts of questions, but first I'd like to hear what you have to say."

"Well, first of all, I cannot emphasize enough the commitment side of things. It's a big commitment, and a life-changing experience, but only one that comes from committing to something almost bigger than you. At least that's how I see it. So let me ask you, is this something you really want to do, that you think you'd be really willing to commit to?"

This was the essence of his communication and the essence of the interview. Was I willing to make a commitment much bigger than me? And I, in the midst of a drunken stupor, had somehow convinced him that yes, I was in fact capable and willing to make this sort of commitment. I'm not sure what I said, exactly, but I somehow convinced this nice man that I was, in fact, a very suitable candidate for an overseas excursion.

"I got the job!" I said to my mom soon after receiving the call, drunk.

"That's um, great," was all that she said, less than enthused.

***"YOU NEVER APPROVE OF ANYTHING!"** I internally screamed.*

*"Feel **good** about it," my dad had said to me.*

*And I did. I felt **great**.* I'd been going to score dope every day. It was friendly—chicken and rib tips and ribs, barbeque joints, garbage, and delicious glass bottles of cream soda they sold in one of the bodegas. I loved hanging out in the streets after scoring my dope and got friendly with some of the locals.

"Shit, man. I see your ass down here almost every day, Dawg. What type of shit is you on?"

"Fuck, G. I'm just tryna get a hit and a beer like everyone else," I replied, laughing.

"That's my guy," he said, smiling as well. His name was Curtis but they all called him Trick. He was little, maybe 5'5", thin, and sometimes brought dope to the truck. He ran when he worked, fists clenched at his sides and enthusiastic.

Suddenly one day after making the drive down and getting to the spot I'd been used to scoring, no one was out—in front of the store or at any of the other corners. I drove around for a bit, up and down various streets but the dope was now suddenly gone. All that remained was this *feeling*, this god-awful, terrible need. I drove for an hour, gripping the wheel and looking for one of the faces I'd grown accustomed to, but no one was there. It was like they had vanished forever. What would I do if the dope was all gone?

I went back to the doctor, and convinced him I turned a new leaf. "Good to see you again!" he said, still smiling and handsome, willing to give me more pills. He wrote me another prescription, more Ambien along with some Xanax and Adderall, and sent me on my way, shaking my hand and wishing me luck on my trip. "You're going to go far..." he said as I left.

*The plan was for each of these pills to get me through the next several days after leaving Chicago with all the withdrawal symptoms I hadn't yet **fully** experienced. There were a few times I tried to kick the dope before I left home but I could never make it more than a couple of hours. Once the symptoms kicked in, I needed relief from the suffering because it was the worst pain imaginable, like a stinging inside of my blood, followed by nausea and puking up bile in the toilet, so I'd come down easy, load up on Ambien and Klonopin over the next several days as the symptoms ran their bell-curved course of misery, anxiety, depression, uncertainty, and pain. I'd do this in Japan as I trained for my job as a teacher of English as a second language, weaning completely off dope over the course of the next seven, eight, nine, or ten days, then completely putting my life back together as I developed myself into an American professional on foreign soil on a mission to educate Japanese children on the nuances of American customs, language, and etiquette.*

The nice man was handling things and making all the necessary arrangements to ensure that my trip would go smoothly, an ambassador of sorts.

And then one day, after multiple interviews and appointments, it was time to depart on my voyage.

They were serving free drinks on the plane. *It must be my birthday,* I thought to myself, as the plane ascended upwards and into the clouds. I'd managed to sneak on the tiny bit of the dope I had left and I snorted the rest in the bathroom. I figured that things would be fine, but then very suddenly they weren't fine at all, and out of nowhere, in a single terrifying instant, I realized what I had done, and then came that terrible need, along with a dastardly realization.

The dope had been lying!

Well yes, Dave. I mean, you see that this was the plan from the start. This IS what I do. I am heroin, after all. This type of thing happens ALLLLLLLL the time, but I have to admit that I didn't think it would work out this nicely. I mean, I of course figured you'd end up at the pawn shop, maybe get arrested or jumped by the boys on the corner, or that you might possibly die—the usual things that happen when naive children like yourself make these types of deals with me, but this, THIS, David, THIS is unsurpassed. I mean, look at you HERE ON A PLANE TO JAPAN! Now don't get me wrong, the jails are bad, terrible actually, but this is a new type of thing. There'll be customs and norms and a JOB! And you see, you've also forgotten that you are a drunk, that before you found me you were drinking to make it all better. YOU WERE PISSING YOURSELF, REMEMBER! AND THE AMBIEN NEARLY KILLED YOU! Well, I've got news, it's all coming back! And in such a strange place. This is exciting! You actually thought you could do it. YOU ACTUALLY FUCKING BELIEVED YOU COULD PULL THIS ONE OFF! Well, much to your chagrin, you couldn't. It's okay, though, right? You've still got the booze! And the pills! But it looks as if MY work is finished, at least for the time being! Good luck, my friend!

I ordered a drink and then took a few pills as the dopesick got worse by the second, twisting itself into its own sort of sinister entity.

HAHAHAHAHAHAHAHA!!!!! Sweet little David, you're fucked! Jeremiah tried to warn you, remember? You really should have listened. I mean, yes it's true that Andrew got robbed, that they almost killed him in fact, but here you are BOUND FOR JAPAN! I mean, I figured that

maybe Cook County Jail would be in the cards, but perhaps now you'll
get locked up overseas. Even better!

Then I drifted away to the land of the lost, coming to as the plane hit the runway.

They sold handles of whiskey on the plane, some sort of duty-free thing that happened on international flights, so I bought one and carried it off. I stumbled and sort of remember some people standing there being polite and accommodating and holding signs, some of them being my colleagues.

Look, Dave, they're waiting for you!
Quite the spectacle you've made of yourself, here, isn't it!?

I was dragging my bag behind me and carrying the bottle. It was heavy, so I perched it on top of the suitcase to make it easier, bumped into a railing, and it fell a story or two and shattered on the walkway below. The people looked up, pointed, and spoke words that I didn't understand. I stared back at them, lost in chaos after riding delusion.

*Fuck. Fuck! Fuck FUCK **FUCK**!* I looked down over the rail, then seemed to float with the ghosts off to some other place.

I awoke in a room a day later, as sick as could be in a puddle of puke. I went in and out for another twelve hours or so, clawing the blanket and hearing the heroin sing, sadistically.

Gone baby gone, love is gone.
I can't help you, sweet David, you left me back home in Chicago!

I tossed around for the next several hours, disgustingly sick as if bugs were marching along inside the grooves of gray matter, and once I had finally awoken, sleep became, very suddenly, impossible. It tore at my brain like a jackhammer. There was itching inside of my skin.

It was raining a soft gentle mist outside of the window and a desk sat in the corner with a lamp that lit the room dimly. I finally got up, walked to the bathroom, and stared at myself in the mirror, astonished at what had just happened.

I finally collected myself and went into the adjacent room. It was evening and each of my colleagues was there—playing games, watching TV, resting and preparing to teach. I wasn't sure who had seen what. *Well don't just sit there, Dave, SAY something!*

I could hear my heart thumping, and the rivers of blood in my veins. There was noise on the outside—the normal sounds of a foreign land—but inside a sledgehammer banged the insides of my skull. There was also a sinister silence that came on in waves, and a feeling of being trapped inside a funhouse mirror hall with a floor made of quicksand and a collapsing ceiling—locked in a riddle, trapped in a scream—psychopomps swirling around. Everywhere I looked, there I was, groaning gutturally and moaning on the inside.

It felt as if I had been kidnapped.

West Side Jail

I was partying at Paul's on the Fourth of July, a month or so after return-ing. I was drinking a beer and along came the need so I headed to TCF bank on the South Side of town, way out on 95th street, the only one that was open in all of Chicagoland. I had taken a break for a couple of days and then soon I was up to five bags before noon. "Lemme get a hundred," I told the teller, laying down the credit card for the cash advance.

"Thank you," the Indian boy said with a smile as he counted the bills.

I was driving too fast, and flew through a light on a mission from 95th, the only open Jewel on the holiday, with the TCF bank that gave the cash advances. I was close to the spot, just a few miles South, almost home-free when I flew through the light.

The cop wasn't mean, politely inquiring, "What are you doing over here?"

"Uhh, coming back from a party."

He grinned like the Cheshire cat. "A party? Over here? Shit, man. What kind of friends you got? Rappers? You a gangster or something?"

I laughed, then he laughed. "No, man. Just passing through, you know?"

"Oh yeah, I know." He was friendly. "Been drinking?" he asked, point blank.

"Yeah, I'm fucked up," I responded, also point blank. I didn't feel like making shit up.

"Get out." He slapped the cuffs onto my wrists, then drove me off to a precinct.

"Blow," he commanded, holding the machine to my mouth. My hands were still cuffed—a jail inside of a jail. I leaned forward, obeying.

"Damn, guy...167. I'm *impressed*. You sure can hold your liquor." He had a thick, blue-collar accent and a roll of fat hanging out over his belt. He led me through the station and put me inside of a cell.

The door slammed shut. The floor was brown-blackish-green. Puke, sweat, piss, other fluids, and infections—Staph, MRSA—had leaked their way into its pores. It was shiny and cold, and moisture condensed its way out from the concrete, then dripped down the walls in beads of sick sweat.

I waited on morning's arrival as the dark, yellowed-light cast dim shadows throughout the cell and I held back tears, needing a fix, stuck on a floor in a cell that had somehow turned cold in the greasy, mean heat of the summer. It had a hard bench, as solid as marble with none of its beauty, and the toilet was filthy and foul. The cell had black bars. Freedom was ringing outside.

A guy, a little bit older than me, was led into the cell. He greeted me. I greeted him back, and he started talking.

"Say, man. Listen to this here bullshit. This motherfuckin' policemen dun' grabbed me and my cuz who wasn't doing shit but hanging out and drinkin' ourselves a beer on the fourth of *July*. And this-here pig comes rollin' up, tellin' us he has a warrant. I looked at him like "Fine, officer, I ain't got shit." But my cousin, he has some weed in his pocket he forgot about, and so the motherfuckin' pig arrests *BOTH* of our asses and tells us the judge will sort it out. Some bullshit man." His skin was dark brown and he had a round face with bright white teeth and big round eyes. He kept talking. "So now I gotta sit my fuckin' ass in here until tomorrow and wait like some sorta sucker." He seemed like a good enough guy.

"That's some crazy-ass shit," I said to him, trying my best to fit in.

"Shit don't matter, Joe, they don't give no fucks," he replied.

A guard stood outside the front of the cell, chatting with one of my cellmates, like they were old friends who'd grown up together.

"Say, man," he pleadingly requested of the guard who stood six inches away, "get me a Mountain Dew?"

"I can't man," the guard responded.

"Aw man, come *on*. I'm a thirsty motherfucker and this here toilet water tastes like shit," he pleaded again, almost demanding.

"You know I can't do shit, man," the guard replied then walked away, creating just enough distance between to get his point across, and the man drank the water that spilled from the foul, soiled spigot.

Nothing made sense anymore.

The morning arrived and I was set free with a couple of papers. The late morning temperature combined with the humidity-drenched summer sun that was pounding the blacktop and radiating itself into the atmosphere, creating ruffled convections of sweltering heat. I got on a bus, grabbing the overhead strap, and headed away from the jail, back toward Cicero to a spot I knew sold dope, exiting somewhere near Lake.

I looked up and saw my reflection in one of the storefronts; and there was Calvin, Dancing with Hobbs on my torn-up old Dead shirt, singing, *What a looooong strange trip it's been...*

A car pulled up. "You looking to cop?" a guy mouthed toward me from inside the vehicle, seemingly wanting to help. I told him I was and got into his car.

He was clean-cut. His clothes were pressed but his skin was a sick, ashen gray. "How long you been doing dope?" he asked.

"Four or five months," I answered.

"Then it isn't too late. You gotta turn back before shit gets bad. I been on this shit for eight years, methadone and everything. That shit's even harder to kick. It isn't too late."

I took it all in; the words struck a chord in my soul. "I hear you," is all that I said.

He pulled over to the side, a couple of blocks down on Lake, trains racing overhead. A kid walked up, handing him a package containing several bags. He handed mine over to me, took out his rig, and nonchalantly began cooking his dope right there in his car, bubbling it up and then slamming it into his arm. I took one of the foils. It was wrapped in a strip of red tape. I sniffed up a pinch and a gurgling cauldron of saliva formed itself inside my mouth. I opened the door up and vomited out the side, more of the green-yellow sick.

"Ah, come on, man." He was pissed.

Sorry, dude. "Can you take me to the impound lot over on Sacramento?" It was miles away, and likely where my car had been taken.

"Alright, man." We drove along, each of us high and relieved. The windows were rolled down and the heat seeped its way into the car.

He dropped me off. The sun shone down as the day grew hotter. The car wasn't there. I wandered off in some direction, eventually making it to a train and taking it home.

It wasn't long after this that I made it to the first of a couple of institutions.

Rehab

Getting the Meds

They gave me suboxone in detox which made it quite pleasant. I slept and I ate and I shit and I caught up on reading, but this meant that it wasn't real. If sleeping's an option, withdrawal is a walk in the park. It's the not sleeping part that will get you, not the puking or shitting yourself or the shakes or the chills. It's that nighttime will come and you'll know of the hours ahead, that you'll toss and you'll turn and you'll beg for just one hour of sleep and then nothing will happen. The boozers come in and pass out, then they wake up refreshed and start eating and putting on weight. Same with the coke fiends and crackheads; they never have trouble with rest. The junkies stand less of a chance on account of no sleep. Dopesick will break you. Dopesick is warrior training. Dopesick makes people suck cock. You may as well be Semper Fi if you live through withdrawal.

They took the Suboxone away when I got to the unit. The guys said the Seroquel worked so I waited all day, through the wake-up routine, over to the smoke deck for coffee and cigarettes, then therapy, more therapy, lunch, and a rest, followed by "group" where all the guys whined about problems, then we had rec and a quiet time where we, a group of supposedly grown men, were forced to put our heads down for an hour before dinner. Then we had dinner and a meeting afterward, then watched T.V. At the end of the day, we lined up for pills before bedtime. I'd waited all day and I hoped that the Seroquel worked.

The Suboxone was orange, the new pills were yellow and round. I swallowed them down, expecting relief, but instead became anxious and wired, and the night lingered into a long, dreary, and uncomfortable wakefulness.

Bed.
Blanket
Pillow.

Pace.

Bathroom.

Bed, again, and then out to the unit. "You have to go back to your room," said the woman on shift. She was kind with blonde hair and had beautiful eyes that were blue and was reading The Bible. *Fuck you, you god-awful cunt.* I went back to my room.

My thoughts were screaming—the court case, the tracks in my arms, and the trip to Japan. I got suddenly sick, staggered toward the toilet, puked out vomit as black as the night, and then shit out whatever was left. Termites were chomping my brain.

I walked *back* out of my room and saw Brett sitting there at a table. He was able to charm the nice lady.

"What's up, kid?" He was gay and had starred in gay porn. *Best oral and best bottom bondage. I was good, real good,* he had said about his performance the previous night, the one that had won him the prize.

"Dude, I'm basically just planning on not sleeping for all of the rest of eternity," I said as he gave me a cookie.

"You'll get through it. Trust me, I been there. This is my fourteenth trip. I've been to all sorts of these places; ended up in the Salvation Army twice. This one's a fucking resort, so make the best of it because you're gonna end up in prison if you don't get your shit together. I had two years clean at one point back in the '90s."

"Dude, what the fuck are you doing going to rehab *fourteen* times? Are you insane?"

"You get used to it. Sometimes the real world is too much. And look at you pointing your finger. You got three pointing right back at you."

He left and went back to his room.

Dawn arrived. The birds sang songs outside the window. My stomach was tied into knots and I hadn't had sleep.

The next night they all cheeked their doses and gave them to Adam who gave them to me, a big fucking pile of pills. It still didn't work. I threw up some more and it felt like my legs were on fire. I wanted to scream and jump out of the window and started to hear little voices. "I'm afraid that I'm going insane," I said to the woman.

"Then you might need to go to the *ward*," she responded, keeping her eyes on her verses. I got what that meant and went back to my room, the voices still haunting my soul. I clawed at the sheets and the pillow, then pounded my head with closed fists, trying to knock myself out. My eyeballs and tongue were dried out from the meds and I started to hear voices.

We have you now, David, they hissed. The next day was worse, and the next one was worse after that.

I finally started to sleep after five or six nights.

The Guys

The campus was manicured perfectly with a ball field and volleyball sandpits. Most of the guys lifted weights.

Jim, a South Side guy who fought fires and who loved to smoke crack, talked about strippers incessantly. "I knew this stripper. She used to come over and fuck me *whenever* I wanted. She had the biggest fucking titties I ever seen." He made a grabbing motion as if reaching for dangling melons. "Ain't nothing like a nice set, am I right?" I laughed and agreed, smiling.

"Oh yeah? Fuck that and fuck you. I fucked my wife's *daughter* before we were married. Fucked them both. My wife's actually hotter and better in bed," Sammy, who worked on trains for a living, a blue-collar coke fiend, chimed in. He used a scruffy, Tom Waits voice, and pretended to grab a pair of hips from behind. He farted all day, thought he was hilarious, walked around grabbing his gut, ate chili for lunch, and smoked Marlboros with the filters torn off—in so many ways, was as hard as they come.

Later at lunch, the two of them started to quarrel. "Yo man, that shit wouldn't fly in the joint." Sammy said, challenging Jim's attempt to throw away unwanted food from his tray. "It's disrespectful," he continued, "they don't have large portions in prison; you gotta eat what they give you."

"Yeah motherfucker, but we aren't in the joint," Jim refuted.

"Right now we're not, but you're one drink away, motherfucker," Sammy said to him, insistently.

Jim got triggered and erupted. His face swelled up red and he stood up and backed away from the table, challenging Sammy and pounding his chest. "What you sayin' I ain't staying sober, motherfucker! Fuck you, man, I'm gonna make it!"

"Fuck you, man," Sammy chided him further, escalating the situation.

"Boys, boys, would you relax?" Brett chimed in with his frail, effeminate wisdom. "I had two years clean and I almost went to the joint," adding his qualifier.

"You and your goddamn two years; it's all that we ever hear about," Sammy refuted Brett's puffed-up claim to fame, shooting him down and directing his attention away from Jim as Jim cooled off.

"Sorry, Sammy."

"It's cool, man." Sammy accepted the apology. I watched all of it, amused, returning to some semblance of normalcy.

We had group every day. There was all sorts of talk about prison: "Yo man, by the time I got out of the joint, five fucking years, the walls were this close to my crazy-ass brain." He held his hands up, less than a foot apart. "It makes you insane if you let it." He carried on, to my enthrallment, "by the end, right before my parole, a few minutes would drive me insane, they'd last like a motherfucking hour, man. Fucked up. You'd better get this shit, man, cuz you wouldn't survive in there, brother. This is my fourth rehab. I don't got another one in me. I'm forty-seven years old. Take a lesson from me."

"Yo man," Jim interrupted, quickly changing the subject away from confinement, "you see that shirt that says 'Biggest gay bar in the world' on it, and it's got a picture of Wrigleyville? That's some funny-ass shit, man." They both were South Side, blue-gray to the core.

"Yeah dude, those pansy-ass faggots are going down again this year, just you watch." Sammy agreed that the Cubs were the worst team in baseball.

"Guys could we watch the language and talk about the solution, please," Steve, the counselor, requested, getting the group back on task. "Dave, why don't you share?"

I took a hopeless breath, collected myself, and started to speak. "Well, I mean what the fuck? How did this happen? And, I mean, I guess that I'm totally *fucked*. My entire life has gone down the drain, and I don't see any way out of it, save some divine intervention or some shit. And that withdrawal was about the worst thing imaginable. Fuck all this shit. The only thing I ever wanted to be was a teacher and that ship has sailed." I shared all of this without the faintest sliver of hope.

"Dave," Steve intervened, "one of the things we want to start being responsible for are our *interpretations*. We can never predict how things will go with recovery."

"Yeah, man. Fuck that. With all due respect, I am having a really hard time believing you." There were four of us sitting around a table. Even with the sleep I was getting, finally, and the food I was starting to enjoy and the girls on the other unit shooting flirtatious glances over toward ours, I was hopeless. I was sick and surrounded by the varying sicknesses of others. For a couple of seconds here and there, there was a respite from it all, but then it came gurgling back. Imagine a place that has taken the vices from those who've known nothing but vices for decades, then disciplines them without necessarily inflicting any sort of punishment. Imagine a war without violence and death. Think of despicable humans being given the chance to talk things out, to get to the bottom of things, to realize the role that their mothers and fathers have played in these great tragic operas that they have suddenly found themselves the characters in. Imagine also that in spite of the collective heinousness that exists in the halls of these units, that are also fluttering instances of hope. There are two or three people who'll make it. There are children who want their mother or father or brother or sister back and who see who they *could* be during visiting hours, and so then assume that the person with two weeks of rehab behind them is who will return to the home. Sometimes they do. Sometimes they return, establish a strict meeting regimen, and do all the things that the others who've made it have done.

Sometimes.

Hilfiger Man

There was this Hilfiger dude, head-to-toe Hilfiger chic. Hilfiger jeans, Hilfiger shirt, Hilfiger socks, donning the emblem across his chest with fancy, black shoes to round out his stellar ensemble. He pulled out a Newport and puffed the menthol through a finely-trimmed, manicured mustache. He had golden-brown hair that was long in the back. He was there to mean business, there to recover. He'd pawned a TV, and told a story of strapping it to the back of a scooter and cruising it down to the west side from Rockford to trade for some pieces of crack.

"The brothers thought I was crazy, chased me the fuck out of the spot. I had to find an all-night pawn shop, and that fuckin' Arabian or whatever he was thought I was crazier." He took a drag, sauntered a bit, and got acquainted a bit with his new life in treatment. The sun shone down on the smoke deck.

"That's not *real* Tommy," Brett opined to a few of us judgingly,

189

suggesting Joe's duds were all knockoffs as he took a slow drag off his Kool and looked the man up and down, then exhaled the smoke out of the corner of his mouth.

"What the fuck do you care, Brett? Mister fucking fashion police over here," Sammy interjected, pointing his thumb in Brett's direction.

"Man I don't wear no fucking knockoffs, faggot." He flicked a butt at Brett, looked like he might have been strong at some point in his life—a street-fighting man before crack.

"Easy now!" Sammy jumped in, defending his friend. They were an unlikely rehab alliance, Sammy and Brett.

"I can spot a faggot from a mile away. I know you wanna suck this," Brett, assertive as always, grabbed his cock and taunted the man who then leaped in his direction before security intervened, de-escalating the situation.

Such was my first trip to rehab. I'd been here a week. I was finally eating—pasta and pudding and meat, bulking up and starting to sleep. The first days were grueling but now things were starting to settle.

There was a fat guy named George. His girlfriend was massive as well. "More to love," is all he said when she left after visiting hours. "I like something I can grab onto," making a squeezing motion with his hands.

"See man, this motherfucker owns it," Sammy chimed in. "We ain't pretending no more. We get to be who we really are when we're sober. Maybe I'll suck Brett's dick now that I'm stepping into my 'real' self," he said, (curiously).

Brett eyed him up and down, "I don't let fatties suck this fatty," and grabbed ahold of his cock.

"Ouch!" Sammy responded.

All of us hung in together—eating ice cream cups with wooden spoons, mixing it in with our coffee, and conducting experiments with the ingredients which stocked the kitchenette. We took three or four packets of grounds, emptied them into a filter, and brewed super batches, the coffee as black as our insides.

We had to line up, like preschool children before recess, grown men standing and fidgeting before getting permission to walk single file to the smoke deck. "Hey dick-faces, you gonna shut the fuck up so we can go outside and look at the eye candy?" Hilfiger demanded; he was fitting in now as a bunch of "new kids" had arrived on the unit.

The Girl on the Smoke Deck

The smoke deck pressed up against the bedroom windows of the girls' unit. There was one, around eighteen years old. She was sexy and curvy and thick, with a big ass and G-string that stuck out the back of her jeans. She stripped as the guys egged her on, hooting and hollering like cavemen. She pulled down her pants and bent over and showed us her ass as she wiggled her hips.

"Take it off!" Sammy heralded, taking a drag and eyeing the bird tattoo on the small of her back, along with her emerging intergluteal cleft.

Hilfiger sleazily snickered, puffed on his Newport, "That's what I'm talking about..."

"You boys need to chill. That girl's like my sister," Brett intervened.

"Fuck you, man." Sammy came back. "This is the closest thing to pussy I had since I got here. Can I *GET* myself a peek now and then?"

"A-fucking-men," I agreed.

"Amen is right. Am I right?" Jim chimed in.

Half the guys left to jerk off.

A few days later, she got kicked out for her exhibitionism, then went and shot up in an alley.

Chores

"Chores! Come on, guys, let's get the chores done before group." George burned his life down to the ground and in a moment of despair and anguish, swallowed a bottle of aspirin in an attempt to end it all, only to end up in rehab with the rest of us. His old, faded KISS t-shirt draped itself over his gut. He wore heavy metal shoes, their tongues protruding, and faded Levis. "We got inspection coming up! Come on guys, let's move!"

Vacuums vroomed through the unit, trash was carried out to the dumpster, and there was a scurrying frenzy as everyone rallied to clean up their spaces before Frank, the beloved albeit somewhat terrifying counselor, arrived.

"Man, I'm kinda sick of that motherfucker. He never shuts up, am I right?" Jim said to me, each of us several days in and getting small glimpses of recovery, myself having slept for a few hours each night.

"Yeah, dude. I'm sick of his shit. He's been sober like twenty days. Imagine what his fatass wife is gonna think when he gets home and she realizes he's been reborn into an asshole control freak." We laughed hysterically.

"Yeah, man. Did you *SEE* that chick? She's easily pushing three hundred. I wouldn't fuck her with *your* dick."

"Fuck you, man." I dusted the dust off the sill. Jim wiped the table as both of us had a good laugh.

Girls

The days moved along. I started to sleep more and more, oftentimes passing out for afternoon naps. I joked with the guys and chased after the girls. The sun shone its light down into the patio area where we ate lunch and had our five minutes with them.

"Why don't you write her a note?" Jim suggested, referring to a hot, blonde 'cutter' I had a crush on.

"I ain't writing her a fucking note," I refuted.

"Why not? You too good for that shit or are you scared? It's one or the other."

"Fuck you, man, " I said back a bit defensively, thinking, very suddenly, of Elizabeth, of junior high, of Colorado, of the fact that I'd lost my license, and of all of the pain in my life.

Frank

Frank was frank. "When I died, I didn't see no fucking choir of angels welcoming me. There were monsters and shit, scary noises, and ghouls. Ghosts and goblins and shit. I wasn't going nowhere pleasant. The shit was spooky, man. And when I woke up, I made the decision to turn my life over. That's why I'm standing here today with you all. I sleep so good at night; you got no clue. This life is the best."

I balanced myself, tilting the chair back as far as I could onto its two rear legs, sitting motionless and teetering perfectly in a zone. Frank was bald with pierced ears, strong but walked with a limp, had OD'd a couple of years prior, gone legally dead, and then been revived and subsequently reborn. He had two years in recovery and had gotten a job at the center not long after waking up in the hospital. He quoted a book, telling us tales of the promises of recovery.

He walked around the table where all of us sat after lunch. "Says here in this Big Book that we will be financially secure if we work these twelve steps here. Says we gotta find a Higher Power. I found mine in a hospital bed; it ain't where you gotta find yours."

I rolled my eyes.

"You ever feel those warm fuzzies? You know when you get that tingling sensation you can't really never explain? That's your higher power talking to you, man. But you gotta work the steps. It's just that simple: work the steps or fucking die."

I'd been here for almost a month but something was off. I was eating and sleeping but something was missing.

I argued, finally speaking up after listening to Frank recite more about God while the others bought into his lies. "I keep this shit to myself. I listen to all of you, rambling your prayers to whatever *MADE*-up friend you've invented, in your bullshit worlds with your bullshit religion and whatever. I feel the same shit in a mosque or a Buddhist stupa. And the Lord's Prayer is offensive to me. I don't get it. What's the big fucking deal with all of this goddamn God shit? I come in here, you shove God down my throat, tell me I have to give up my will, that I'm powerless. You are never powerless; that's just some shit that they make you believe"

"Hey man. You're entitled to think however you want, but this ain't no religion."

"I feel like I've been here for weeks and heard nothing but God bullshit. It's fucking offensive. Take your Lord's Prayer and shove it, like seriously. Have you paid *any* attention to the state of the world?"

"Have it your way," he didn't fight back, "anyone got anything for our friend Dave here?"

Sammy chimed in, "Dave, man, you're a smart guy. Probably *too* smart. Too smart for your own good. And I heard you when you first got in here, bitching about the God stuff. All *offended*, like that's your job, to be nothing *but* offended. You see where that gets you, my friend."

George had a similar sentiment. "Dave, I mean really, you got some nerve saying the stuff that you do sometimes. You traveled to *Japan* in a goddamn blackout, *THEN* made it back, living to tell the fucking tale!? And you sit here, claiming there's *fucking nothing*! You ever think that you just might have guardian angels?"

"Listen to these guys here, Dave. They're your brothers now," Frank said, winding down the afternoon.

Getting Out

Frank pulled me aside. "You gotta get outta here and get straight to a meeting. It's the first thing you gotta do. Then clean out your phone, and get rid of all the bad numbers. Get a new one, or do whatever you gotta do to stay sober. All these guys here, they're your new brothers now. You gotta call them if you wanna stay alive."

"Yeah, man. I hear you. I got a plan."

He stood cockeyed in front of me like a mangled Heavenly messenger. He probably knew I was lying. How could he not? His job, after all, was in dealing with liars all day.

There wasn't a plan.

I got home, went upstairs, and lay on the bed. I felt like a martian, like some sort of alien life form, sent to a planet with no hope of learning its ways. It was September and the long, weary hopelessness had not left the places it rested.

I fell deep into sleep, waking hours later, as lost as before I went in. My parents had gone out to dinner and hadn't removed the wine from the rack, assuming that I would be cured. *There ain't no fucking cure,* Frank had repeatedly said. There was no place to go. I had nothing to do; and the foreboding shadows still cast themselves out through the house, leaving me nowhere to hide from what I had become. Nothing made sense.

Incomprehensible Demoralization

*Newport Nightmare—Fill-Ups—Cook County Jail—James'
Resurrection—The Abscess—Probation—Cat Shit—A Spot off of
Laramie—Drinking Mouthwash—Boo—The Restaurant—
A Spot off of Lake—Staying Sick—The Bed—Cubs Game—
Eating Shit*

Newport Nightmare

The *original* plan was to steal and then pawn my great-grandmother's ring. The cigarette plan would work better.

The streetlights reflected off the windshield as I drove down Roosevelt, past several gas stations, then onto 290, exiting at Cicero. Again. I made left and right turns as abandoned lots sang vacant melodies. He came up to my car at a corner; his skin shining black in the light. He was maybe sixteen and as desperate as me. It was warm, early September, still a warm summer night in Chicago. A breeze wafted through and we looked into each others' eyes.

"Lookin' for blows," I told him.

"I got 'em, dawg," he replied, looking over his shoulder and leaning up against the window, flicking his cigarette ashes.

"Will you trade? I got smokes," I asked.

"Newports, dawg? Ain't need no bullshit Kools or nothin'."

"*Hell yeah, I got Newports*, plenty of these motherfuckers," I answered, pulling the carton from the bag.

He pointed down another street and told me to wait by an alley. "Meet me over there in three minutes."

"I-ight," I agreed, and headed to where he had pointed.

I got to the spot and backed into the alley. The light from the streetlamp shone down on the dashboard, an eerie yellow, with flashing blue lights in the distance. The late nights were different down here, silent but cursed, like the quiet as storms approach sailors at sea, or the terrifying boredom of soldiers who wait between bombs. A rat scurried across the street in front of me, its shadow extending itself in the light. The darkness here lacked the peace that it had in the suburbs. The filth of humans in poverty had taken the evening's sacredness and left it for dead.

He returned and I gave him two packs for a bag. I took a taste, could tell it was good, and told him to get me some more.

"I-ight, dawg," he said and walked off down the alley.

The streetlight cast friendlier hues. Now I'd feel the hot night with the wind in my hair as I drove the truck back to the burbs with the windows rolled down. I'd keep a few packs and I'd have a few smokes. Maybe I'd call an old friend.

And then there were several more kids who'd surrounded my truck.

"Give up the Newports, motherfucker," one of them ordered.

"Chill out, I got 'em for you," I said, casually reaching over toward the passenger seat as suddenly it felt like a brick hit my face.

"Get him!" one of them yelled as I, very suddenly, realized what was happening.

I slammed on the gas, plowing the truck through the crowd. One of them grabbed my lapel and then fell in the street. I made a quick right as my heart started pumping, feeling death giving chase from behind! The expressway was just a few blocks away and I knew I'd be safe when I got to the ramp, but then the engine sputtered and died. I had run out of gas! I opened the door and sprinted as fast as I could, hurdling a fence and rolling down an embankment through broken glass, dirt, and debris, landing on the side of the Eisenhower inside a gasoline rainbow. Then I ran more—like a child fleeing bombs—screaming and waving my arms as dark magic carried me swiftly along without thought. Cars hurried by and left tracers. The street lights lit up the expressway.

"HEEEEEELLLLLLP!" I sprinted as shrill cries made themselves known, running as fast as I could. The scene was a medley of colors and streaks as the Sears Tower watched from a distance, the west side now off to my right. I finally stopped and my hands hit my knees. I breathed a safe breath and collapsed on the side of the road.

A Camry pulled up.

"What-chu crazy, boy?" he said with a confused grin through a rolled-down window, wondering what had just happened. "Get in the fucking car."

I jumped in the car and spit words in his face. "These kids tried to kill me! Drive, motherfucker! We gotta' get outta this bitch!"

"It's cool, dawg. I got-chu man. I'm Kelly."

"I got a credit card. We can party," I told him, and off we drove back to where I'd just left.

Fill-Ups

"You gotta watch your back, dawg," he said assertively, then continued, "always be watching your back down here. You never know what these gangsters be plottin'. They be robbin' and shit; kidnap your dumb-ass and take your shit back to the suburbs, then rob your parents at gunpoint. You can't be flashin' that credit card shit up in this motherfucker and not be expectin' motherfuckers not to be noticing that shit. So you gotta stay with me, you dig?"

"Alright, man. I hear you," I said from the passenger seat, settling into the scene that had seemingly, suddenly found me. We drove a bit, arriving at a gas station a couple of minutes later, the night suddenly supercharged with electricity.

He flagged down his boy. "Yo, Tyree!"

"Yo whaddup, G! Long time no see, Kelly, my brother! What's up with you?" He was strong with dreadlocks and wearing a black hoodie with Jordans on his feet.

"I got me a gas card," Kelly answered from underneath the gas station awning, shouting out to his friend as he stood near the entrance.

"You doin' fill-ups?" Tyree inquired, "How much, dawg?"

"We'll fill that shit up for forty."

"Nah, dawg. I ain't payin' more than twenty."

"Fuck that shit, nigga. Thirty then."

"I-ight dawg, fill that shit up." He continued, "and have the white boy here pump that shit."

"I ain't pumpin' yer fuckin' gas," I told him.

"I'm just playin', dawg." He smiled and we had a quick laugh.

We took the money, repeated the hustle, and went to a spot to score, then went and got high on the side of the road near a park.

We pulled off the scam for the rest of the night until the sun rose up over the lake in the east and we didn't have the cover of the night anymore.

"Yo Laney! Wassup, sistah!" he shouted at a prostitute crossing the intersection.

"Kelly is that you?" She smiled, moving toward us both. "Goddamn, it's been a long time!" Her gut hung down over the waistband of her biker shorts and she wore a faded old t-shirt.

"Baby, I got me some goods but we ain't got no place to party."

She eyed me through the window. "Damn, I see you got a friend with you *don't* you?"

"Oh, this here is Dave," he said introducing me, "Dave here got himself a gas card. We got us some treats; you feel like having us over?"

"Don't mind if I *do*," she agreed, eyeing me still.

"How you doin," I said to her, glancing a bit.

We got to her house. There was a table, a couple of chairs, and a dresser. A mattress was thrown on the floor in another room and the blinds were drawn. She ripped off the crack pipe and blew the smoke out through her nose.

"DAYUM that shit is some fire!" she screamed as she tore off her clothes, stripped nude, and gyrated in front of a mirror; then bent forward, palms on the dresser, raising her ass in the air. Convulsing, she demanded I spank her. "Hit that fat-ass! Hit it!"

The sun had come all the way up. Kelly laughed. I spanked her as hard as I could.

"Harder, baby! Hit that shit!"

I spanked the poor woman, harder and harder, almost raising myself off the floor in the incomprehensibly demoralizing situation I had found myself living inside.

"I wanna suck yo' fucking dick," she proclaimed. "Kelly, baby you gots' to go. Gimme a piece of this fine, sexy white boy."

A part of me wanted her, another part firmly said no. He drove me back to my truck. The windows were broken. I drove myself home to the suburbs. My parents were waiting.

Cook County Jail

You realize you're caught. There is no harder truth that you've ever ingested. There's sinking and pain in your chest. There's terror and screaming inside, then surrender, and then suddenly things you are sure of, the first of course being that you are not able to move—when you'd like or to where. You are also sure that you are no longer someone but someone's. You are owned; and reason, something you suddenly realize you've taken for granted, no longer applies. You had all your chances with reason so you don't even bother. There are cuffs, then a car and some processing, then you finally get sat in a cell. It smells and it's foul, but you were looking forward to it—to the cage—because it meant there'd no longer be handcuffs. Instead of being bound to a chair awaiting processing or fingerprinting or a long and unreasonable wait because of the officers' whims, you'd get to sit down, take a semblance of rest with your back to a wall and your knees in your chest, hanging your tired head between them. You don't know what the others inside of it with you did to arrive here. You're afraid, and your arrest has a way of making you see all of your choices by viciously removing them. There are people who care but your friends—anyone who is not a brother or sister or mother or father or anyone immediate—will get on just fine with you stuck here. Friends aren't family; you realize this; they're great and all, but they won't sit up worried, begging a God who won't listen before a judge does.

There are lawyers you suddenly need. They understand phenomena most people never consider—like which judges are up for reelection and the sentences and penalties you are likely to incur as a result. They might know you're fucked but they'll still take your mother's life savings. They're fine that your dad went and got a home equity loan on the small chance you'll get to return to the house you grew up in. They're fine with their lies. They're good at hearing the thank yous from the ones who hired them to hopefully free you, and at pretending that they did their best.

All of it's fucking corrupt and you know it.

I rode the Metra from the suburbs, sitting in front of two chefs who talked about football—this was what normal people with normal lives did; went to work and talked about sports. I stole a bottle from my parents' wine rack before the ride down, drank the whole thing, and threw it up seconds later. It looked like blood staring back at me from the toilet. I needed my fix even more.

It was October and a day I will never forget, both for its sheer horridness but also for the memory, *the experience* it afforded me. I was wearing a hoodie. It was blue; it seemed like every junkie could at least get his hands on a decent one. The cold hadn't come and I remember the smell of the platform: stale urine, liquor, and unwanted trash. A candy wrapper drifted around in the wind and brushed against a fire hydrant below. Cars sped by. Police car doors slammed. A guy named Bill, a junkie I bummed around with, and who I later heard died, gave me free shit near the corner on my way from the spot.

"Jesus. Thanks, dude." I extolled, delighted, then bent down and placed the dope in my shoe.

This happened once, so not all junkies are bad, selfish, scared, terrible people with demons swimming around inside them. Dope had its own sacred selfishness, but it must have been good and he must have been perfectly high, forgetting he'd need more for later.

I was *trying* to save it for Starbucks, just a few stops west on the green line, but needed my hand on the fix. I was high, but not in the deadliest sense. I'd shot up a few minutes prior, but it was best to be close to the edge, in the death zone, dancing with demons disguised as angels. I reached down and pulled out the foil as a strong man suddenly appeared in front of me.

He didn't have a uniform or anything, but I knew right away it was bad, and that I was fucked, more so than I'd ever been. He and his partner were waiting, watching the west side from up on the platform for people like me to come through. I should have known better. There were lots of white addicts down here, but not many well-dressed, together-looking, strong, white men with guns and handcuffs under their jackets who hung around the El stops on the west side of Chicago.

"Excuse me, I'm with the Chicago Police Department," he said, very politely, half-smiling and knowing my fate, casually but forcefully moving in my direction. I felt a sudden chill run through me, then clutched my aching heart as the day became gloomy and sad.

"Yeah," I politely responded, my entire being shrinking, realizing what was to happen.

"What ya' got in your hand there?"

I froze, then showed him almost instinctively the blow I'd pulled out of my shoe. It sat in my palm, exposed and almost telling on itself, and he took it and bound my wrists in what felt like the same motion, then handed it to his partner who placed it inside of a ziplock.

"Please, *you don't have to do this*," I pleaded, shaking and terrified, knowing they knew I was scared. This wasn't my first time in cuffs, but this time was different, and a morbid darkness descended on the platform.

If only I'd listened to Frank, I thought, very clearly, and now I went into the murk, begging that they change their minds.

"This is the only way you'll learn; *we're doing you a favor.*" He smiled smugly, feigning concern, and held me in place while his partner frisked me. There were people around, all of them black. They looked at me, shrugged nonchalantly and understood as the train I was supposed to be on, the one that *would've* taken me to Starbucks arrived and then moved onward toward Oak Park. It was cloudy and gray. Bottles rolled in the street below and the sounds of the train echoed off the buildings as it vanished. The temperature dropped. A pigeon took flight from the edge of the platform, fluttering its filthy wings and then vanishing into the city, free.

"I wanna go home," I said desperately to them both as they led me away, my feet shuffling almost involuntarily beneath me, physiologically resisting it all.

"We can't let you do that," one of them responded, politely enough, then continued, "what's your name, boss?"

"Dave," I answered as if I'd forgotten and then in that second remembered, shaking, and now being led down the stairs by the scary, strong men, one on the right and one on the left, each of them gripping an elbow with merciless hands.

"I'm sorry, *Dave*, but you're coming with us," the bigger one said. He was strong with red hair and a mustache.

"Yeah, *Dave*. Now you'll know what *not* to do," the other one chimed in, smirking some more.

Well, this is more as I'd planned. You've been to Japan and now
you are going to jail! The adventure gets better and better!
Just the two of us...

My wrists hurt from the cuffs as I shifted around, trying to get comfortable, locked in the back of the squad car with a hard, mesh screen separating us—a little cage of its own. It was an unmarked, "transit-detail" cruiser, sort of undercover, sort of not, like the cops who had taken my shit. The seats were navy blue vinyl. I looked out toward the varying forms of freedom effortlessly expressing themselves—walking, talking, drinking, playing, eating, tying shoes, and each of these trivial things, these things I had taken for granted, meant so much more than they had just a few minutes prior.

We drove up and down Lake for an hour, and onto the various side-streets—Kostner, Kolin, Kildare, Kilbourne, Maypole—looking for more desperate fools. I felt oddly and uncomfortably *safe*, like all that could touch me suddenly had, and that the worst that could happen just did and that I was okay.

"So what, you guys just drive around, looking for junkies like me all day long?" I inquired, having accepted my lot, pleasantly high and gazing out the window.

"Dude, you really shouldn't have taken the shit from your shoe. You were basically home free, boss" the smaller one said as he adjusted his glasses in the rearview mirror, driving.

"Fuckin' a," I responded, "I gotta be done with this shit. Ya' know I was a teacher back home?" We drove past some tenement structures; a prostitute crossed the street in front of us, sick in her own right. The officer, the bigger one sitting shotgun, waved like he'd seen her before.

"A teacher? What the hell's wrong with you? And where's home?" The other one said. They were both sort of nice.

"Colorado," I answered.

"Oh, they got them big fuckin' mountains, don't they?" the bigger one with the mustache, asked in a thick Chicago accent.

"Yeah, man. They got mountains and rivers and all sorts of fun shit to do." I answered him, remembering. *How in the fuck did this happen?*

"Well then what the fuck you doin' on the west side of Chicago?"

"Fucking up my life," I answered bluntly.

"Apparently, boss." I wish I had waited to take the dope out of my shoe.

"A teacher, that's a first," the smaller one said as I forced out a nervous, odd laugh. "So we got ourselves a smart one here."

They brought me to a precinct on Madison, sat me in a chair, and locked me to a steel bar so I couldn't go anywhere, then walked away. The cuffs hurt my wrist and the chair was uncomfortable, as if by design. I could hear them messing around and joking with the other cops in the station.

Bears are gonna whoop on the Cardinals. Leinhart's a bitch.

Yeah but it's football. You never fucking know.
Mister fucking optimist over here!
Fuck every last one of you.
Da Bears…
Da Bears…

Another came back and entered my information into a computer, hunting and pecking the keyboard, a broad-shouldered cop, about six-foot-four with a beard.

He took my I.D. and looked at me, "So Mr. Kehnast, let's get this underway."

"How in the fuck did you pronounce my name right the *first* time?" I asked, regarding his anomalous reminder again, of the person I *was*.

"Common sense, right?" He continued, "I never was too good at typin', so bear with me," he added in a self-deprecating way.

"Well I'm a teacher, I can help you with that," I said, oddly cooperative. "Hey guys, we got ourselves an educated junkie here!" he yelled down the hallway and joked. I laughed a bit too but was dying inside, seeking out whatever humor I could to lighten the situation. He led me away.

Another cop forcefully and robotically gripped my hand and smashed my fingers into the ink.

"So you learn your lesson yet, dawg?" he asked.

"You know it," I replied, very agreeably, and continued. "I'm fucking done with this. Fuck all this goddamn bullshit."

"Boy, you best not be takin' the Lord's name in vain in my station, you hear me?" he commanded.

"Sorry, man," I answered agreeably again, laughing a bit, and not really noticing that this sort of *agreeableness* in regard to *the man* would be noticed by others. Stockholm Syndrome might get you killed in Cook County.

"You find yourself a God, or let God find you and all of this will vanish." I imagine he offered the Lord every chance that he got.

"I'm done, man."

"You sure?"

"I'm sure."

"Positive?"

"Yes. I can't live this way anymore. I'm done with it, all of it. Totally fucking done."

"Watch the language at my station. Do you have a mother?" he asked, concerned and curious.

"Yes," I answered, thinking of her as my head went rigid. My eyes shifted to the floor, to the walls, to the ink pad. I whimpered a bit, bewildered and sad, and thought of my father and sister and brother as well.

"Then why you puttin' her through all this bullshit?"

"Hurry it up!" One of the cops from the back shouted up to him to hurry me along. There were others.

"I know, man. I fucking know. Can I make a phone call, by the way?"

The cops grinned, cynically. "No," one of them flatly exclaimed from a desk behind us, smirking. Rain was now pelting the windows outside of the station.

He pressed my fingers into the fingerprint machine, one at a time. He had dark brown skin, a round face, and bright white teeth, and was gentle and doing his job. He was shorter than me and shared that his first name was Michael.

"That's my middle name," I told him, remembering again.

"Well well, then, the greatest of kings and the greatest of angels! So you done then, ain't you, David Michael?"

"Done."

"I had a brother who used to shoot dope. Dude died in an alley out there on MLK Drive. Left behind my niece and nephew, now they ain't got no daddy, all for a couple of blows; and their mama be smokin' them rocks. The kids done been abandoned. This shit ain't no joke, boy. You gotta get your shit together before they send your dumb-ass downstate, and a pretty white boy like you wouldn't do so well out at Menard or Vandalia or wherever they send your stupid ass."

"I hear you, man," I responded. He was smiling a bit, grabbed my arm, led me through the station and past a desk littered with disordered papers, and then into a cell where I'd spend the next seventeen hours.

This was the worst day I'd lived. Jail, like everything else, was fine if you were high. I remember I started an exercise regimen after the door shut and doing some push-ups and squats; *this could be a new beginning*, I thought for an hour or two. But when the dope wears off, the walls close in; you throw up and see shit smeared on the walls and the floor, and the smell permeates into places without asking permission. It was filthy and crude, an *actual* prison, and minutes were different from what I had known them to be—hours and days and lifetimes of sad reflection on the animal I'd become, pointing out that everyone I loved was gone and that alone had never meant so much. I contemplated my life and childhood, my crime, my existence, and my addiction, all the while burning inside, needing the dope that they took. I was ten, kicking a can on a firefly night and the pool was right down the street waiting for me to climb the high dive and descend fearlessly into the water below. Then it was fall and we pulled out our sweatshirts and jeans, relieved that the heat was receding as the leaves started to show the subtlest signs of changing colors. And then I was starting fifth grade and looking forward to seeing girls for the first time. I wanted it back, to go to the womb and start fresh and to never see jail. I remembered the magical summers and drifted back through the years, into the summertime mornings and bug-zapper nights, while shaking and crying and needing and begging police from inside my sick brain.

*You got the wrong guy. Really, you must understand. I'm not sure how I can explain but I'm not a **bad** guy. Most of the guys here are **bad** but this is not me. I'm not one of **them**. I'm here to do good. I'm here to enlighten young minds. I taught children and sang in the choir! I'll prove it to you that I'm good if you'll just let me go! I won't hurt a fly! Please. PLEASE! **PLEASE LET ME GO!***

I am not my crime! My heart is kind!

Our family took family trips in the summer to Hilton Head Island, and to the shores of New Jersey and Florida. I had a BB gun and the only thing I killed was a Bluejay that I suddenly remembered descending— dead—demonstrating morbidly the preciousness of life. *I remember the way that it felt.* I cared for the world and the creatures of God but forgot this because of the drugs. I thought of the boy who I'd been and the life I had lived, the mountains and rivers, The Mish and the places I'd worked, the girls in Fort Collins, the parties, the music, and drugs. The drifting through fields of fresh powder and the nights in the kitchens.

Was it that bad? The cell I was in was actually, in so many ways, a lot safer than the experience in Asia. I knew where I was, after all, and I knew where I was going, mostly. I could make out the grid of the city inside of my mind and walk home if I needed; if they, having had a sudden change of heart, had decided to free me, having realized that inside of this criminal, deep down, was a soul who was terribly sick and who needed a rest. I wasn't that far from my home, not the thousands of miles like that *other* prison I'd found myself in. But by now it was *all* one big cage. At what point did all this go dark? *At what specific point did I start making the decisions that ultimately led to this confinement? Back on the playground in school? At Hawthorne? In the middle of one of the trips?*

The deputy walked by. He was short with a mustache and looked like a superfan guy, wore a Bears sweatshirt over his uniform shirt, and waddled a bit when he walked. A big ring of keys hung from his trousers. I asked him when I would get out.

"That's a decision the judge will make."

"When do I find out?"

"What did you get picked up on?"

"Possession."

"Possession of what?"

"Heroin."

"Tomorrow."

"You know where I'm going?"

"The county."

"26th and Cali?"

"Yes."

"You sure?"

"Positive."

"Alright, can I get a paper to read?"

"No, and don't ask for anything else."

There was a phone in the wall. Pressing the buttons took all of the strength that I had.

"Where *ARE* you, the caller ID says jail!" My heartbroken, agonized, tortured, and worried mother had answered, pleading and needing my release more than I did.

"I got arrested. *Don't worry.*" The dope was wearing off, rapidly, and the cold, heartless reality of withdrawal was burrowing into my bones.

"We'll get a lawyer. W-w-w-we'll get you out." She was shaking but what could I do?

"I'm *fine.*" I snapped back, irritated, like the self-centered trash that I was, and I hung up and sat on the bench.

I had a cellmate. I looked at him, not knowing what to say or do, or who to be, and I didn't know if I should greet him or leave him alone. He didn't seem sane, had crazed eyes, a dirty beard, and ears leaking wax that heard voices that weren't in the cell. I hadn't yet noticed his stench; and the nightmare minutes were punishments unto themselves spanning out into odd, melancholy eternities.

This was *ALL* so eternal in nature.

My joints started aching; the concrete and steel hurt my bones. I was thirsty and tired and sick from the junk wearing off, and I knew that the nighttime had come, picturing a cold moon rising in the autumn evening outside as minutes kept ticking away. There weren't any bars; it was a thick door with a narrow window and hatch they opened once during the night to put sandwiches through to nourish us with bologna, which seemed specifically designed to rot out the insides of prisoners.

The sounds the keys made stood for freedoms that I didn't have. The water shot out from the sink which was part of the toilet; it wouldn't go into my mouth, and my cellmate had his hands on it so it was covered in shit and piss because he was filthy and insane. It all went so slow and was painful with craving and tears on a concrete bench I was forced to make into a bed; my pair of brown Vans that my mother had bought me, the pillow.

He stacked up the food on the toilet, using it as a table—settling in, having his dinner—and his smell made me gag and want dope. He called the cops racist vulgarities and screamed words that didn't make sense; and this was my only companion: a racist schizophrenic who ate bologna off a toilet, then shit and didn't wipe himself and was safer in jail than out in the streets. I don't know what he was picked up for, perhaps loitering or otherwise offending society in the so many ways his very existence was capable of.

The minutes meticulously multiplied, each new one identical to the previous hundreds. If the jailers had suddenly freed us, bestowing an act of providence upon each of our suffering spirits, it's not likely that he would have left. He seemed like he'd found his new home.

We didn't have rights. A man at the end of the cell block was scream-ing—his voice screechy and whiny and desperate—all night that he had to go to the hospital. I can still hear the way that he begged. *"PLEEEEE-AAAAASE……"*

I have never heard please mean so much.

He thought he was going to die and kept crying for hours. I could tell he was weak and in need, and not a strong man, just a sad soul who'd turned the wrong way as I had. I imagined the hoodie that *he* probably had and the mess that his life had become.

"Shut. The. *FUCK. UP!*" the blue-gray machine shouted back, laugh-ing while he could have died.

I don't know if I deserved this, but this is all part of the story.

It is me.

I am jail and God and drugs. I am Heaven and Hell, rolled into surfing with angels down waves of despair and redemption.

It made me insane—the boredom, my cellmate, the filth, the toilet, the sounds of the sirens outside, and the blue-collar accents I heard down the hall. There was freedom so close, just a few feet away, but I was locked up in the cage.

I waited all day and all night—the worst fucking day of my life. At four-thirty in the morning, they loaded us carefully into another cell and handcuffed us together. It was dark and cold and stunk of death and crime.

"Anyone need any meds?" the officer shouted.

Methadone? I thought, but no one said anything, as if any type of cooperation at all was forbidden.

"Alright then, gentlemen! You're all gonna walk real straight and nice and get into the bus without incident. You understand me?" Everyone nodded like zombies, then moved, single file toward the paddy.

They drove to the different jails, picking up crooks from all over the city, driving as if transporting cargo. We kept falling down in the dark, and were bound at the wrists, cramped and miserable, having nothing to do but stare out into a putrid black belly. There was no way to put up our arms, so we fell on the floor, awkwardly rose, and reconfigured ourselves on the bench, angry and powerless, shaking and cold. I was squeezing my bowels, trying to not shit in my pants, and my body and brain were on fire. I wondered what crimes were committed by each of the others, be they of desperation, lust, madness, or revenge.

We got to 26th; they unloaded us out of the paddy and onto a stairwell. I was in front. There were bars in front of me and the reinforced garage door behind us was shut; there was no getting out. And I knew, almost instinctively, that the entire complex was surrounded by barbed wire, that there were towers with gunmen who wanted to fire their weapons, and that this was as bad as it got. All of the others were black, had been caught on the south and west sides, and I had to stand there and wait, pretending I'd been there before—terrified, weak, afraid, and caucasian.

A cop from behind started yelling. "Alright, motherfuckers, court's at 9:30, and we don't want any problems, so as long as you shitbags cooperate, we'll get those of you who are going home out of here as soon as possible! And those of you who aren't are pretty much fucked anyway, so you may as well settle in and cooperate."

9:30, fuck.

"Any of you steps out of line and it slows the entire process down. You understand me? We're taking the cuffs off and each of you cocksuckers is to keep your hands behind your back at all times. *BEHIND YOUR FUCKING BACK, YOU HEAR ME?*"

There were a few quiet utterances.

"I SAID, DID YOU HEAR ME!?" he demanded, continuing, *"I WANNA HEAR 'YES, SIR!'"*

"Yes, sir!" We responded in unison. It was six in the morning or so. I'd slept for a couple of minutes.

"Correction, gentleman! One of the judges is sick, so bond court's not until 1:30. Sit tight, it's going to be a while."

Fuck! I didn't know how I'd survive. *The lawyer will hurry this up,* I thought optimistically, but then realized he could do nothing. Cook County had its own time. We were caught up inside the machine, the blue and the gray. Human cargo. The laws of the jail were outside of the laws of the world.

I thought about slavery and chains, the Jews and the gulags and all of the things prisoners see; and how each is the same in one very particular way by the fact that he is incapable of leaving the position he finds himself stationed in. Find me a prisoner who's able to leave and I'll show you the keys to the kingdom. *You can't leave,* and along with this immutable fact, there is the sudden realization of all of the things that might happen as a result of not being able to get up and go where you'd like:

Because I can't leave, there might be a beating.

Because I can't leave, there might be a rape.

Because I can't leave, the officers might commit torture.

This is a Hell in itself.

We walked, single file, into a big holding cell, and another cop, a big guy with black leather gloves, walks in and starts yelling.

"Alright, so each of you motherfuckers gets to decide how it goes for you here in this shithole. I wanna get through my day, go have a drink, see my kids, and then fuck my wife, you hear me?" He smiled a bit, then continued.

"So gentlemen—each of you, take off your shoes."

We hurriedly complied.

"So this is your last chance. If any of you is holding anything—any weapons, any drugs—this is your pass. Take that shit out and put it here in this bag. If we catch you later, you're gonna catch hell, you hear me?

You'll be charged. You understand? The charges will be exacerbated. You hear me?"

No one admitted to anything.

"Now pick up your shoes and bang them together hard. NOW!" We pounded the souls of our shoes as the stench filled the cell, wafting itself out and blending with the colors and stains on the floor. "Harder, gentlemen! HARDER!" We primally banged them together. I had such little strength. It took all that I had and the sick mildew smell filled my nose and I almost threw up. I wished for it all to be over, and realized how filthy I was—how exhausted and desperate and sick. By now it was seven o'clock. It seemed to be lasting forever, as if I was trapped in a peculiar darkened dimension, pending salvation.

A few minutes later, another cop came into the cell. His job was to count. Each prisoner was accounted for and given a number. The cop was the same age as me but had made different choices. He was a captor and I was a slave.

The bullpen was shoulder to shoulder. I stood in the same spot, not moving, shivering, shaking, and scared, arms pressed close to my sides, needing the thing that had gotten me here. It had been almost twenty-four hours. There were people passed out on the floor, men on the benches, and a filthy toilet in the back all enclosed within the foreboding, confining walls. I needed to go to the bathroom so badly and thought that I might have an accident. A man got up, stumbled past me and a few others, and dry heaved into the toilet, retching whatever contents remained in his stomach.

"Damn, motherfucker's dopesick," another one said, matter of factly.

"Best not be gettin' none of that sick on me or I'll be fittin' to handle your ass," another man said, angry and cold.

There were a couple of other disgusted grunts and comments, and then the same peculiar quiet settled back in, speaking only the things that strange silences can.

I thought about things that could happen. *What if I have to throw up?* If I needed to puke, I'd have to navigate the crowd as the other man had. In the process of this, I might bump into or otherwise offend one or more of the inmates, which might then result in me having to fight or defend myself, which might then result in the guards coming in and spraying the place down with mace, which then might result in the overall attitudes of the men in the cell being turned against me, along with associated plots for the things they would do to exact their revenge. I thought about rape and the terrible things that had happened inside the walls.

I stood in the spot for six hours. It spanned on forever, it seemed.

Some lawyers came through, carrying briefcases, dressed professionally, and doing their jobs. The public defender was an attractive woman about my age, and I kept thinking about her kitchen, the nice bottles of wine she probably had, and her freedom. She had wavy brown hair, glasses, and a beautiful figure and smile. The inmates clawed the mesh door like animals to get her attention. Some knew her name, and she, theirs, and the line between cops, criminals, liars, lawyers, and thieves seemed blurry and thin. I wondered who was who.

A number was drawn on my hand and the hands of the others, and at some point, finally, they started calling them out. "77, 54, 43, 61, 25, you're up!" and the men who'd been marked with the numbers in question filed out into the hall, awaiting their turn in front of the judge, who presided from the other side of a television screen. After several others had gone, it was finally my turn, and from the station where I stood, looking at the screen, I peered into the courtroom and saw my pitiable mother standing there with the lawyer my parents had hired. I have never felt more ashamed to be the person I was than I did at that moment. Here I was: the most despicable and disgusting display of all that it could ever mean to be someone's son, staring through a screen at the back of the head of my desperate, terrified mother and the lawyer she hired to save me.

The deputy handed me the phone. "Hey bud, how you doin'?" The lawyer, a man who was instrumental in all of this journey because of his sobriety, called from the courtroom.

"Not so good, man."

"Yeah, I can imagine. Okay look, we're gonna try to get you outta' here and I think we got a good chance so you just sit tight and we're gonna see what we can do, okay bud?"

A good chance? What do you mean, try?

"Okay."

"Sit tight, talk to you soon," he said as I hung up the phone, returned my hands behind my back, and waited my turn.

The guy before me, a black man whose last name was White, and who I'd ridden in the paddy wagon with, was accused of kidnapping a woman, binding her arms and legs with duct tape, and throwing her in the trunk of his car. She'd been discovered when the officer pulled him over for throwing the tape out the window, and it was after discovering this as the result of hearing his arraignment over the television, that it was made known to me, as the result of *my* television appearance, that I could leave shortly as my mother had posted the necessary bond. Then I got cocky and made the mistake of trying to flirt with one of the female police deputies who was talking about the pharmaceutical drugs she had at home with the other officers there in the hallway. I chimed in with my old charm, making a dosage recommendation, and the sergeant unloaded on me.

"ARE YOU FRATERNIZING WITH ONE OF MY DEPUTIES!!!" She reeked of cheap perfume and cigarette butts; her teeth were a rotten brown-yellow, and her eyes were like windows set in frigid stone walls. She could take me away to the back where the tortures had happened years prior. I knew this but more importantly, *she knew it* and wielded her power violently like Mengele.

And there was the sudden and terrifying realization that these people—these other beings, these different expressions of what living means—owned me, my life, and my soul; and although my time in their confines was brief, this realization will stay with me forever. *I have been owned. I have been held. I have been captive. And I understand, if only in a brief sense, what bondage does to the soul.*

Every prisoner's the same.

"LISTEN TO ME YOU GODDAMN MOTHERFUCKING PIECE OF SHIT JUNKIE!!! THIS JAIL ISN'T MEANT FOR PEOPLE LIKE YOU!" STAY IN THE SUBURBS WHERE YOU BELONG AND DON'T EVER COME BACK TO MY JAIL!!! IF I SEE YOU IN HERE AGAIN, I'LL MAKE YOUR LIFE A LIVING HELL, SO HELP ME GOD!!! DO YOU UNDERSTAND ME!?!?" I nodded the humblest nod that my spirit could muster. "LOOK ME IN THE FUCKING EYE AND SAY 'YES, SEARGENT!'"

"Yes, sergeant," I said—chin to my chest—my browbeaten eyes glancing hesitantly upward at hers.

"Now get the fuck outta here!"

Those of us heading home were moved to another cell. It had multiple benches and each of us got a sandwich and juice, some high-fructose garbage they fed to the dregs of the earth, then we were handed our belts and shoelaces and led out a door, then through another door, and into the lobby of the courthouse. There were lawyers and cops, metal detectors, badges, guns, and my mother. The span between freedom and bondage was just a few feet. It was late afternoon. The sun was beginning to set.

James' Resurrection

Somewhere in the midst of this mayhem, I remembered James, one of the most obnoxious expressions of party culture I ever encountered. There were days in those first years of college when his life was devolving and he was flunking out and making himself such a nuisance to me and all of the others around that I wished he would vanish forever. And then he did, very suddenly.

"He's reborn or some shit," Andrew had said as we stacked empty Busch cans into a pyramid on his counter one night a few years later.

"That's too bad," I joked in response and we all had a laugh. *"Where'd you hear this?"*

"Cheez said he called him up to apologize or some shit. Fuck him and his God and his bullshit."

"Echo that, motherfucker. He ain't nothin' but a piece-of-shit rat."

This was a couple of years after James and Andrew and a few others had stolen a bunch of shit from a Radio Shack with the intention of pawning it for drug money. They'd been caught on camera and James had then ratted on all of them to avoid prison time, alerting the police as to the whereabouts of all of the stolen merchandise, which one of the culprits had stashed underneath an old rotted-out halfpipe in Andrew's backyard. This unfortunate unfolding of circumstances had happened in conjunction with James having gotten a second D.U.I. while driving without a license, then being caught hitchhiking down Route 53 with an ounce of mushrooms while on probation. They made him a deal and he took it, and he had somehow, in the midst of all of the shitstorms that he had created for himself, found some sort of Higher Power to surrender himself to and then gone on a rampage of apologies to those he had harmed, somehow excluding Andrew and a few others, including myself.

I remembered his parents' phone number from memory *somehow* and left them a message, having instinctually known he could offer me something, but not really knowing just what. A few days later, there was a message from James, who had vanished almost a decade prior, on *my* parents' machine. He spoke in a tone unfamiliar, almost giggly. There was joy in the words that he spoke, and in all of the years I had known him, I'd never seen joy. I'd seen humor. I'd heard horrible impressions of Hispanics. He'd grunted to Beavis and Butthead in his dorm room, bong in hand. I'd even seen tears on occasion as James was a sensitive guy, but I'd never seen joy, and so the voice of the man on the answering machine was not one I immediately recognized. I listened, again and again, having finally deduced it was him, and then called him back and he answered, and a man who was foolish in all of the years that I knew him no longer was. He was some sort of spiritual being. He was caring and kind and he listened to all that I said. *He was sober.* I spewed my words through a discord of laughter and tears and he took it all in, neither judging nor really even caring. He was just sort of *being.*

He came and got me and brought me to "one of those meetings," which I really didn't care for too much, then we went to his house, a house which he shared with a wife who was also sober. He had children as well and immediately began fixing a sink in the house, having promised his wife he would do it. *"I told her I'd do it and I've learned how to honor my word,"* he said. This was after he got me situated, told me to sit on the couch and make myself comfortable, and brought me some water. I took a sip and forced down a couple of saltines, again, I remind you, just a few days after he flashed through my head and I recalled his old number from memory.

I sat there and suffered. My life was a mess.

He answered the phone every time. He was not the person that I remembered.

The Abscess

I'd been to the doctor to have an abscess drained. My bicep gave birth to a swollen, disgusting, golf ball-sized pustule in a spot that I rammed with a needle. It stunk of death, was purple and green, and protruded outwards, stretching my skin like a fleshy balloon. It poisoned my body, leaked pus from its edges, and oozed through the pores in my skin. I tried to pop it but failed. It burned. Like campfire ashes or the sting from a bee or a wasp, and grew bigger each day as if living a life of its own. It hurt while I moved and I had to hold still, as each breath told stories about what could happen: *blood poisoning, it spreading, my arm falling off, it eating my body and stealing my blood, surrounding me in a fleshy pink bubble, forcing me to breathe the infection's gaseous and poisonous fumes.*

"So what seems to be the problem?" asked the doctor. He was friendly, adjusting the pens in his pocket.

"Uhhh, so my girlfriend stabbed me with a pencil and I think it got infected. I'm not sure what the hell I did *this* time but I think that I must have upset her."

He laughed in a dry-humored way. "Well, you must have some sorta mojo," he said, then gave me local anesthesia, grabbed a scalpel, sliced swiftly into my arm, and drained out a teaspoon of puss, which stained and saturated the gauze. "Do you think you'll rekindle your romance or let this one go?"

"I'm not sure, doc. I thought she was a keeper. I don't know, man. What in the hell is going on with all these women anyway? It's like they all want something but they never tell you what exactly, and then they stab you in the arm with a frickin' pencil."

"Tell me about it, I've been married for twenty-six years, but I keep all the pencils locked up."

The nurse laughed and joined in. "I'll keep this in mind the next time my boyfriend acts up."

"Can I get something for pain?" I asked, guiltily.

"I suppose I can write you a prescription," he said agreeably, then squeezed out the rest of the puss with the forceps, stitched it up, and wrote the prescription. I kept the bottle, after taking them all in a day, knowing it might come in handy.

I could take the bottle and show it to Megan, my probation officer, and she would then record that I was legal, that opiates were good, and that I didn't need jail if the judge wanted it for me.

Probation

I got put on probation and had to report once a month, to the same building my ordeal began months before in a filthy, shit-stained cell the color of bile and bowels. Cook County justice had blue-collar vices itself—smokers and drinkers and philanders. South-Side, Irish police with their neighbors and relatives manning clerk's desks—making demands, filing paperwork, smoking and swearing, enjoying their freedom and hot cups of Cook County coffee.

"Take off your belt," the cop ordered bluntly. I laid it on the conveyor, alongside my shoes.

A cop stood there rambling. "So I says ta-da guy, get yer fuckin' hands on the car or I'm gonna smash your' fuckin' head in. You hear me, cocksucker?" He smirked and adjusted his gun and his belt.

"Atta' boy," the other cop nodded along, laughing, as I moved through the metal detector. A lawyer stood next to them with his briefcase, smirking, wearing a long, navy raincoat.

"So did he put his hands on the car?" he asked.

"Well, I mean, he didn't wanna get shot, now did he?" All of them laughed. Steel doors and old, rusty cages waited in the background.

I dreamed about prison, often and recurrently, the gray of it all, the concrete and steel. The colorlessness. The shit smell stinking in the cell-block after meals, and the forced sexual advances by strong, dominant alphas. I saw it lucidly and then woke, feeling terrified and familiar, like an abusive home was waiting to teach me dim lessons when I got there. The evil dreaming and merciless waking blended into a long tunnel of decrepit misery.

The probation floor was downstairs, beneath the jail and courtrooms, and was littered with cubicles, a massive, manila-folder metropolis. Megan, my probation officer, was nice, maybe twenty-seven, and probably doing this work to make some sort of difference. We chatted a bit, mostly about the judge and how funny and firm he was in his dealings with criminals. His name was Kirby. Kirby was just.

I had an upcoming meeting and had used dope that previous day; getting caught would mean prison downstate. I needed a dark, dreary miracle and a cup of clean piss.

I thought up the story and how I would tell it: there were black kids that chased me down Polk, threw me down, then kicked me and punched me for coming through on the wrong day. They'd decided they didn't like junkies. The bruises were proof. I ran through it all in the mirror, rehearsed, and went over my lines. She'd understand, jot down her notes, and the judge would excuse me from jail. I'd show her the bottle I'd saved from the doctor as well, more proof that I had been hurt!

But I couldn't connect as the Samurai did with Seppuku. I needed a hammer, or a strong man's fist, a real-life beating, a bat or a pipe or foot, but I picked *safe* tools that wouldn't leave bruises or scars. Still, I smashed at my face and my head with an empty Coke can, the T.V. remote, and *my* fist, not the fist of another, hoping to leave real marks.

I spent all day punching myself, thinking that there would be marks; that the three hundred limp-wristed floggings would at least amount to something, a real black eye, a contusion, something *convincing*. It just wasn't working; I couldn't cause actual harm. I found an old wrist guard from skating the following day, put it on as a prop, then saw some bruises appear, faint, yellow and bluish, and thought I'd completed the costume. Now it will work. My plan will succeed!

"He was on fire today, sending guys up the river," I said to her, recounting my experience from the courtroom.

"He was in a bad mood at our meeting," she replied, referring to briefings she had in his office before her day had begun.

"I have a prescription. I kind of got jumped." I handed her the bottle and adjusted my wrist guard. There were faint bruises on my forehead and around my eyes.

"Well that's too bad. I'm glad you're okay." She took note of the prescription number. It was inconsequential, my efforts had all been in vain. She didn't care. Prescriptions fit into the system.

"I'll need a drop and you'll be good to go." She handed me a cup.

"Uhhh, so I'll have to go upstairs and get some coffee first if that's okay." It was embarrassing; needing to explain this each month until she remembered and expected to hear it, then eased my concerns as much as she could.

"Go get some and then head over." This was all she could offer; the law was her job. I suppose she had pity. She kept a picture of her dog on her desk, and one of her husband. She was roughly my age, pretty, and offered as much compassion as her job allotted her.

I stood staring at the wall, squeezing and trying my hardest to force it out. *Please just a cocksucking dribble!!* I screamed on the inside, but nothing would happen! So I had to go back and drink more.

"Cook County's startin' to crack down on them possession charges," one of the cops said to another in the cafeteria line.

"Tell me about it," I chimed in, making a joke to the cop.

"Was I fucking talking to you, shitbag?" He laughed with his partner, then ordered some food for his shift. "Give me one of them hot dogs, sweetie."

"Only if you ask real nice."

"I called you sweetie, didn't I?" he answered, smirking.

She giggled, then shot her icy eyes in my direction. They both walked away.

"May I please have a large?" She poured me a styrofoam cup.

I slammed it as fast as I could, and ran down the stairs, explaining to the court officer that I needed a while, that I wasn't ready to go.

"Man, I can't go. I got stage fright," I said to him vulnerably, mumbling.

"You gotta try anyway, boss," he responded, politely encouraging me, "focus on your breathing or some shit."

His job was to stand there, watching parolees and people on probation piss. Finally, after ounces and ounces of Cook County criminal coffee, I squeezed out the tiniest bit. He gave me a fist bump and a hint of a smile.

I had to repeat the humiliating ritual once a month.

Cat Shit

It made me safe in deadly situations. There were days I went up to the crack house to sit among rats and cat feces, dirty needles, crack pipes, and trash, feeling safe from shooting deadly poison into my blood. It was like I was back in the womb, there on a mattress inside of a crackhouse where filthy things had been done, watching the guy next to me nodding out, motionless, lost in delusion, and on the edge of drifting away forever and having life not hurt anymore. If no one had loved me the way that they did, I would have been fine dying here.

I'd rest a few minutes, nod for a bit, then float through the neighborhood, back to the train, and out of the city to the refuge of suburbia. The cops didn't care anymore. None of the junkies, the really bad ones, seemed to get fucked with by cops; they just blended in with the dirt and the grime and the rust. I'd ditch my rig, hide the dope in my shoe, walk into a rib joint, and order some food through the thick, bullet-proof glass. Some of the people would smile. I sort of felt like I belonged. I had track marks and bruises and scars, some sort of street smarts, and a needle exchange card. I knew certain people by name. Some of them, dealers. Some of them, hookers. Some, I'm sure, cold-hearted thugs who saw me as a mark.

A Spot off of Laramie

I knew all the spots by this point. There was one off of Laramie, in an alley I crept into undetected, where I once met a white dude named Ben, probably from somewhere near me. We ended up in some apartment, somehow, not far from the train, with some *other* dude, a black guy who Ben said was cool, who would let us shoot up in his place if we bought him a 40. And so, all of a sudden here I am in this *room*, with these people, in this neighborhood, hearing the train in the distance, wondering what I was doing, and having how messed up things had gotten suddenly dawn on me in peculiar moments of clarity. The dude, the white dude named Ben, who brought me here, who was "doing me a favor," shot his dope into his neck, as if this was normal.

"The veins in my arms are shot," he said matter of factly, as he jammed the rig in, and moved it around until feeling it nick on a vein, which he then attempted successfully to pierce with the needle, completing the ritual in one of the more sickening ways that I had seen.

"At least you ain't done your dick yet," the other dude, the black dude, who now had a 40, also said matter of factly and so then, all of a sudden, this deeply perverse and disgusting act was now a distinct possibility if things didn't end. This guy—his skin gray and sick—hadn't yet, but he talked as if someday he would, and I think that it was in hearing these things and being caught up in these odd, peculiarly familiar places, that I started to subconsciously make my decision. I think this was 2007. Spring would arrive soon enough.

Drinking Mouthwash

I remember the sun, and that it was cold—wintertime—one of those cold sunny days.

It was 52 proof, over twenty percent, with a white, plastic shot glass screwed on. *How could I never have known?*

I drank it and puked in the sink, cinnamon down, cinnamon up—candy for breakfast on Sunday.

I drew a hot bath, sunk in the tub and went piss, rinsed in the shower, put on some clothes, and then thought about what I could steal to get money for dope.

Boo

Boo was the shit. She flagged me down at Cicero and Chicago, got in my car, and took me to get better shit than the boys on the corner were peddling. We'd go deep into places where people like me weren't allowed, past tracks of dilapidated housing, down into alleys, and into vast neighborhoods and blocks that seemed to be hidden from all of the rest of the world. It felt like a different planet. "You make sure you call me when you get your skinny ass home, you hear me, baby," she'd say, and I would. There was plenty of good in this woman who made her own way.

But sometimes these times would get scary, like I was in over my head, once meeting a couple of crackheads in Boo's kitchen, getting high and thinking they were cool—both big, strong black men—then them asking me for a ride, and ending up in some housing project deep in the ghetto. I didn't really know where I was, had sort of forgotten how I got there, and then started realizing that maybe they wanted to rob me or kidnap and kill me. It all suddenly began to sink in, that maybe they were accomplices, pulling a heist, the heist being *me*—to beat me and leave me to rot in the street with dead rats, but then somehow managing to squirm out of harm's way again.

I don't know when all of this happened, this deeper and more demented part of the story, before or after I'd been arrested, or before or after probation started. I remember the warmth of it all and the heat. I remember the freezing cold winter. But all of the rest of it's blurry. All of it's scary. All of it's murky and gray. I can't believe these things that happened inside of this life, *my* life. What if these guys, the guys from Boo's kitchen, decided to take me at gunpoint back to the suburbs, then ransack the house after tying us to chairs and torturing us? Maybe raping my rapidly aging mother? What if Kelly had plotted some similar thing, and had been gathering intelligence each time we met? And he and the hooker, the other hooker I casually met and knew, the one who I spanked in the kitchen, colluded to kidnap and kill me, assuming I had lots of money? What if Kelly's antics had, the entire time, just been a plot to inevitably commit a robbery and murder, to seize all of my mother's jewelry and the money they thought they could get? The prisons are full of these types—two-bit murdering criminals who figured they'd make a few thousand, and who knew about prison and didn't mind taking the risk.

I suppose that the angels were watching.

With that said my friends could do nothing. Miles, who introduced me to the needle years before, gave up on me after I got arrested (there were a couple of other minor ones on top of the major one). There was nothing to say. He was as lost with me as I was. The guy who shot pills in my vein for the first time years earlier gave up because he fell in love and graduated out of this phase and into marriage and family.

"I got arrested again." I felt guilty with my confession to my old friend. We'd both done some serious drugs. We'd been awful with women and in so many ways had been failures. I'd never felt guilty about anything I'd ever shared but now things were, very suddenly, different with him.

"Super Dave, I don't know what to say to you anymore," he said to me in a way that I heard. He had given up junk for a girl. For some people, it works like that; they stop drugs and escape, and wake up from nightmares to live normal lives. I was dying, *and how do you hide a dead son?* Sometimes I go to wakes and funerals and there is happiness and reflection at long-lived and fulfilling lives, at accomplishments and achievements, at successes and the impacts those people had on the lives around them. There would have been nothing to celebrate at mine. Nothing but darkness and tragedy and lost potential, shot up with everything all of them had ever wanted for me.

The Restaurant

The owner had lived through the Vietnam War, or the 'American War' as she called it, and saw things most people have never dreamt about even in the worst hours of their darkest nights. The money she made helped the orphans she knew back in Asia.

I pounded a bottle of wine and then started my shift.

"You get the tea and I'll set tables," Scott ordered politely.

"On it," I said, then fetched the hibiscus concentrate, mixing a batch and getting it into the fridge.

Hillary walked up, taking it all in stride. "I got the napkins and silverware."

"Hell yeah. Let's rock this shit tonight," I said to them both.

Scott nodded. "In theory, if the reservations show up *relatively* on time, it should all work like a well-oiled machine," he assured us as he dimmed the lights. "Can someone get the music working?"

I looked at Hillary. "Death Cab?"

"Death Cab it is," she agreed, then put the CD in the tray.

The music came on—an organ or some sort of keyboard, and each time we played it, I went to a place inside my heart, and a dark, cold and beautiful sadness gave me peculiar moments of reprieve.

Scott pulled me aside. "So, uh, Mykha told all of us to watch you. She doesn't want you drinking anymore, or smoking on shift."

"No problem," I answered, agreeably.

I went outside and lit a cigarette. The last remnants of the subtle wintertime warmth had dissolved as the sun sank and the gray shadows of the evening emerged. The wind whipped frigidly against the frozen frost of the restaurant window. The patrons were starting to show. I put the butt out in the gutter.

"You take table six," Scott ordered me upon my return.

"I'm on it." I approached them and read them the specials, a good-looking family of four. "Tonight we'll be serving not only braised Chilean sea bass but also fresh Maine scallops, broiled to order, each prepared with Mykha's touch, that touch tonight being a medley of imported edible flowers and a light Vietnamese teriyaki."

"Which do you recommend?" The man asked, leaning in and adjusting his tie just a bit.

"Go with the sea bass."

"Too oily."

"I hear you. Then go with the scallops. Did you *really* need my recommendation then?"

He laughed. His family was laughing as well. "We got a comedian here, I see."

"I try," I replied.

"And bring us a festive merlot, waiter's choice."

"I got you covered on that. Sit tight and we'll have a complimentary appetizer out shortly as well."

"Thank you, kind sir. And what might that be?" he asked, folding his menu.

"It's a secret. You have to hold tight. I promise it won't be too long and I promise that it will be an exquisite culinary masterpiece." All of them laughed. The night was off to a good start.

I managed to get to the wine when no one was looking—emptied the bottle into a styrofoam cup and set it behind the register, then came back and slammed the whole thing in the couple of seconds I had. I was a genius at this sort of thing and *also* always managed to pull in the most tips as well.

"You did it again," Scott would say.

"I didn't drink shit."

"No, the tips, man. How in the heck do you do it?"

"Hillary rakes them in too," I said, making eye contact with her.

"Leave me outta this," she replied.

"Outta what?"

"Never mind. By the way, I want you to tell me a story one of these nights, the one from Japan, or the one about jail."

"Okay then. Hang tight, one of these nights."

We worked well together. We got through the shift, the night winded down and we all got our shift glass of wine. I was already wasted, having slammed the remainder of the glasses off of all my tables all night, and pounding a bottle or two. I was starting to *need*, and had planned on catching the 9:40, it being an early night. On my way out the door, Hillary grabbed me.

"Tell me the *story*," she demanded flirtatiously. She was cute. A good Christian girl from Wheaton College, who I, through all of the sickening addictions, had managed to have a crush on. And here was my chance to impress! We went back and sat down at a table. The restaurant was empty of patrons.

"Alright. Here goes. Several months ago, I got hired to teach in Japan…."

"Oh wow. I have a friend who wants to do that."

"I wish I could advise her, but my experience was a total fucking shitshow," I said somewhat belligerently.

Her energy shifted a bit as I told her the story, herself having only known me in a professional sense up until then, and having only heard snippets between Scott and me. She was *good*, and the story I told her was not the type she'd planned on hearing, but I still thought that I could impress her. But the more that I spoke, the darker the dining room got. She wasn't smiling. It wasn't funny. There was nothing impressive about my adventure because it wasn't an adventure at all—just vain words about a tragic event in my life with no resolution. I got lost in the middle. It didn't make sense. I wanted for it to be glorious, like a fistfight at a rock show, but rather it was filled with pathetic and desperate words that trapped and exposed themselves as I spoke them. The story revealed little regarding the series of events but far too much about the person telling them. I got embarrassed because she didn't like my obscenities, and they were all I had. The story was *supposed* to impress her, but I was a drunk, nothing more, and she suddenly knew this. Nothing was funny or redeeming. It sounded the same way to both of us.

By now, I had missed the train and was needing my fix more than ever.

I finally left, just in time to catch the next train to the city, which was important because it was the last *inbound* train I could catch to be on the final *outbound* one after I scored, which was 12:56. This gave me an hour.

There weren't many times I went to the ghetto at night, but the dope from the morning wore off and I needed a fix; so I needed to get to Oak Park, where I'd catch the Green Line, then walk six blocks to a place that I hoped would have dope, then rush back to the El so I could catch the last Metra back to the suburbs. I had just worked all night and was tired and drunk from the shift, but my real job, the actual reason I lived, was staying high. That meant going into the worst neighborhood in America, in the middle of the night and in the dead of winter, to buy drugs that made pain go away.

The train was delayed, stuck because of a freighter. I finally got to Oak Park and the Green Line and then took the El into the dark.

I got to the spot around midnight.

The streets were deserted and lonely; no one was out and the usual dope spots were barren. I had on my dress shoes from work. They were no shelter from the cold and provided little traction on the ice and snow that doesn't go away during Chicago's February. The wind blew through my pants—light khakis—and into my bones. It was snowy and quiet, and I was a ghost in the shadows; wandering, scared, sick, shivering, and desperate. A cop drove by, cruising the streets, looking for junkies and whores, and I had to duck out of the streetlight and into a playground in the snow so I wouldn't be seen. The snow then went into my shoes, and my body hurt more as my feet became blocks of black ice.

I wandered around for as long as I could. I was freezing and sick and the wine that I drank had worn off, only a dry mouth and headache remained and I needed to piss but was frightened to stand in one place. I made my way back to the train after almost an hour, barely catching it back to Oak Park in time to get back to the burbs.

I got nothing that night.

So I had to spend *more* for the train, and then take it back to the burbs. Then plan B to get sleep and get up to go back in the morning. Not copping burned like hot lava and there was ten dollars wasted on a trip into the urban tundra.

My dad had an Ambien prescription; I knew this because I kept track of all pharmaceutical transactions.

I knew where dad kept the slip.

I needed to steal it and fill the prescription, to sleep that night; six or seven of them would do the trick, so I called into Walgreens from the train on the way back. I needed to walk to the pharmacy and commit forgery to get the prescription filled. It was a controlled substance, so they only refilled every 30 days. This was the 29th day, so I begged them to make an exception.

"I have a serious case of insomnia and need to work in the morning. Please, I need them."

"We can go ahead and fill it for you."

"Thank you so much," I responded politely, desperate and insane.

It was two thirty in the morning when I got home and passed out. When I awoke, the bottle was gone, which meant I left it on the table and my parents found it, which was fine because I could go back to the ghetto now that it was morning; the dealers were out and ready for business.

I'd wasted two bags worth of money on my trip the night before, so now I couldn't be as high that day if I didn't steal more to stay ahead of the sickness. I was completely insane.

In the end, before I surrendered, I saw people I grew up with and looked in their eyes and saw pity. A semblance of me would stare back through dark eyes, accepting their judgments, knowing that I was grotesque.

I glanced up and saw my reflection one morning in the window of one of the churches on Cicero, which was nothing more than a small room with a keyboard, but happy and dripping with God nonetheless. I was wearing a bright purple fleece with no shirt underneath, one of my mother's knit hats, and a pair of flooded khakis, exposing my ankles with no socks, and a pair of bedroom slippers. I had just grabbed whatever and left, taking the train, then scored the dope, got to feeling normal, and looked up, accidentally. I hadn't shaved in a week, was skinny and weak and malnourished, with bruises all over my body. I shot dope in my arms and my knees and my shins and my hand. It was such a strange moment, seeing the pale reflection, the ghost of a beautiful boy staring back through dark eyes at the filthy mosaic my life had become.

I'd had *multiple* abscesses drained. They burned like a scorpion sting, and came from using non-sterile syringes, massive infections with accompanying lies as to how I got them. I was drunk all the time, stinking of death; alcohol mixed with heroin, blood, and pus, and hopelessness, with fear oozing out of my body.

Spring was coming. One of the days as the weather got warmer, I got dope that was wrapped up in tape, and that I needed to make sure was real, so I started unwrapping the package in front of the kid. This made him mad and he threatened to hurt me, not letting me move, and kicking my skateboard away, just enough out of my reach (I rode my board into the spots, got my dope quick, and then skated away. It was quicker and easy and safer to move on my board). Another kid came on a bike. I recognized him from past buys.

"Man, I just wanna get my shit and go home," I said to them both, scared and afraid that they'd hurt me.

"Let him go; he's cool," he ordered the one who had wanted to beat in my brains. It was gray; spring warmth wafted itself through the alley. There were brown bags and bottles, graffiti, garage doors, and trash. All of the kids were in gangs. The gangs controlled all of the drugs. The junkies all needed their fixes. Many would kill to get drugs.

Anything you need can take you to dark places in its absence.

A Spot off of Lake

I remember the springtime of 2007: birdsongs and lilacs, squirrels in the driveway and trees. I was scarred from probations, judges and lawyers, dull syringes, vodka pints, nightmare sleep, and thievery. The warmth wafted in, an unusual seasonal warmth: April heat, April hustle. Give me poison. Help me die.

Mom opened windows and tried to pretend. Dad read the paper and Bible and loyally drove me to all my probation appointments, waiting on California outside the courthouse near 26th.

My skin had turned gray. My teeth ached and sweated. It was sunny and warm, shining gold light through the house. I had vodka or wine inside a brown paper bag. The conductors all knew me by name.

I still saw beauty—after the junk went in—and glimpsed the magnificence of the west side community: a whore in a doorway, shriveled and black; needing like me. Dead cats and abandoned, burned-out cars, stranded for decades. Crime and needles and misery, crack pipes and brown paper bags. Bottles and trash, old tires and rotting, rusted jungle gyms sitting in abandoned schoolyards. Wandering souls, drifting down Cicero then onto the side streets, begging for dollars, small sips of liquor, and cigarettes, hoping for shelter and places of peace. A planet, oozing stale heat with blotches of light seeping their way through the darkness; and children dancing through hydrant rainbows and grasping at semblances of innocence. Lots vacant of housing, humans, and decency, strewn over with weeds and overgrown grass. Rats eating shit and moving through alleys. This place was a kind of home—its pulse and its heart and its guts—and although someone could mark me and steal my life, I found myself gazing at billboards, observing its ways, its history, and its changelessness. The progress reserved for the privileged wouldn't make it here. It couldn't. The people who lived here would kill it.

It was beautiful.

There was a spot off of Lake, just east of Cicero, off to the side of the sidewalk, a grass-alley patch between buildings, littered with needles, corroded aluminum cans, broken bottles, and used condoms. It was hidden by bushes—a secret nook—forgotten and filthy, perhaps a small lot that got bought but could never be sold, and where hookers brought johns and where junkies convened to shoot up. A guy named Aaron was there as I whacked through the bushes. Another guy, a black man named Drew who politely introduced himself, reclined himself in the clearing. The whole scene was pasty and rotten.

"That's my brother's name," I responded.

"Well I like your brother already," he said warmly, smiling, as birds fluttered through, singing songs. There was beauty that morning, like God spewing grace through the junk. We sat in the dirt and the weeds.

"So what's up, Dave?" Aaron asked. He was just a blur of lost eyes and thinning, brown hair turning gray. His teeth were rotting and his skin seemed like nothing more than a drapery over a sunken skeleton. "I thought you were kicking this shit."

"Soon enough, man. Soon enough." I responded, defensively.

"Bull-fucking-shit. I'm already planning on dying out here on these streets. Found a cool-ass building to sleep in last night in Villa Park, though." His eyes were sunk back in the sockets, staring out, confused but disturbingly clear all the same. I could see that his molars were missing.

"Man, I got HIV from this shit," Drew stated nonchalantly, resting on his elbows, "ain't no fucking joke, so you best get your ass into treatment." He was dirty and gentle, and had a kind heart, I could tell. I don't think that he'd hurt a fly and was easy to talk to, raised in the hood but exactly like me. He seemed more at peace than I was—like he had surrendered and found something serene in the dirt. "It sure is a bea-u-ti-ful day," he observed, continuing, "it's basically all we got; you know what I'm sayin', motherfucker?" Then he smiled and laughed. He was missing a tooth in the front.

I laughed, feeling something I'd forgotten, and smiled back. "Yeah, man. I think that you're right, but who the fuck knows, bro? Right?"

"Ain't nobody know but God." He smiled again.

"Take that God shit and get the fuck outta here," Aaron jumped in. He was tall, always conniving, missing a front tooth as well, and starting to look like a corpse.

I grabbed an aluminum can, flipped it upside down and emptied my smack, cooked it, and blasted it into a vein on my knee. I was used to syringes by now; some days sharp, fresh from the white Walgreens bag, and sometimes leftover dull ones, and looking for veins that weren't dead, using a spot until it hardened and scarred, leaving a track mark behind. There were bruises all over my arms and my shins and my knees—yellow-blue splotches, inked in my skin like tattoos, and hardened arteries and veins—solidified bumps and reminders that wouldn't go away. Squeezing the plunger, releasing the poison through highways of blood, into muscles and marrow and teeth, soothing the soul of the soiled, sick junkie I was.

Staying Sick

It took everything, staying sick. It wasn't the flu: lay there and dream, have water and soup, rest, watch T.V. and get better. It was work, full-time, all-consuming, and dragging me around into chambers where monsters sat waiting. Wellbutrin sat on the sill, spring air wafting past it, used occasionally as something to swallow in hopes of effect; a placebo like the Neurontin, an anti-seizure medication, 600 milligrams, whose dosage I often quadrupled in search of relief. Non-addictive, I found how to make myself need with nothing else near me to cling to. I made pills into potions that held magic spells, giving reprieve from the nuisance of each waking hour.

They call it disease, and that's what it was: a lack of all ease and normality—in breathing and walking and speaking and sleeping and living. My breaths needed venom; oxygen wasn't enough.

The Bed

I lay there all night then the morning came through with the god-awful chirps and the sun. It turned afternoon. I squirmed, fighting the blankets and sheets—the way that it went when I didn't have money for junk.

You could stop if you want...the pestering thought that occasionally worked its way through.

But you know that you need me....just the two of us....remember...?
The voice that at first seemed so kind.

It was spring, normally cool, but the sticky rot of summer struck early that year and the air convected in warm, wavy currents of sweltering heat. The AC went out and it made it all harder to bear. There were children outside, younger neighbors shooting hoops. The ball thudded down on the pavement. *Thump, thump, thump, whoosh, thump.*

I grasped at the pillow, slamming my head. The sun shone its way through the blinds. It was hot and I couldn't stop sweating, but then I'd get cold and start shaking without the warm blanket. It twisted and turned in my arms, mocking the blanket I had as a child in the same bedroom decades ago.

Cubs Game

Andrew showed up. He had a new girl. I thought she was great from the moment I met her.

"Any friend of Andrew's is a friend of mine," I said to her in between sips of Skol as she drove us all over the city. We were headed to the Cubs game later that day. "This one's a keeper. Don't fuck it up, dipshit."

"I'm not gonna fuck it up," he assured me, looking back from the passenger seat.

"You'd better not!" She said, smiling and laughing. She was sweet with brown hair, *better* than him, I guess you might say. He'd been in Montana for the last several years, doing the mountain-town thing, and somehow he'd landed a gem.

"They say that you don't lose your girlfriend in Montana, you just lose your turn," Andrew said, laughing.

"Same shit in Steamboat, but I had plenty of turns," I said. All of us laughed. Megan was one of the guys.

"I'm not your fucking turn, *Andrew*," she said, sort of smiling and scolding. From the moment we met she was gold. Andrew was different when she was around; smoothed out and funny and kind. He'd follow her into a war. We hung out all day, getting hammered with Jeremiah, then went to the game. I shot up in the stall at Wrigley and nodded out, lifting my eyes to pound beers.

Cubs win! came the announcement and we filed out together, engrossed with Wrigley in the usual summertime mayhem, sticky and hot, tasting victory.

"I gotta run to the bathroom," Megan said, slamming the rest of her beer.

"I hope everything comes out alright," Andrew said, and both of us laughed.

"Beware of the Wrigley Field cling-on! Them hot dogs are brutal with summertime heat," I added, a bit louder than I'd anticipated, and a girl in a jersey looked up, disgusted, then walked down the ramp to the exit below.

"Gross, you guys!" she snapped at us and walked into the restroom. Jeremiah smirked then headed to the bathroom as well.

Then I looked straight at Andrew, and spoke the only clear thought that I'd had in a year: "You gotta marry that girl, bro. You'll never do better."

"Ya think?" He seemed to be taken off guard.

"I *know*, bro. Trust me. Don't let this one get away."

"Hmm," is all he said, but a couple days later he proposed.

This day was the last I recall of the mess. If there was a memory, a day to remember as the last before everything changed, I suppose that this would be the one. Of course there were more, but I'd categorize *this* day as fun, a sort of respite from the nightmare.

Eating Shit

A day or two later, I went to the west side to score. I was still on probation and headed to prison if caught doing anything bad. There were cops everywhere, and I had too many close calls to count, but I knew all the alleys by now, along with the varying getaway routes.

I got to the platform, the same one where I had been caught, and a man started moving toward me, eyeing my movements, it seemed. I swallowed the dope that I had, wrapped in a small plastic bag and got on with my day, not having money for more. He walked past me without incident, carrying a camera, and I was pissed but had learned just enough by now to know that this had been a smart move. I'd just have to deal with whatever was next.

*I'm never lost to you anyway. I am **inside** after all.*

And this is what junk makes you *do*: this is my last memory from inside the heroin dream, of the train trips and freezing cold nights and the sweltering days, of the judges and courtrooms and lies, of the torture inflicted upon those I loved and the impact of all of this mess.

It sat in the water, well-formed, a regular piece, not the usual soup, and stared back from the bowl. It was light brown and normal, like some sort of twisted foreshadowing of Light in my future.

I was used to loose stools, and years of illness and misery by now, like my insides gave up and spewed liquid each day out of habit. But this one was *different*. Its smell engulfed me, telling me what was happening. I whiffed my fate—my filthy, fowl, and disgusting destiny. There really was no other option.

I picked through the piece, wearing a blue rubber glove, and dug out the bag that I'd swallowed the previous day after pacing all night. I opened the foil and looked at the dope, glistening and congealed, with little pink sparkles of filler. It seemed brighter than usual, as the sun shone its light through the bathroom window.

Every junkie has a story like this, and each of these wretched and prodigal souls is a setting sun in his or her own disgustingly beautiful expression of what living means. Some have been whores. Most have been thieves. Some pick through shit and then shoot shit-dope into their veins.

This was my life. This was my war. We all have our battles to fight.

In so many ways there is no greater love.
I like to think all are forgiven.
Love is *supposedly* blind, after all.

Rebirth

*Detox—Ain't Too Proud to Beg—The Pool—Cat Fancy—
Undercover Angels—It Came Shining Through—Getting Swoll—
The Mattress on the Floor—The Good Times—The Fracture—
Freedom Rings*

Detox

There was a counselor named Mike, referred by the doctor who gave me the pills months before. He'd gotten me onto a list for the following stint.

"This disease got me stabbed," he told me, very matter of factly, as I sat there on his couch, nodding in delirium.

"Oh yeah?"

"Yeah. The pain is unbearable, and in prison it's nothing but aspirin. Two aspirin for knife wounds. Two aspirin for cancer. Two aspirin after a surgery."

"Shit, man."

"Shit is right, so consider the fact that I got you onto their list a gift."

My roommate's name was Anthony, a Puerto Rican gangbanger from Humboldt Park. The two other white guys, the ones in the adjacent room, were racist and ornery shitbags. All of the others were black; most of us all got along.

"I seen you talking to them black motherfuckers. Only thing worse than a nigger, is a nigger-*lover* as far as I'm concerned. And I think I'm looking right at one right now," Nick said, accusingly, after mincing very few words. I'd really just stepped into his room to say hi—us having the western burbs in common.

"Would you like me to go and grab a few of them and let them know how you feel?" I asked him, quite sincerely, an offer he didn't take me up on.

"Whatever, man, but don't *act* like you didn't sneak out."

"I didn't do shit, motherfucker," I argued back, not really liking him at all initially, but then even less by the second.

"Why you getting all *defensive* over there, *Dave*? The door in the back was wide open," the other one said, some guy named Alan who shared the same sentiments as Nick.

"I *told* you I didn't do shit."

"Relax. Nobody gives a fuck anyway." He'd been bumming around the suburbs with the rest of the riff; this guy Brian Bluecloud and another guy Jimmy, both alcoholics, not junkies. He drank beer, never liquor, and his skin was as red as a lobster on account of being homeless and passing out in the local forest preserves during daytime. "Just ditch the fucking bottle so we *all* don't get in trouble. Or don't. You think them eight-dollar-an-hour motherfuckers really give a shit anyway."

Doubtful, I thought.

And it was true; I was lying. On the second night, I'd snuck out the door in the back of the hallway, down a metal staircase, and then down the alley. I purchased a bottle of rum and snuck back into detox, guzzling my last sips of booze in the summertime heat.

For reasons I cannot explain, I'd said yes to my mother's sugges-tion a few days earlier to check myself into this dump. There weren't any meds—no Suboxone or Seroquel, no Hydroxyzine, no Tylenol—nothing to make it go easy. I curled up, accepting it all, and sweat out the next several days.

There was a black kid named Adolf—six foot eight, a hundred forty pounds. I can still hear the way that he laughed with his guts, deep and brilliant; his smile could light up a room.

"You gotta be the only motherfuckin' brutha named *Adolf* to ever live," a guy we called Tyson, on account of looking just like Mike, was joking with him out back in the alley during 'quiet time,' the slang term for cigarette breaks.

Adolf stood up against the brick wall, smoking. "I'm Adolf Hitler's long lost great grandchild or some shit," he said, laughing and picking his hair. He sold dope at a spot where I shopped. He recognized me and so this meant he *might be* my friend.

"What kinda sadistic, motherfuckin' momma name her *black-ass* child *Adolf!"* Tyson came back.

"I guess them Nazis sent my great grandma to the right or some shit, then I got named after his racist-ass cause they spared her."

"What in the fuck are you talking about?" Tyson asked, confused.

"Motherfuckin' holocaust, G. Did you *not* pay attention in school."

"Man, there wasn't no niggas in *Germany* back then anyhow. We was diggin' them ditches on chain gangs and shit down south when that big-ass war happened," Reggie chimed in.

"Runnin' from rednecks and them nooses," Adolf agreed, chuckling a bit.

"Uh-huh," said Tyson.

"Yep, yep," echoed Reggie.

"The only shit you niggas be huntin' is rocks and you know it, so don't trip," the counselor chimed in, "now spare me one of them Buglers."

"Mister fucking counselor over here bumming smokes," chided Tyson, laughing.

"We can end the quiet time right now or ya'll can bum me a Bugler."

"I'll do you one better. Have a Newport, dawg," Anthony walked over, handing him one.

"That's my guy." He took it and nodded, content, and we smoked another and went to our rooms for the night.

Once inside, Anthony watched me working diligently on a Sudoku. "How in the fuck do you do them things all night long? Them boxes and numbers don't make no sense, dawg," he asked me antagonistically, impressed.

"You figure it out eventually. It's a challenge like anything else," I told him.

"You and your fucking *challenges*." He lay on his bed, on top of the sheet that was over the one made of plastic.

"Dude, these things are fucking badass. The shit's from Japan but you don't need to know Japanese. It's nothing but numbers," I shot back.

"Sure, man, *numbers*. Whatever, just keep on *reading* too, I guess, mister smart-ass, caucasian motherfucker." He grinned. "Speaking of numbers, what we got five or six nights down in this bitch? So let's bust out another thirty."

"Something like that. Just try not to piss the bed," I said to him, laughing, then we counted out push-ups together.

"These fucking rubber-ass sheets are making me mental as a mother-fucker," he said as we finished, sweaty and sick but accomplished.

"Fucking tell me about it."

I mastered Sudokus. I read Dostoyevsky. I paced the hall, with its dirty black and brown checkered floor, and eked out what push-ups I could with my partner. I jerked off in the shower after flirting with some of the black girls, then sipped on powdered Gatorade and nibbled peanut butter and Saltines—a couple of days after I'd picked up a toothbrush and forced the cruel instrument into my mouth as the dirty mirror stared back, reflecting my filthy existence—the very first step in the agonizing *reassembly*. I puked and I shit and I sweated and swore. I curled up, I cried and I begged for an angel to save me. I cursed the hot nights but I twisted them into my allies. There was something inside, the spirit of some sort of warrior that sought its expression. It seemed to have something to prove, and had been there for all of my life, I realized suddenly; and once I made contact, it took all the pain and transformed it. All of the horror and imminent death became something I chose to transcend.

Each of us has our own warrior that lives in our bones, and when it awakens, we see it was there all along.

Click your heels

Use the Force

There's no place like home....it reminds us.

"We ain't got no washing machines up in this joint," the counselor had told me when I arrived, so I got in the shower with my clothes on, washed my shirt and shorts with a dirty bar of soap every couple of days, then hung them up in front of the box fan pressed up against the window. It hummed like a choir of dusty, war-torn angels.

I didn't sleep. I didn't plan on it. *I didn't resist.* Each eternal evening was its own rite of passage.

*Something **clicked**; like I'd accessed a part of myself I'd forgotten about. A spirit from some distant past life? Perhaps it had been there that day on the Dead lot, hovering over the bald, wailing man at Soldier Field that hot afternoon. Perhaps it was there as I rode through the fields of fresh powder, or spoke sense to my soul in the bars, occasionally whispering things I eventually heeded. Perhaps there were angels and demons above me—fighting as all this ensued—each of them seeking to capture a sad, lonely soul and offer it something less purgatorial and more **permanent**.*

We were kids when we started this stuff, and almost two decades had passed, all in the blink of an eye. They made us feel good but then made us do things that were bad. I think that the Devil exists for this purpose, but I'm not exactly sure how he benefits when he traps you. How could anything get off on something as twisted as the suffering and sickness of others? I think there are eternal truths buried somewhere in these types of journeys, but how do we know when we're entering gates that firmly shut themselves behind us, forcing us through and into places we never should have gone as part of what may, perhaps, serve us in the long run? What sick, evil paradox exists in the lessons I've learned? Or the more sickening ones I was spared from? Would a beating in prison have actually taught me lessons, albeit "tough-learned" ones? What's in it for you when you make the mistake of your life? There are Deadheads rotting in prison cells still to this day. Are there books they should write that inspire us all in the end?

Some people came in giving talks every evening, just like the ones Frank doled out on my previous stint. I listened—there was nothing else better to do—and then suddenly, when one of them didn't show up, I *missed* her, as if something about her appearance made sense; the sense I was suddenly missing. *The only sense.* And I flashed back to what she had said the previous night from the table that sat in the front of the day room, a Big Book—navy blue—in front of her.

"The only thing you dumb motherfuckers need to change is every motherfucking thing," she more or less preached to the zombies. "It sounds simple, right? But it's the hardest shit you'll ever do. Recovery's like opposite day. *Every* day is opposite day for me and because of that, you see, my life just kind of *works*." She smiled, then snickered and laughed. "So you don't like prayin', kneel down. Don't like your husband or boyfriend or whoever because of some shit *YOU* probably did, make amends. Don't like police, stop getting arrested."

"Don't like the clap, stop fucking hos from the south side," Tyson chimed in, in perfect rhythm, unable to resist, and we all laughed as hard as we could.

"Ladies and gentlemen, *please* quiet down or we ain't getting no quiet time," the counselor commanded, barely smirking and taking control.

She laughed some more with all of us, then continued, "I'm the first one to tell you all that I can be the *BIGGEST* pain in my man's ass. It's a miracle he puts up with my shit, but, you see, I live like it's opposite day, and because of that, life just works out. Make sense?"

It did. *Each* of us searches for sense and we suffer without it. *You* might call it purpose, or something else; but to *me* it is sense. A purpose can help us *make* sense, but sense is the thing that we seek when we step into purpose—purpose being just one of the access points we can harness to help us get clear. If you go out and live your purpose, your days will make more *sense* than most of the days of your friends, but it's the *sense* that we seek, the *sanity*. And this woman—*this African American Angel*—made sense to me and a few of the others that evening because she was living *in* service and *with* purpose, and so life to her *made* sense because of this; and so suddenly, the teeniest tiniest *something* now made sense to me. These meetings were suddenly *sensical*, and suddenly I was more *sensible*.

I'm giving this shit a try, I thought—the first thought that made sense in years after she'd failed to show up and I recalled the previous night, and the subtlest feeling of freedom presented itself.

In the absence of the messenger, the message sank in.

"We're set to head out early tomorrow," Reggie informed me regarding the van that was supposed to drive us to Cornell, a treatment center in Woodridge I'd been assigned to as one of the terms of my probation. I had gotten onto a waiting list for the place as the result of a chance introduction I had with the therapist. Had it not been for him, I might have ended up somewhere less *desirable*, because I was in fact, so completely lost in delusion, that I hadn't even known that treatment—long term treatment—was in fact a requirement and term of my probation.

"Sweet, dude. And so we begin the long haul," I said, smiling.

"Dude, we just came through the longest haul possible if you know what I'm saying. Shit's downhill from here if we want it to be."

"True-dat, my brother from another mother."

"Who'd a thunk I'd make friends with a white boy," he smiled, fist-bumping.

"Racist-ass motherfucker," I replied, smirking. He laughed.

Adolf walked up, joking and smiling with Tyson. "Both of y'all needs to bunk up together or some shit; get a room, if you know what I'm sayin'."

"Nah, man. Dave likes the *sisters* if you haven't noticed. He ain't going for the likes of no Reggie," Tyson chimed in.

"Never say never," I laughed, joking around, fistbumping Reggie again.

"Whoa! Easy now, my friend. It ain't *that* kind of rehab!"

"What kind?" Asked Adolf, laughing, "Reggie's jokes never make sense. You ever notice that shit?"

I laughed. "Totally. What, *gay* rehab Reggie? Have you been?"

"Fuck both of you," Reggie said, laughing, defensive, and slipping his way into sanity along with the rest.

"Quiet time! Three extra minutes for a Bugler, seven if y'all got a Newport!" the counselor shouted. "I got you," Anthony said, handing him a menthol. We went out. The alley was littered and a sweet, subtle breeze blew off the lake.

I'd been here two weeks, *another* eternity. I was sleeping and smiling and laughing and looking forward to what was next, having gained fifteen pounds, less afraid and willing. *I bet that there's hot chicks in recovery. I bet they got meetings all over. I should probably try sober living. Just a few months and I'm free!*

Ummm, remember…just the two of us…Dave?

Dave?

Dave?

At four o'clock I awoke, jostled up out of my sleep, suddenly. *Already? They're loading the van really early,* I thought, groggy. The light was on and the counselor stood there. I looked at him, waking and smiling a bit, "What, is it quiet time already?"

"We're searching your room. Somebody said you were drunk." I immediately thought of the bottle then started to panic, remembering, very suddenly, that I had in fact *forgotten* to remember to stash it, as Nick had suggested. *Motherfucking, cocksucking, racist-ass snitch!*

*And here you thought you were **leaving**, and if I remember you've still got a twenty in your wallet. I do know everything, after all.*

There wasn't too much I could say. It was sweaty and dark. Anthony rustled a bit and woke up, rubbed his eyes and smirked knowingly, not really judging or caring. The box fan was blowing. The light hurt my eyes. He'd started to search through my bag, and a few seconds later, there he stood, holding it up to the light, his white rubber glove gripping the neck of the last bottle I ever drank. "Hmmm, what do we have here?" he asked, not laughing or smiling at all.

I started to panic, the same way I did on the platform, but back then there was nothing like hope having crept in at all, and something had happened the last several days in the hallways and showers and meetings, during 'quiet time,' and in the hanging of clothes on the fan. In the listening, and the subsequent sense that ensued, I became willing to give up the fight, but the fight had come back like a monster set free from its cage.

Pssst! Look on the bright side. We can get back together!

"I got no fucking clue," I answered.

"What, this isn't yours?"

"I dunno. I was fucked up when I got here. Please, man, just give me a chance. I *finally* want to stay sober." I was pleading, shaking a bit, but I also knew I wasn't drunk.

Another man walked in, short, with tattoos and thick-framed glasses, and someone who I hadn't met, holding a breathalyzer machine. "Blow," he commanded, seriously but nonchalantly, and I did, obediently.

They looked at each other, each raised an eyebrow, and the one with tattoos gave a nod to the one who I knew, then looked at me. "Somebody probably ditched it or something."

"In *this* boy's bag?"

"I mean, It says .00, but you'll have to wait until our supervisor gets here. She'll make the decision," he said, looking at me but talking to both of us.

Ain't Too Proud to Beg

She got there at six. The sun had come up, and it cast golden beams down the hallway. She came to my room with the others, peeked in, and then walked away, down the hall to her office, *tip-tap…tip-tap…tip-tap*. A few minutes later, the counselor came in and got me, then led me down the hall, walked me in and placed me squarely in front of Ms. Jackson.

She spoke. "Listen, I know what happens here in this place. I'm not stupid. Mostly the people who come through won't change, but sometimes, just *sometimes*, they do. Which are *you?*"

"I am a person who's changed," I told her, but answering more for myself, as if I was speaking a new language with words cast from some other place.

"Prove it to me, then, mister educated one. This guy here says he's always seein' you reading, and doin' them funky-ass number puzzles from the newspaper, but have you *changed?*"

I fumbled around in my mind, searching around for a lie but then landing on the truth. "All I know is that the meetings make sense, finally. I know it's a long-ass road but something feels different this time," I pleaded, entreatingly. "I can't really explain. I never went at it cold turkey before. This time was different. That's all that I really can say. I mean, I'm sure you hear this kind of bullshit all the time, but I finally want it. I've done too much damage. I want the god-awful nightmare to be over."

"Alright, fair enough," she said, agreeably, then went on, "all I'm gonna need from you then is for you to get down on your knees and beg."

"Beg?"

"Did I stutter?"

"No ma'am."

"Okay then. I need you to say 'Please, Ms. Jackson, please let me go to Cornell.'"

"That's all that you need?"

"That's it, but I need to *feel* it."

So I got on my knees; and beneath her sturdy and powerful, statuesque frame which loomed over me like some sort of gate-keeping Seraphim, I begged her with all of my soul.

"Please let me go to Cornell, Ms.Jackson."

"I can't hear you, David."

"PLEASE, let me go to Cornell, Ms.Jackson!"

"One more time." By this time the others were up, and a small crowd had gathered outside the door to her office—witnessing, watching, and waiting.

"PLEASE let me go to Cornell, Ms.Jackson!"

"And now so that everyone hears it," she ordered, so calmly and sure of herself.

*"PLEASE, **PLEASE,** Ms. Jackson! **PLEASE LET ME GO TO COR-NELL!"*** I had started to sweat. The counselor was leaning up against the inside of the doorway, arms crossed, poker face on. The man with tattoos stood inside the office, the slightest hint of a smile poking through.

"Now get up and go get your things," she ordered again.

"Okay…" I answered, and started to walk toward my room, unsure.

"You can go. And I best *NEVER* see your ass in here again," she yelled down the hall as I walked away.

"Jesus, thank you Ms.Jackson!"

"Don't take my Lord's name in vain!" she said, smiling, "now get in the van with the others and leave me alone!"

"Yes, ma'am!" I replied, rejoicing.

The Pool

The trips to the pool were the worst.

Lloyd was driving. Johnny turned around in the van's shotgun seat and instructed us before we got out. "Listen here, you dumb mother-fuckers. I catch any one of your stupid asses talking to the lifeguards or looking at the lifeguards or smiling at the lifeguards, whatever with the lifeguards, we're getting back in this here van, driving back, and doing treatment assignments. Keep your eyes and your hands to yourself, you hear me. Is there anyone who doesn't understand?"

All of us nodded, some more eager than others to get out, then walked single file to the entrance.

I was standing behind Lloyd. "We're here with Interventions," he said to the girl working the desk, who immediately knew who all of us were and what we were doing with our lives. It was a hot July day, sticky and damp, like so many others.

Mike looked right at her. "How you doin'?"

"You can go in," she said bluntly, not looking up from the pad in front of her.

"Mike I swear to fucking god if you fuck up the trip to the pool I'm gonna beat you bloody in front of her," John told him aggressively as soon as we got into the locker room.

"Don't hate a player," Mike responded, rubbing his goatee, and look-ing back toward the girl.

"You ain't no motherfucking player and you ain't the game. And that girl ain't but fourteen years old, so stop rubbing that prison-pussy of yours while you're staring. You *know* I got a daughter," John responded, laughing but angry, as the sounds of kids playing echoed out from the pool and into the locker room. I whiffed the chlorine, feeling uncomfort-able feelings with associated memories.

"What in the fuck's a prison pussy?" he asked, rubbing his goatee some more.

"You gonna find out soon enough, *Mister molester*, and that pretty little mouth of yours will get *used up*, I assure you."

"Oh," he responded, the slang sinking in, "fuck you, just cause you can't grow a beard you talk shit."

"I can, too!" replied John, rubbing his cheek and chin, "I just like my shit *smooth*."

"Scientific fact," I agreed with John, laughed, and got a fist-bump, "you gotta shave that shit off anyway if you're using it to try and bang fifteen-year-olds."

"Dave here knows what's up," John said, agreeing, "ain't no goatee-ass-having white boy gonna ruin my trip."

Johnny chimed in, scolding us all, "We'll turn this field trip around right now if you boys can't behave."

"It was Mike," both of us said at the same time, laughing.

"Snitches get stitches," Johnny reminded us, grinning mischievously. We walked to the high dive. I did a few backflips.

"Damn, Dave. Didn't know you had it in you," Scott exclaimed, impressed.

"What do you take me for?" I responded, a bit defensively.

"You're just kind of a hippie, that's all," he said, scratching the hair on his gut.

"Get up there, man. Give it a try, Scotty boy," John, who had done a few backflips himself, chimed in, challenging.

"I'm good, man," Scott responded, looking to his right and his left, then over at some moms near the kiddie pool.

"Oh yeah, you *good*. I get it, Scotty. It's all good. I know they didn't have no high dives in southern Illinois back when you was growing up," John jeered as I laughed. Scott believed he had marked me for some sort of weakling, but I *watched* him. He didn't do shit. He had a formidable wardrobe of fashionable workout gear but always got 'nauseous' at gym time.

We all did a couple more splash dives and flips, then Johnny came over, ordering us, loudly and in front of the lifeguards, to file out and load up the van. *"I got some good news and some bad news, gentleman,"* he'd say as he commanded we cease whatever fun we were having, but there was never any actual good news.

There is little more degrading than for a grown man than to be chaperoned. I'd been there for over a month.

Cat Fancy

"Yo Dave. So looks like Erin's taking off for a sober living. You gonna miss sneaking literary sips of his cat fancy periodicals?" Matt asked, jokingly.

I laughed. "Dude literally knows all different varieties of catnip and shit, total cat lady."

"Right, a *she* now," he said, "Aaron is now *Erin*. I mean, I'd figure he'd want to switch it up a bit, maybe name himself Madonna or something."

"Right, or Cleopatra; get extravagant on that shit," I added.

"Totally. Or Marsha, bro. Give herself an old-school seventies name."

"He's the easiest roommate I had so far in the two fucking months I've been here, though," I replied, reflecting and puffing a smoke. "I guess he blew all the money for his operation on booze, like literally." (Erin was kind. He slept every chance that he got and kept to himself, waking early, methodically combing his hair, and then reading his cat magazines, which he kept meticulously stacked on his nightstand in the order of their release dates).

"That shit's fucked up, man. Can you imagine drinking a *shopping cart* full of fucking vodka?!" Matt said in genuine astonishment.

I laughed again, "I got mad respect, straight-up, for her or him or whoever. I'm gonna miss him."

We both laughed some more. Matt was smarter than most; that was why we got along. We talked about books and music and had our own theories about the counselors.

I bet Lloyd watches porn in full surround sound.

Totally, dude. On his days off it's just him and a bottle of Jergens.

Takes off his parachute pants; kicks back and orders a pizza for a Stormy Daniels marathon.

Pretending that Suzie's there with him.

Who in the fuck wears motherfucking parachute pants non-ironically anyways?

Lloyd, that's who.

Apparently.

How about Theo and his CO-caine?

Dude straight up accentuates the first SYL-lable of every SEN-tence.

Let me bum a smoke.

Mooch.

Whatever.

We had the same sense of humor, and no one else read. He was also a drunk of epic proportions and had *also* almost drunk himself to death, once sharing hilariously and disturbingly, how he'd converted a rolling chair into a makeshift walker to get him to the bathroom. *"I was totally fucking atrophied, dude,"* he had said, making light of it.

"Just imagine, all this time, the dude was basically a cat lady trapped in the body of a man, not some hot-ass supermodel—a cat lady," he said ponderingly.

"I know! Dude, I keep picturing him in a house-coat, cats and cat shit everywhere; passed out from vodka in some shitty-ass west-suburban apartment complex, then the HAZMAT people arriving in rubber suits."

"Very sadly, I imagine it ending that way—litter box crunchies all over with Erin dead in a puddle of puke, wearing a mu-mu," he said morbidly, as both of us laughed even more.

"Nasty," I agreed.

"It's funny cause it's true."

"Neither of you fools is above that shit, so don't you forget it," Johnny interjected. He'd been standing behind us, eavesdropping. "And at least he, I mean *she*, is courageous enough to be who he is," he continued, trying not to laugh, but then all of us did. It had been a long summer and hints of autumn were starting to whisper themselves through the breeze. He continued, "Besides, he's leaving us today for sober living, so y'all better wish him well and say some prayers. And we're moving Scott in with you, Dave, to make room for the new guys down the hall." He pulled out a Kool, adjusted his tie, and addressed me some more, "and we got you on the waiting list for Serenity House. You're getting outta here soon enough too, brutha-man, but it's probably gonna be at least another month."

"Right on," I said flatly, un-elated. I'd become sort of used to this place—to the lines and the weights and the cigarette breaks, to all of the ways that treatment had helped me avoid things. *Out there*—the world, the normal people who hadn't destroyed their lives, the fact that I didn't have a license and that my probation would last another year. All if it felt like too much.

I took a deep breath and sighed, feeling a bit uncomfortable, and looked at Matt. "Bum me another?"

Undercover Angels

There were these spiritual guys who came in, the same type who came through the detox. They weren't the most traditional-looking gurus—no beads or yoga regalia, no Bibles or advanced Buddhist texts, nothing *fancy*. They smoked and they swore and they looked just like Frank from the last place.

"So what's it gonna be *this* time, guys?" one of them asked, looking right at me, then continuing, "You gonna pull your heads out of your asses, take the suggestions on sober living houses, and finally make the decision to do this?" It sounded rhetorical the way that he asked, almost like he knew what most of us were going to choose. He had a triangle tattoo on his arm with a circle around it and held a blue book, the manual to the anonymous program he represented, and one I had become somewhat used to seeing. "This book here holds *PRECISE INSTRUCTIONS* on how to recover from the *hopeless state of mind and body* that has afflicted each one of you. *PRECISE!*" he emphasized, almost shouting. His name was Steve, and he sat on a chair in front of us in the cafeteria. There were a few others on either side of him, all holding the same book he was, nodding. "So what's it gonna be, gentlemen? You gonna keep up this Groundhog's day bullshit or are you gonna get it this time?"

"For me," a guy named Theo chimed in, "it was all about the next bag of *CO*-caine, a bunch of vodka and hookers, and blowing every cent I made, which sure as shit wasn't a lot. My life was in ruin and I was living one great big lie. And then, one day, *I made the decision.* I gave it all up and I called this man to my right *and I admitted to my innermost self how insanely powerless I was.* I had a spiritual awakening, *as the result of the steps*, and it saved my life. What did I have anyway? Case after case in the system. Car crashes. Lying as if it were the most normal thing in the world. Heck, I'd steal your money, *then* help you look for it." We were sort of transfixed. There was something about the convictions that all of them had. Believers, and this one reminded me of myself—about my age and a kid from the suburbs with parents who loved him. He spoke powerfully, as if guided by something beyond. "I wish I could say it's all roses but life isn't fair. *Life happens.* For god's sake, *I got dumped again last week!* True story! And I have actually *spoken* to another man about it. I had to rid myself of every last resentment because resentment kills. All of us are angry. Everyone in this room is crazy and don't try to pretend that you're not."

John fidgeted, smirking, and glanced in Big Mark's direction. Theo went on, "But now I got tools to deal with it all. I got honest with myself and so I can be honest with you. Any of you ever get vulnerable, like truly honest and vulnerable with anyone ever? Most of you all have never been honest with anyone, including, most importantly, yourselves. That's what this shit's about—honesty, *and life on life's terms*, and if you choose to just simply start doing the next right thing, you **will** have a life beyond your wildest dreams. I've seen it happen way more times with way more people than I would have ever imagined." He was thin with brown hair and glasses, and was living the sober life out in the suburbs. The other guy, Steve with the tattoo—the de facto leader of the bunch—was older and employed the majority of them with the crawl space sealing company he had.

I listened. This place was basically the same as the last one I went to, only with crappier coffee and food, and no girls. The things that *these* guys were saying, were identical to the things that *Frank* had said, and to which I paid little attention. The chores were the same, and there were two of the same guys from my previous stint.

I want to say that the consequences—the prison sentence hanging over me, the humiliating urine analyses, or the Cook County system— had something to do with it all, and it is true that the consequences of our actions oftentimes have a way of forcing our hand regarding certain things, of beating us into submission, but something inside me had shifted. Perhaps this came as the result of the mercy of that sweet albeit frighteningly powerful woman who had granted me clemency. Perhaps it was the horrifying cold-turkey detox I had survived. I was now *different*. I'd become willing, and along with this willingness, there were all kinds of associated thoughts.

*Maybe there actually **is** a God...*

Maybe recovery isn't as bad as I think.

Do I really need drugs to survive?

*I bet there are **girls** in recovery.*

Perhaps sober living is best.

The willingness helped me to hear what I had previously disregarded, like a spiritual propulsion system. The message was always the same. *I* was different.

It Came Shining Through

The institution—Cornell Interventions, located behind the Wal-Mart in Woodridge, Illinois, to be exact, was *medicinal* in nature, the kind of medicine that requires a spoonful of sugar to even *think* about ingesting. It wasn't for comfort. The food tasted bad. The mirrors were made out of metal and they barely reflected—like trying to see yourself in a steel refrigerator door. Lloyd, my counselor, was just kind of absent, staring obliquely in my direction during our one-on-one sessions. The entire staff seemed disgruntled, and I imagine, now, the battles that each of them faced as they woke up each day to the place that employed them.

"Heads down before dinner!" Laura had ordered, and each of us went to our rooms. Mine, the one I had shared with Erin and who I suddenly shared with Scott, was at the end of the hallway.

Scott was asleep and the stench of his gas was wafting out from underneath the blanket he had wrapped himself in. I pulled out a book, "A Brief History of Time" by Steven Hawking, remembering the time in the woods with Andrew and Cheez: *A light year is the distance light travels in a year, which is 186,000 miles per second times sixty seconds in a minute, times sixty minutes in an hour times twenty-four hours in a day times 365 days in a fucking year. It's like six trillion fucking miles for one fucking lightyear! And the Milky Way is a hundred thousand of those across, dude!*

It was odd that it sat on the shelf here, and the material was *mostly* over my head. I wasn't supposed to be reading. *"Naps are important,"* Laura had said, almost sadistically, to me one day as I protested, so to pull out a book was a gamble.

This is precisely the way that I remember it: very unexpectedly, there was this *word*—this assembly of letters—positioned intentionally, it seemed. It was there on the page, just for me, sitting in the middle of a sentence, in the middle of a book I was barely comprehending, and that I wasn't supposed to be reading.

What it said was: *"It would be very difficult to explain why the universe should have begun in just this way, except as the act of a **God** who intended to create beings like us."*

And at that moment, there at the end of the hall, this God—this Being or Deity or Presence or whatever—that I had been insistent regarding the *nonexistence* of up until then, became suddenly *ALL* that there was.

The blinds were coated—a thin film of dust—and the particles suddenly jumped up and danced through the room, like electrons freed from a nucleus that bound them. Golden rays of the late-afternoon sun lit up each little speck, glimmering.

Electricity shot through the veins that the needle had stabbed just a few weeks prior, transforming my filthy, old blood.

I breathed a clean breath and then wept for the span of an hour.

This was the time I found God.

"Naptime's over!" Laura shouted. "Clean up for dinner, then group!" I stumbled back onto the unit, reborn, having seen[1] Bill and Bob's Burning Bush.

---

[1] Bill Wilson and Dr. Bob Smith are the founders of Alcoholics Anonymous, the first meeting happening at Dr. Bob's house in Akron Ohio several months after Bill had a white light, Burning Bush type of spiritual experience in a hospital bed.

Getting Swoll

Sweat dripped off of the rusty old barbell. My palms slipped a bit as I pounded out another rep.

"Look at you, dawg," Big Mark observed, impressed. "You was barely pushing up the bar when you got here in June, and now you throwing up plates *on top of* plates."

"Scientific fact!" John chimed in. He'd gotten himself together and salvaged his soul from the infinite wreckage and soon would be leaving, off to the same place as Erin, a sober living facility in Addison called Serenity House.

"Thank God for the weight room," I said to them both, sweat dripping from my forehead and onto the floor.

"You been getting swoll as a motherfucker in here," Mark agreed. He was throwing up over three-fifty. I had just thrown up one eighty-five and started wearing tank tops.

*You want me to get you **what** kind of shirts?* My mother had asked when I told her about the new duds I had suddenly wanted.

"Now if we can just get Dave here to start rushing the net, his ass gonna be looking like a superstar when he gets outta this motherfucker," John said, laughing and giving me shit, fist-bumping Mark.

"I was born to ride boards, that basketball shit ain't my bag," I replied, a bit defensively, thinking about Colorado.

Mark came back, "Yeah man, but you give that shit everything you got. I see you out there, teacher. That's all that matters."

"Says the brutha who calls foul every chance that he gets," John riled him a bit, and I laughed with him.

Mark wiped the sweat from his forehead. "Fuck both of y'all."

We went in to shower and eat.

The Mattress on the Floor

Scott was a jackass. At night, I'd drag the mattress off the boxspring and into the bathroom, shut the door, shove ear plugs into my ear canals, and eke out the few hours of sleep that I could.

"You're just gonna have to deal with it," is all Laura said when I'd asked for a room reassignment. She hated my guts for reasons I never quite understood.

But this was all part of surrender. I was living in opposite day.

The Good Times

Big Mark was six-foot-eight. He weighed about three-fifty and had a fat gut that hung over his belt. He took the nastiest shits after dinner and sang the blues on Friday evenings, when our weeks were finished while another guy played the guitar. He had worked himself up through the penitentiary ranks during his several stints in the joint. "I put in over a decade up in that motherfucker. Never again. Recovery is real for me now," he said at one of our candlelight meetings one evening before bed. "And you," he said, looking straight into my eyes, "teacher man—my white-bred brother from another mother—your job on this Earth is to teach, and *I* know that *you* know that God put you here for a reason. And this here recovery shit is real, dawg, so you better get some of this wisdom that's being so graciously offered free of charge up here in this motherfucker."

"I hear you, man," I said back, agreeably, "I wouldn't survive in the joint anyway." The three of us sat on the couch. Another guy, Rudy, was across from us in a chair. Everyone else on the unit had gone to bed and we'd gotten permission to stay up so long as we were working on something relating to recovery.

"You'd do just fine in the pen, dawg" John opined. Both were my friends by this point. "You carry yourself like a man and ain't' nobody's bitch, always respecting everyone. I see that shit."

"God sees it too," Mark rhythmically chimed in.

"You a man, dawg, but fuck that shit anyway. You ain't fittin' to end up with none of that mess."

"Scientific fact," I agreed, somewhat hesitantly.

"Proven in a court of science!" John declared, giggling, his bright teeth and smile lighting up the room. He was part of the P-Stone Nation, raised on the south side. A straight-up, motherfucking gangster but so much like me it was eerie. Same jokes. Same books. Same tastes in so many things and the same sort of soul.

"Only motherfucking science this motherfucker *thinks he* knows is the science of how to end up with some nappy-ass, beat-up-from-the-feet-up lookin' baby mama," Mark riled him a bit.

"Nah, man. I'm a *love* doctor, you dig? I study the science of pussy, and I get the quality shit. I know that you know this, my man," he said, mostly to Mark.

"I like the butt," I added, smiling.

"See now, Dave here's a pimp, I can tell, he's just into them fine-ass European bitches."

"Dude, I don't know no bitches from Europe. I'm from Glen Ellyn, bro."

"Same motherfuckin' difference, white boy." His eyes were mischievous windows, eternally amused and brilliant. And *each* of our eyes those evenings were soft pools of understanding for one another.

We laughed. There were good times we had at Cornell—pizza and movies on Friday nights when we stayed up later than usual, the outside meetings we were allowed to attend with the recovery guys, and these candlelight meetings we organized ourselves, which were sacred.

Rudy was generally quiet but suddenly spoke up, very vulnerably. He was thin with feathered brown hair and a pointy nose, and wore polos he tucked into blue jeans. "I mean I know we're all joking around a lot of the time, but this shit is deadly fucking serious, and sometimes I think you guys joke around a little too much. It's easy to forget what it was like a month ago for me and how bad it had gotten. We get here. We eat and lift weights. Some guys get *swoll*, others get fat. Whatever. But this shit ain't no joke. I didn't leave that shithole for like four months after my fiancé left me; and here I am now, a year after that, stuck in here. *This is my fourth fucking time.* When will it end? A part of me knows that I'll never get clean so why bother? And that part talks the other part, the part that wants it, out of it by putting these sick fucking thoughts into my head. These candlelight meetings are nice and all, but the real world is out there waiting for all of us, ready to pounce with a quick dose of reality as soon as life happens; and for me, it can be anything. My triggers are never-ending. Good days. Bad days. Weddings. Funerals. Whatever. And when I get completely honest with myself, I know I'm not finished. I'm headed back to my apartment, alone. I surrender."

We sat there, feeling the weight of his soul. I remembered the way that I felt my first time around. I remembered the hopelessness and the *knowing* that I knew I wasn't done. *I'll just get one more,* I had thought, over and over again for my entire previous stint; and I hadn't realized, yet, that something about *this* one was different, that something had changed without me even realizing it had. There had been, of course, that day at the end of the hall, but there'd also been the grind—the lines for cigarette breaks, the bullshit with the counselors, and the morons like Scott I had to deal with. *I knew that he'd never be sober.* I was now a believer, but the day-to-day shit—the litany of simple repetitive realities—was the same and all of it made me forget that a Higher Power, whatever It was, had come in and started to work.

"Fuck that," I said to him, looking straight into his eyes. He was from Wheaton and had nearly killed himself with cocaine and cheap vodka in some cheap-ass motel out in Downers Grove after being caught red-handed with a hooker by the woman he had chosen to wed, who then took his house. "Dude, it's all about surrender, which I've recently come to realize is very much the opposite of giving up. That shit you're talking there, bro, that ain't surrender. *It's giving up.* It's hopeless, bro. It's giving up *everything.* This surrender shit is totally different, I'm seeing. It's what the former crackhead said to me back in detox about living in opposite day—which is *just* finally starting to really sink in for me—*that's* surrender, frickin' opposite day. Surrender is doing a bunch of pain-in-the-ass shit you don't wanna do. Surrender is the shit hole detox I was in for two weeks and begging *something*, God I guess or whatever, for the strength to get me through it. *Surrender is active*, it ain't sitting around and waiting for something to save you, or cramming some dope in your arm. It means you'll start living differently. It's like '*Fine, God, you win. I'll go to those stupid meetings till I'm blue in the face.*' I'll work the twelve steps. I'll go to a crappy-ass sober living facility *after* my three months in treatment and do all *their* motherfucking chores. More counselors. More piss-cups. Whatever. It means that you'll go do the thing that you *don't* wanna do so that you can have the life that this God—He or She or It—or whatever has in store for you. I'm *stoked* for Serenity house. *I hear they have fucking lobster*, and that you can lift whenever you want. There are girls, too. I'm giving this shit a shot, bro."

Everyone sat there in silence as the candle flickered. Rudy adjusted himself on the couch.

"Spit that shit, teacher man," Mark said quietly.

"Scientific fact," Rudy said, glancing in my direction a bit.

"Scientific fact," John added, leaning forward in his seat and fist-bumping Rudy, who died a year later, his funeral, unfortunately, not standing as a catalyst for any sort of revolution. We were all so old.

The Fracture

Weights were Mondays, Wednesdays, and Fridays. We had basketball Tuesdays and Thursdays. The weekends were up in the air—sometimes we went to the weight room and sometimes we chilled. Things were clear. I had a routine. I'd accepted that this, *all of this*, was going to take a while, and couldn't wait to get to Serenity House.

"I'm headed to a halfway house after this," I had told my brother and his girlfriend.

"That's what mom said," he replied. They were back from Colorado for a summertime visit and had come in to see me.

I played my heart out at basketball. Someone would pass me the ball and I'd dribble a second, freeze, then pass it as soon as I could to someone who'd then charge at the net. Mark sometimes dunked. John hit jump shots effortlessly from outside. Another guy, Dean, had played in college and did these stealth passes, looking one way and hucking the ball in another direction to someone who'd go for a layup. Autumn arrived and leaves fluttered themselves across the court. I'd been here since June and it was suddenly mid-September; the sun was starting to set earlier and an entire season had passed. And then one morning, while jumping up for a rebound as the result of getting bolder and bolder, I came down and something went *snap*, and I hit the ground hard, writhing in pain and clutching my ankle.

"Shit man, someone call Suzie," Mark ordered as they led me over to the grass, my ankle throbbing. One of the counselors came over and they loaded me into the van.

I'd broken a bone in my ankle. They gave me some crutches, an ice pack, and some ibuprofen. Laura picked me up.

"Damn, dude, you didn't even *TRY* and get no painkillers?! I'd a' been all over that shit, like some sorta motherfucking *free*-lapse," John said, impressed.

"I thought about it. I can't really say that I even wanted them, though. It was weird," I told them, surprising myself with my words, then Laura walked up and called me into her office.

"So I'm afraid that I have some bad news. I just spoke to Serenity House and they have a new policy, and they're not going to let you in with a broken ankle." She sounded pleased, almost sadistic. She knew how long I'd been here, and despite whatever personality conflicts we had, there was no evidence whatsoever that I hadn't been toiling away.

"God-fucking-dammit, that's bullshit!" I yelled.

"Please keep your *voice* down," she ordered, passive-aggressively, adjusting her Cubs hat.

I calmed down a bit and somewhat composed myself. "I've been here three fucking months. Those were the terms of my probation."

She nodded a bit. "Actually, there aren't any *terms* regarding the actual length of stay. You go when you're favorably discharged and this just seems to be a deterrent to that." I could feel the sway that she held, just like the woman back in detox, and I knew that I had to shape up, right then and there. It felt like a test, and in this moment an opportunity presented itself with something unseen whispering soft messages I chose to heed.

I composed myself in the chair. "Listen, I'm sorry. I'm just not too stoked to be here, suddenly on crutches and gimping around. I know I can cop an attitude, but I finally want this shit. I want to get out and get on with it. *I actually want to be sober.* I am totally not bullshitting you, I swear."

A wave of compassion seemed to come over her, and she looked at me genuinely. "Look, I don't want to keep you here forever, contrary to what you may be thinking, but their policy is their policy."

"It's been a long fucking road is all," I pleaded, feeling defeated.

Someone came into her office with some pressing matter she had to address. "Talk to Lloyd. Maybe he can do something for you." The suggestion here was that, although *she* could do something, she didn't really want to, and so she would delegate the decision to Lloyd. "And we're going to have to suspend rec as well while you heal," she added as she walked out, knowing full well of the impact that this would have on me.

"Okay," is all I said, keeping the anger contained but still feeling like a prisoner.

Part of all of this predicament was the fact that I was "on paper," meaning I still had the system to deal with. I'd only been on probation for a few months, and this *institution* made it easy to forget about court and the cops, and the judge. This new variable—this fracture—this new life event that had taken the way I had planned things to go and shifted them very suddenly into another direction, as often happens in life, either to evolve us to keep us stuck in a pattern. So was it, perhaps, a subconscious act of sabotage to keep me stuck in an environment that I *said* that I hated but had grown so accustomed to that I was afraid to leave it? After all, Cornell managed everything. Cornell made the calls to my P.O. Cornell saw to it that my visits to 26th and California had been suspended. Cornell made things easy in so many ways: wake up, line up, shit, shave, and shower, then sit in a room and discuss how you feel for the day.

So had I 'broken my own leg' or was this an act of providence, hiding seemingly in disguise?

"Fuck all this shit," I ranted to them both in the weight room, "I'm gonna be stuck in the bitch for another six months if that horrible woman has her way."

Mark laughed sympathetically. "Man, you gotta relax. God's just fittin' to find you a *better* place to live. You gonna see, dawg, that this all works out for the better. You're always bitching about the suburbs anyway. Maybe you can find a new spot in the city?"

"Whatever. Fuck all this shit. And she tried to tell me I couldn't lift weights, made me call the fucking doctor to get a note. Fuck her too."

"Yeah, man, that bitch don't like you no-how so fuck her and fuck her fat ass. You're fittin' to fuck some of them white bitches when you get out cause you're a pimp anyway, dawg," John chimed in.

"Yeah, man. I'm not sure what her problem is but she's gonna see when I'm sober ten years from now," I said to them both.

John nodded, smiled, and looked in Mark's direction, "Man, I wouldn't fuck that dirty-ass pussy with *Mark's* dick."

"Leave my big-ass dick out of this," Mark replied, smiling his Cheshire grin. All of us laughed.

"Dave, man, listen," Mark continued, "I know you're upset, man, but I *been* to the penitentiary, spent years of my life up in that motherfucker, and this here ain't shit. So chill the fuck out, read them books you like to read, and trust in God's timing, cuz he got it all figured out and you're a part of his world now, G."

"I hear you," I said, agreeing, and threw up the barbell.

Freedom Rings

I went to my meeting with Lloyd—pleading—to see if there were any strings he could pull.

"Dude, I gotta get out of this place. I can't handle this shit anymore," I implored, somewhat desperately. "It's been like a hundred days, dude. The new motherfuckers showing up are crazy as fuck and Mark and John are leaving. And Laura's got it out for me and you know it."

He just sort of stared, saying nothing, then finally uttered a little bit of his brand of peculiar and awkward wisdom. "You *can* handle it, you just don't *wanna* handle it. The only thing you *can't* handle is death."

What the fuck, Lloyd!!?? A pair of Oakley blades hung off his collar, resting inside of the tether his badge hung from. He was skinny and balding and spoke with a squeaky voice, and was seemingly useless as a counselor.

"You're goddamn right I don't wanna handle it! I don't wanna handle these crutches or this bullshit cast either."

He stared again, a bit cross-eyed, creating another awkward silence. "Sounds like you're angry," he finally said, stating the obvious.

"Ya' *think?*" I retorted, infuriated. The meetings with Lloyd were the worst. We had our sessions and he'd sit there and stare. "Can you just call that place in the city, The Rez or whatever it's called?"

"Do you think it's a good idea for you to go to the city?"

"Why in the fuck wouldn't it be?" I asked, argumentatively, annoyed.

"There are more ways to use in the city. There are all sorts of triggers you can't anticipate."

"Dude, yes, I hear you, but they got way more meetings, and I'm doing the fucking meetings. AA all the way."

He seemed more concerned with what he was having for lunch than the fate of my soul, but told me he'd make a few calls, hearing me out nonetheless. I picked up the crutches and hobbled my way down the hall.

A Life Beyond My Wildest Dreams

*Rogers Parker—Serving the Homeless—Smitten—
Happy Birthday—The Job—The Sherwin—Jim Called—
California—Andrew's Celebration—Hope*

Rogers Parker

My dad picked me up, patient as always—reliable, helpful, and kind, then dropped me off. I'd *thought* that Wrigley Field was north and that if you ventured beyond, past Lakeview and up to Andersonville—'Girl's Town' as they called it—that you'd be as north as could be. But Rogers Park, home of Men's Residence North AKA 'The Rez,' and my new home, was even farther than Andersonville, an eccentric bohemian enclave on the shores of Lake Michigan.

I walked in mid-morning and unpacked my things—a beautiful day in the fall. I'd started in June in the sweltering heat, and October was now nearing its end. The leaves drifted down, a perfectly crisp day like the ones I remembered from childhood. *First day of school. Markers and pens. Folders and scribbles and stars on the sides of the papers. The girls and the new teacher. The card with my name on my desk.*

There were men coming and going, and moving about through the house; racing to jobs, carrying backpacks, and trying to stay in good standing. A guy checked me in, very casually, made me piss in a cup, and led me to my room, which looked out into an alley and the kitchen of a restaurant. I looked out the window and saw a rat scurrying away from a dumpster. *My new home,* I thought with a chuckle.

I took a long walk, at least thirty blocks. The sun shone through the crisp autumn air. Cars sped by. Bicyclists raced down the street. There were hipsters and tricksters, and beautiful midwestern girls wearing tight, faded jeans. Taxi cabs, diners, and places for slices of pizza—a graveyard, a church, then a bar. Chicago, alive. A season inside the abyss had now come to an end; my winter, my desperate lost weekend, had come and then finally gone. The dark night was seemingly over.

A familiar old voice hissed in my ear.

Hey Dave! I've been waiting for you to get out!

I walked to a meeting and called someone I knew in recovery.

Serving the Homeless

"THAT'S NOT SERVING THE HOMELESS!" He seemed so nice when Ed had first introduced me to him.

"Sorry, Terry. I mean I thought we were *all* serving the homeless," Ed replied, pathetically.

"WE ARE, ED! WE ARE ALL SERVING THE HOMELESS! SO GET YOUR HEAD OUT OF YOUR ASS!"

Things had gotten strange and codependent amongst the ranks of our team and our leader. It was late fall and the seasons were changing, with frost blanketing the small patches of grass and urban plots around Andersonville in the mornings. The leaves were changing—from green, to orange and yellow, and then brown, finally falling and blowing around in the streets. I'd ridden twenty miles the previous day.

"You see here Ed, *DAVE* wants to serve the homeless. *DAVE* is on board," he screamed as I awoke and made coffee. You stand outside smoking. You haven't showered in days, and I can smell the stench from your dirty-ass beard over here! WHY DON'T YOU SHAVE, ED!? I quit being a lawyer after seventeen years because I wanted to *STOP* the abuse in the system. What the fuck did *you* do, ED!?"

"Terry, Terry...c' mon...I thought we were working *together* on this" Ed replied, weakly, asserting himself the best that he could. "I don't want any friction. I want to save the homeless too!"

"We're not *SAVING* them, Ed! We're *SERVING* them! SERVING them so they can save themselves! No one needs saving except you!" He spun around in his chair, turning his back to Ed. The room took on the same awkward silence we'd grown accustomed to.

The phone rang and he answered. "Serving the homeless!" A faint voice came through from the other side of the phone.

"Yes. YES!" He perked up, shifting his demeanor. *This* was the man who had answered the phone for Ed and then showed up to greet us, offering each of us jobs. "Well, I *live* to serve the homeless," he began, then meandered his way into the story about quitting his job as a lawyer to serve a higher calling, this calling being to support the poor souls of Chicago who didn't have housing.

"I finished the stickers," Adam chimed in, in an attempt to break the tension. He was working like I was, doing his best to stay on the right track. Ed had been on Craigslist a month or so prior at The Rez, answered an ad, and then grabbed Adam, a Jewish kid from the north shore and recently recovered crackhead, and brought him to Lakeview to meet Terry, along with myself.

"Good, now get them into the bags, and let's head out. Remember, everyone gets a sticker and a 'Thank you for serving the homeless,' I don't care if they give you a penny; they get a sticker and a thank you and a reminder that they're serving the homeless."

He bought us all bikes which we rode to various intersections all over the city, collecting money for the charity he had founded in big woven baskets at various intersections.

It was getting closer to winter, and colder. I'd been sleeping on the floor of the office in Andersonville only to find out that the charity he formed was a scam. This came as the result of a driver pulling over and informing one of the girls on the crew I was running that he had in fact been disbarred for gross misconduct as an attorney, hadn't quit, and then had thrown together this bogus charity in an attempt to pay his bills for a handful of months. I'd left The Rez after arguing with one of the counselors who had woken me up at four o'clock A.M. to scrub a toilet that he said hadn't been properly scrubbed the previous day, and I'd had it. It was bullshit, and there, in that moment, I forgot about opposite day.

And so Terry had become quite abusive, having me there as a subject of sorts, always promising to pay me but not following through. "Remember Flowers for Algernon, Dave," he said one night as I left for a meeting.

"I'm not some motherfucking retard, dude," I responded, "please don't suggest that I'm slow."

"But you go to those meetings, *EVERY DAY*, Dave! It's just you and your hobbled friends and your meetings. Three yesterday alone by your own calculations! You disappear from here, this home that I gave you, and you come back late. I don't know where you've been!"

It was true. The previous day I had been to three meetings—one downtown first thing, then a "nooner" in Lincoln Park at lunch with another one in the evening called Pacific Group, which was really more like a party with hundreds of people from all walks of life and from all over the city. I was *surviving* on meetings by this point—some had donuts, all of them had strong, black coffee, and there was one way up north that had peanut butter and jelly sandwiches, cut into triangles with all sorts of chips and refreshments. They basically kept me alive, and I rode the bike

Terry bought me all over the city, often from one to the next, to the next, all day long as the work he was giving me was drying up. These meetings were in a lot of ways, all that I had.

"You think he's gay for you, dude?" someone had asked me out front of a church after I had explained my living situation to him and the subsequent challenges.

"Definitely gay-*ish*," I'd responded, laughing uncomfortably.

Despite my shortcomings, the fact that I gambled and left the safe house (which wasn't all that safe in the first place), I worked my recovery program and met hundreds of people. Ed later died, OD-ing on a lethal concoction of Vicodin, vodka, and internet porn after leaving The Rez himself.

And then it was suddenly winter, as often happens in Chicago, freezing cold, and I was essentially homeless, sleeping on the floor of this office. I'd been sober for over six months, taking it all very seriously, however, and unwavering in my commitment to stay clean.

One day his friend, perhaps his *only* friend—a sweet woman named Mariam—emailed him about a building she found on Craigslist that had an apartment for rent. It was all the way north, a few blocks from Evanston, and sat on the shore of the lake. We drove in Terry's Jeep from Andersonville. A woman named Janet with frizzy, dirty-blonde hair met us and let us into the building, and then into a ballroom just off to the left of the entrance, which immediately captured my attention. There were chandeliers hanging from the ceiling, and an old phone booth sat off to the left with the receiver still attached by a cord.

"Woah," I exclaimed, somewhat awestruck, not really imagining, until now, that such a place could even exist. "This is *seriously* beautiful."

"I know," she said, "we get that a lot. It was built in the 1920s, and used to be a hotel."

"Looks like one of Al Capone's hangouts," I added, joking.

"So goes the rumor," she answered. "Here, I'll show you the beach."

Terry then went into his spiel regarding his retirement from the law profession and the charity and all that crap and I dismissed it as he proceeded to capture this woman in the same way he captured everyone. He was charming at first to most of the people he met, handsome and strong with neat hair.

I walked away from them both, through the ballroom and then out to a veranda, which was a hundred feet wide and overlooked a beach, blanketed in snow; and there was the *lake*, beautiful and vast with a couple of birds floating on the surface, bobbing up and down atop the gentle waves that were rolling in. The city sat off to the south.

She walked up, led us out, and then gave us a tour of the boat room it had in the basement. It had icicle-looking stalactite formations dripping from the ceiling and a damp, musky odor. There were kayaks and wind-surfing boards stacked up on racks and resting against the walls.

"This is where we keep the windsurfing gear," she told us as she led us into another room that had sails hanging from the ceiling on hooks.

"Woah. I've always wanted to try that!" I said enthusiastically, trying to contain my excitement, with the insistent words of the guys in recovery from the previous months echoing in my head—*You can have a life beyond your wildest dreams*—suddenly making sense, along with the fact that I'd broken my leg, which had healed.

"Well, this building is kind of a mecca," she said. "We've all been windsurfing here since the 80s. There's plenty of hand-me-down gear lying around."

"Hmm, so might one of these units come with a windsurfing lesson?" I asked, kidding a bit.

"Perhaps," she answered, smiling, "but I only have the one unit. I do have a friend, though, who I think is renting one as well. I'll give her a call. Terry, you're the one who contacted me first, so you get first dibs on mine, but I'll call her today."

"Okay, please do," I said, as politely as I could, then waited a couple of days, trying as hard as I could to let God do his job. *"If it's meant to be, it will be,"* one of my new friends said to me outside a meeting as I explained the situation.

A woman named Laura called a few days later and showed me a room at the end of a hall. It had no kitchen, just a hot plate, and there was barely room to throw a mattress on the floor; it being the bedroom of a one-bedroom she had converted into an 'efficiency unit.' But it had a beautiful view from the seventh floor looking southward toward the city with the Sears Tower towering in the distance, extending into the sky like some sort of cosmic compass needle. The lake sat off to the left and there were various jetties and piers extending outward into the water, seemingly lined up in rows all the way down to the Loop. It was perfect.

She was short with brown hair and a little bit cunning, wanting to get someone into the unit as soon as possible. "If he doesn't call me by the end of the day, I'll give you a call and we'll square it away," she told me regarding the Loyola student who was supposed to take the place. "I'm asking $550 a month."

"Okay," I said, trying to contain my excitement, then waited a few more hours for her call.

I moved in a couple days later, continuing to slowly and surely piece my life back together from the shattered mess it had been just a few months before. There will never be words apt enough to describe the love that I had, and will always have, for this tiny room at the end of the hall; God's reward for my surrender.

Smitten

She taught me to fuck, and loved cocaine and not eating. Her cat's name was Lily. She loved the cat too. I saw her at one of the meetings, then stalked her on Myspace. She invited me down to the Gold Coast Galaxy high rise her parents had paid for. I don't think we got out of bed for a month. She lay there before me; I thought that forever had happened.

She had four months; I had about seven. It was sick even though I'd been reborn.

She had a stuffed lamb-doll named Marge. She was nine on the inside but looked seventeen. She was twenty-three.

I loved her.

Happy Birthday

It was snowing—a gnarly spring dump, grimy and brown. A small splotch of sun made its way through the clouds as I trudged through the snow, my front tire slipping and constantly re-correcting all the way to the courthouse. I was used to the routine by now—*belt and shoes off, arms to the sides, wanded and patted, cops all around, jail in the back of the building for those who fucked up.*

I was covered in splotches of mud—soaking and cold. I'd been clean for nine months and the first day of spring had arrived; my thirty-third birthday. It was seventeen miles to the courthouse from East Rogers Park, north going south—Sheridan, Touhy, then Western for most of the ride. I made it with time to spare, unwilling to ever be late.

Judge Kirby walked in, carrying a Burger King bag, situated himself, offered his clerk a hashbrown, then looked at my case. "So what brings you here?" he asked bluntly, vaguely recognizing my face and my case after seeing me several times.

"Probation," I responded.

He looked me over for a second or two, the sight of me sinking in."You're covered in mud!" he exclaimed.

"I rode my bike," I answered, honestly.

"From where?" he asked.

"Rogers Park." A puddle of frigid water had formed at my feet and I shivered a little.

He continued, "Why didn't you take the bus?"

"I don't like to rely on public transportation," I immediately responded, sure of myself as could be. "Also, I like riding my bike."

"In the snow?" he asked, somewhere rhetorically, continuing "but what if you got a flat tire, and that then caused you to be late?" He was smiling a bit, and glancing down at my case file.

"I have a spare."

"But what if that took you too long?"

"I figured that into my time estimation, plus I have money for a cab."

"What time did you leave Rogers Park?"

"By seven."

"Two and a half hours ought to do it, I guess," he said, agreeably, smiling. Then he closed the folder and looked at me abruptly. "You know

I ride a bike," he said, then paused dramatically, throwing his glasses down onto his desk.

"Oh yeah?" I replied, confident for some reason.

"Yes, an *indoor* one. In my living room. Because it's freezing outside. And snowing. You must be insane."

"Definitely a little," I answered, trying to not seem smug.

He got back to business. "So you completed treatment, it says, had several clean urine tests, and rode your bike over fifteen miles in the snow to get here on your birthday, arriving on time."

"Yes, your honor," I responded truthfully.

He paused, looking around at the various defendants. The courtroom was dreary, lit with fluorescents. "Cook County doesn't need people like you in the system. It's a waste of our time and our money. I'm terminating your probation, effective immediately." He paused again, then spoke, addressing the courtroom. "Take a look at this man. No excuses. No bullshit. Just an honest guy who made some mistakes. This is why he leaves today and hopefully doesn't come back." He focused his attention back on me directly, then smiled. "Good luck, David. I hope I never see you again."

"Thank you, your honor," I said, silently rejoicing.

It was thirteen months before my probation was set to be over. All that I had was the fact that my life was now different, that I'd worked to transform my existence, and succeeded by taking the Steps which some others had taken.

It was all about opposite day.

The Job

I answered an ad on Craigslist a month or so later. The winter had passed and I'd been selling bicycle reflectors for John, and having moderate success. John, who was very obviously mentally ill, and myself, being less insane as my recovery became more and more solidified, slowly faded into the background of my existence, finding others who lived in the building to hassle and bully.

I updated my resume, which had not been half-bad before all of this happened, and sent it in to the ad, receiving a call a few minutes later.

"Hey, this is Jon from AvePoint. I just got your resume and I was wondering if I could ask you a couple of questions." He spoke professionally. I guess you would call him a company man.

"Sure," I answered, excited, not having expected so quick of a response.

He got right down to business. "So tell me about this job you did the last two years, *First Capital Funding*. Can you describe to me more about that?"

I'd made up a job. I don't know exactly what I was *thinking*, but figured I'd be able to slide it past someone. "Oh, that was selling shell corporations with their associated lines of credit," I answered, having overheard two guys on the train talking about this a few days before.

"Well that sounds *interesting*," he replied somewhat antagonistically. "So then how do I buy a corporation? Like from where."

"Uhh, they have a website on the internet," I answered, squirming and blushing a bit, which he seemed to sense through the phone.

"Well, I have my computer here in front of me, why don't you tell me which one?"

I froze. I had nothing, and an uncomfortable silence made itself known through the phone.

"You know what, I'm really not buying it," he said, breaking the silence, "but what the hell, why don't you come in for an interview? Can you come in later today?"

"I can," I answered, hanging up. I banged on my neighbor's door, another guy in recovery who lived in the building, and asked him to borrow some clothes, which he lent me enthusiastically.

I got to the office. It looked strangely familiar. He kiddingly drilled me a bit more about the job, not asking too many *serious* questions, and then finally offered me the job, a no-bullshit salaried position in sales.

"There's just something about you," he said as I signed the offer.

I met with my sponsor the night before starting the job, going over the list of the people I'd harmed. There were all sorts of people to make amends to—my parents, obviously, the woman who owned the restaurant, and the nice man who'd hired me to go to Japan, just to name a few.

"You're just going to pray for willingness at this point. Don't worry about making the amends just yet," he told me as we went over each of the names, and when I arrived the next day for my first day of work, I realized what it was about the office that seemed so familiar. Just as the realization hit me as I was walking into the bathroom before my first day of work in the brand new life I had worked very hard to create for myself, *I bumped into the nice man who I'd fooled into hiring me for Japan.* There he was, looking right at me with faint recognition but not fully realizing who I was, then walking past on his way to the urinal. The office I was now working in, was on the *same floor* as the one I had interviewed at to go to Japan!

I wish I could say that I knocked on his door soon thereafter, but on advice from my sponsor I waited, and then one day he no longer worked there, and my attempts to track him down a couple of years later were unsuccessful.

"You tried, and that's all that matters," he said to me after. "It's all in God's hands at this point. If you're meant to make amends to this man, it will work out when it does."

This particular event, this coming full circle of things in a way that I could never have imagined, along with the other events, including the ones involving me ending up in the apartment at the end of the hall, are all of the proof that I'll ever need. I know God is real, and that what transpired in that room during naptime that day, the moment I became "reborn" was as real as the eyes that are reading the words on this page.

I just call It God. You can call it whatever you'd like. I felt Him laughing that day.

The Sherwin

*"One of my least favorite pieces of writing advice is 'Make the setting
into a character.' I admire the vivid rendering of time and place as much
as the next bookworm, but the conflation of a story's location with the
people who populate it has always struck me as lazy and inaccurate.
Character is character and setting is setting. A protagonist has a personality and a will that gives the story momentum. Setting, the authentic
depiction of an era and a locale, is crucial, too, but should serve the
function of stage, not actor. Or so I thought before I met—yes, met—the
96-year-old, eight-story Italianate edifice holding court as regally as
a royal in exile at 1205 West Sherwin Avenue. The lakefront building,
imposing and unmistakably the stately eccentric of her windswept block
in Rogers Park, made me reconsider my bias."*
~Kathleen Rooney, *Chicago Reader*

Nina walked up, demanding. "You have to move your windsurf board.
It's blocking my locker." By now she was bald and we'd somehow made
friends with each other.

"Alright, I'll do it," I answered her, begrudgingly, smirking and
glancing at Kevin.

"You have to do it now. I don't want it there when I return my shit
later." Her words had a way of enforcing themselves, forged in Mid-
dle-Eastern iron. She also spoke French and smoked Marlboro Lights.
Her skin turned dark brown in the summertime months at the Sherwin. I
got up and moved it and then she said thank you. We both had a smoke.
Her children were running around with a bunch of the others.

Nine years went by. There were days when the residents, the "Sher-
winites" as most in the neighborhood, themselves included, referred to
them, would pull out the beach recliners and sit together. They'd watch
the sun move from over the lake in the east, all the way across the sky as
the day passed, disappearing behind the building at five when we'd jockey
for position with our lawn chairs to catch the remaining swaths of sunlight
before evening descended. Sometimes in mid-July, the dragonflies would
number in the thousands, coloring the sky with the reflections of sunlight
that shone off their wings, buzzing mystical ancient melodies. We all sat
in wonder—surrounded—the bugs coming close, often flying beneath the
seats of the chairs and the sand, but never quite touching our skin.

"Where in the hell *are* we?" I said to Kevin, who sat next to me with his wife.

"It is truly a magical place," he answered, his wife nodding in agreement. "Summers are sacred. Hopefully we'll have a good fall and winter this year." They'd been here for decades and Kevin had taken me under his wing as a surfer's apprentice, throwing me his hand-me-down wetsuit, along with a pair of old mitts and an even older pair of booties from his locker. He took me along with him to catch my first waves behind the steel mill in Miller, Indiana around Thanksgiving a couple of years prior. That day, *my first day*, was cold, and we'd hiked for over a mile to the break as snowflakes trickled down through the cloudy and gray, midwestern late-autumn afternoon. (I'd looked out my window the previous winter, not long after I had moved in, and seen someone in the water on a surfboard, which was odd because of how cold it was, and also because of the fact that it was a lake and not the ocean. He turned out to be Kevin, a close friend to this day. Kevin taught me to windsurf, then surf, along with another guy, Larry, the following summer and fall when the winds picked up from the north. Suddenly, I was flying across the beautiful freshwater sea on a twelve foot board, sail attached, then gearing up for the winter surfing season, committed to learning to surf).

Jim Called

Jim called. Jim had made drums for the Dead back before I was born. His first-floor apartment, which sat just off the Sherwin's veranda, was cluttered with various relics and untuned guitars. I'd been buying creatine from him which he'd ordered in bulk through the connections he had in China, himself being Chinese. I don't think the creatine worked but I mixed it in yogurt. "Care for a smoke?" he would ask, courteously, and I'd always say no, but this was not the reason he'd called me that gray afternoon.

It was one of those days in the part of the year that would go on forever—nothing but the cold, awful February colorlessness. There were crows on the wires. The snow had turned black and the lake was a sordid collection of tectonic ice plates. Off in the distance, a boat from the fire department was smashing itself through the ice. A helicopter swirled overhead and there was a general commotion around the snowy bank of the lake near Pratt Pier. This was the time of the year when it felt like the city was covered in ice.

And there it was, the dog that he'd called to tell me about, stranded, and making its way along the frozen plates about half a mile out on the lake. "You have a wetsuit. You have to go get it," Jim said, almost demandingly. He was nice and I'd always liked him and so I was prone to oblige even though I was scared. I put on my wetsuit and mittens and booties then went out and grabbed one of the kayaks that sat perched against the building. I plowed through the ice near the shore, feeling the frozen sand beneath my feet, and paddled through a clean channel of water that had formed just beyond it, making my way toward the dog.

It wasn't that big of a deal, really, and I was totally unaware of the people on shore who'd been watching. I had no clue that there had been cameras and that the news people had found a big story. I was simply a guy with a wetsuit who knew what to do. I had fallen in love with the lake and I knew she would protect me. I got to the dog; he was running along on the ice. I clapped with my neoprene mitts as I reached for his collar amidst all the flurries of snow fluttering through. He growled and attempted to bite me then swam to the shore.

Suddenly I was surrounded. The anchorwoman was tall, taller than me by a handful of inches, and asking me all sorts of questions.

"How did you know how to handle the danger?" I clearly remember her asking, and by this point, I talked like a surfer.

"It really wasn't that big of a deal. I've been surfing for years on the lake, so...um... like...I just paddled out there and got him," I answered, surrounded by cameras, police, and all sorts of firemen, along with the Rogers Park citizenry—always a colorful collective.

The story had made international news by the time I got back to my apartment. I felt like a hero that day.

This happened a few years before I decided to move.

California

There'd been a DVD in a discount bin that I found in a used record store in Fort Collins shortly before I left. "Riding Giants," was aptly named and it chronicled the lives of such big wave surfing legends as Gregg Noll and Laird Hamilton, among several others. I was transfixed, having never surfed but having ridden a handful of waves at the Jersey Shore as a kid on a boogie board. There was of course skateboarding and riding on snow as well; from the first time at Hawthorne, that night in the spring of seventh grade after experiencing my first broken heart, it felt like I was born to ride boards. Water was part of my bones growing up. So I'd stare at the scenes in this movie, from inside the heroin nightmare, and imagine myself in Hawaii, almost as if a part of me knew that I'd make it there someday. I had never imagined, however, that my baptism would take place in Lake Michigan during the frigid months of winter, and that what distinguished me and the others—whose footsteps I followed into the icy waters—from the big wave legends were the icicles that formed on our wetsuits after just a few minutes in the sub-zero temperatures and the commitment, not to riding the biggest waves ever surfed, but without question, the coldest ones.

I remember crying to myself on the couch in the basement and thinking that surfing would make it all better, which is a fair enough but also delusional thing to think when one is addicted to drugs. It *did* sort of save me but more in the sense that it helped me to put my thoughts back together after I'd gotten some clean time under my belt and had secured shelter and employment. This was about the time when I'd looked out the window and seen Kevin out on the lake.

The waves in California come from thousands of miles away, originating in the Aleutian Islands in wintertime, creating the famous north and northwest swells responsible for the iconic images reminiscent of Waimea Bay or the famous Banzai Pipeline in Hawaii. In a good year, these monstrous swells will work their way into southern California just enough to give us a taste of what those in Hawaii experience but without all the impact or intensity—mostly waves that are chest-high to a few feet overhead but which often get bigger, exciting each of the dedicated many who arrive before dawn in hopes of scoring a handful of life-affirming rides. There are very few days where I'm thwarted because of the size, but occasionally I stay on the shore, watching the others who exist in the next category up from me do things I do not have the courage to attempt.

Surfing is so many things—strategy, intuition, precision, dominance, and spirituality to name a few—but more than any of these things to which a chapter itself could be devoted, for me, it is freedom. In the same way that the lords of the highways extoll freedom's virtue and how it expresses itself on their Harleys, so is it the same for me on whichever vessel out of my quiver I choose to ride each morning, and at which spot. On the faces of waves there are moments of peaceful perfection. I forget about all of the mess that I made years ago. There's no rent to be paid and no heartbreak or pain. For a handful of seconds, the past and the future fade away into the spiritual anomaly that they are, and all that is left is the present.

On the face of the wave, I am free.

Andrew's Celebration

It was Andrew's celebration. Everyone was there: Jeremiah, Joslyn, Jared, Craig, and I, and the kid who did a handful of years in federal, as well as a whole bunch of others.

Andrew had all sorts of friends, and I was so happy I'd seen him a couple of months before the celebration. He and Megan were visiting SoCal and I was so mad at him for wanting to go watch the Padres that night and suggesting I meet them there. I was cursing him all the way down to the stadium from Oceanside, it being a Friday afternoon with the traffic and all. It took almost three hours but we met, hugged, then went to the game, and we laughed and made jokes about the big lesbians that kept showing up on the screen, and so Megan was giving us shit. They came back and slept on the couches at my place that night and the next day we went to the beach. I surfed and then suggested we all get a picture and just kind of had this strange feeling when we departed from one another.

They were going to Guatemala to teach English and I guess he had a heart attack. He basically died on a sidewalk in front of a bar.

Everyone drank and cried and cursed and I sang him a song that I wrote. I'd been off the booze for twelve years, but everyone besides me got hammered and sort of turned into their spirit selves and floated around the party, laughing and crying and remembering. A couple of hundred turned out, saluting the brother who'd fallen, leaving his Megan and mother and sister and brother and the rest of us behind.

I worry about Jeremiah and how he is handling it all. Still.

Sometimes he visits my dreams. One time it was 1997 or so in a Wicker Park hotdog joint, the kind with the dirty brown tile and the dirty black grout. And there he was, wearing his Indians hat and sort of half-smiling and smirking like he always did. And I knew that I only had a moment with him there and I begged him to stay but he left. Too soon.

I woke up in the bedroom of the trailer in the trailer park where I'd been living and felt him around me. Then I sent Megan a message and called Jeremiah.

I was crying as hard as I could. I loved him with all of my heart.

We made jokes about Jeremiah. There were jokes about each others' moms, jokes about each of our friends, and jokes about things that we knew people thought about us. Specialized jokes. Jokes no one else understood. Jokes with one word. Jokes which were nothing but smirks and eye contact. Filthy jokes about dead children. Jokes that we laughed at on the inside and felt bubble up and go down, which we later discussed with each other because perhaps they had to do with something we could not be seen laughing at.

We gossiped like girls. We talked about teachers. We hated the whole fucking town.

He never had weed. He didn't get jobs. I drove him and drove him and drove him all over the world. Sometimes I hated his guts.

I guess I wasn't born to lose, that there was something inside me that couldn't say die, some sort of morsel of light, some sort of truth that had always known it would prevail; just something I knew—knew the whole time—just like the part inside Andrew that knew that he'd die. I knew that he knew, way back in high school and then in Colorado and then after that, even after he'd met his wife and I was the one shooting dope. I just sort of knew he'd go first. I think he knew too. Deep down, I think that he knew, and now all that's left is a feeling for what it was like back when we were just kids. Fucking around. Playing with fire. Running with scissors. Cheating death.

Hope

There was this moment just after Cook County Jail, lying in bed in my room in the midst of it all. My insides were screaming; my soul was a blazing inferno. The pain was too much; paralyzed inside a nightmare. I got into bed but the nightmare sleep never helped (*if* there was sleep, which there wasn't unless I had dope). There wasn't escape. This was 2006, the worst year of my life, an eternity really, caught up and stuck in a Dantean realm of foreboding turmoil, surrounded by evil. That which could never be love, which hoped love would die in the most painful ways, surrounded me thickly inside a blanket of fear. I lay on the bed and cried out. "God, if you're real, please help me now! Show me a sign that you're there!" It was begging, a desperate, destitute pleading to have the pain stop. And I remember, so specifically, in that instant that something subsided; like a pressure valve opened and things got less bad. Just for a second, something became *less worse*; like every moment had been worse than the previous one and then, all of a sudden, things were just *less worse,* and less worse was better than how things had been. And this was the best it could be in this moment, *less worse*. **And there was a light**...It kind of went *"ting,"* like a soft, ringing bell, and this tiny relief breathed the tiniest breath of redemption into my sad soul.

So what was it? A Cherub or Seraphim being? Some sort of Angel of Mercy? A guide who'd been faithfully watching as all this unfolded? This was sure a long way away from the end of this dreadful debacle, a point at which my soul hadn't yet decided, but there was *something*— subtly, softly, and mercifully proving Existence beyond this sick world, proclaiming that *something* unseen was in fact there to help. The subtlest hope.

None of the story could have happened if *all* of the story hadn't happened. It *ALL* matters. Every last bit.

If there hadn't been the piñata, or the associated fit, then where would the story have gone? I mean, think about it; how might things have looked had I seen the candy I had not agreed with, been perfectly guided by parents who were perfectly raised, then chosen to *not* throw a fit, to have gone back to the party and to have learned that "that's the way the cookie crumbles" at age three, then applied that lesson reliably each time that life took an unfavorable turn?

I'd be one of those well-balanced adults; who would have made *rational* choices and sound financial decisions. Surfing *might* have happened (on weekends). Maybe I would have *tried* marijuana, once or twice. Maybe even I would have talked to my parents, who would have not had knee-jerk reactions to drug use, and maybe we would have decided together that it was a bad idea after a nice, adult, and rational discussion. That would have made for a really great memoir: "The story of a well-guided and well-balanced child who turned into a healthy adult." I see those kids at the reunion every five years and they have a whole different set of problems. No thanks.

And what if Japan hadn't happened the way that it had? Would you have read any further? If it didn't have sizzle, then would it have sold? It seems to me that something stranger than fiction had to unfold for the story to go as it did, and to make it a story worth telling.

But then what if the bottle had smashed in the skull of a newborn? There'd be nothing to salvage from infinite wreckage and sadness. It wouldn't have made for a tellable tale had there been *actual* horror and death. Still, the events which *could* have happened will haunt me for the rest of my days. Please do not think that I take all which *didn't* happen for granted. Several events which transpired could have killed me or worse (I know of a kid who was kidnapped and tortured for days; caught stealing from a dealer, feeding a need that placed itself in front of his life, which every drug addict has done). What's worse, there are others who I could have killed, and knowing this, like really getting it in the deepest way possible is not something I can live down. I know two people who have murdered, albeit by accident, but committed murder nonetheless—there were humans alive and then humans who died because of them. Each of them has made the necessary amends, and all of those I know who are in recovery and who know them understand. They were totally out of control, possessed in the most literal sense you might say.

Furthermore, things would have made sense had I landed in jail, having accidentally committed a homicide similar to the one just described, or gotten caught buying drugs one more time. Judge Kirby was clear with the defendants who entered his courtroom. If they fucked up, he would send them to prison. His firmness and fairness spoke volumes to all those who entered. I could have been one of them, could have easily been picked up and locked up once more, this time for more of a stay. And it would have been just, a justice of which I would have been very deserving. But then again, this would not have made for much of a story. "I was wasted for years and then, finally, I did something so stupid that somebody died. And now I'm really sorry and feel really bad and I'm locked up in jail and life sucks. The end." Happens every day. There is a very fine line between a hero's journey and a horror story, between a classic Greek tragedy and something that really inspires. I don't have much clue as to why I'm entitled to any sort of life, much less one that exists beyond my wildest dreams. I guess it was all in the cards.

Was there anything heroic in any of this, after all? Perhaps the recovery part, but leading up to it? Did Luke Skywalker slam a bunch of cocktails and take a handful of pills before blowing up the Death Star? He'd been abandoned, afterall. Did *he* turn to drugs? It seems as if there will be eternally unanswerable questions to much of this story I've told.

So, instead of all of the god-awful things which *could* have happened, we get hope, a hope which was facilitated by surrender; surrender being the doing of the long list of things I did not want to do, beginning with a gut-wrenching experience in detox followed by four months in rehab and then the narrow spiritual path I walked and still walk. Hope prevailed in the face of all of the things that could have gone wrong. This is what makes it just that, the expectation that everything terrible might happen but then doesn't. Hope happens when you kind of expect things to kill off protagonists but know that they're not meant to die. Deep down, there was a knowing that it would work out, and an expectation that things would eventually change for the better. Everyone dies in the end, either way. Hope can prolong things but never does anything more than postpone the inevitable when you actually think about it.

If I hadn't met John, how would the Sherwin have come into being? And then how would my surfing have surfaced?

It could have gone no other way. And I owe everything to him and his racket, to his bullshit and lies and abuse, and to his cruelty and kindness.

There's a name for people like this: they come into our lives and our lives become different. They can be lovers or bosses, or parents and police. Sometimes they hurt us and we scream at God, or beg for their deaths while we know them, smash fists into walls and whisper and cry in dark, beautiful curiosities as to why we met them.

Perhaps they are angels.

So I guess It was all in the plan. All of it sat, waiting to happen and find its perfection. I can't really explain any of it, while at the same time being able to explain every last bit. It's like it's 1. All perfect and divinely ordered with God-like perfection, or 2. It's just some cosmic anomaly which ultimately means nothing is going anywhere and matters to no one. This is why nihilists aren't any fun; they see all of this as just some stupid coincidence, a great big nothing going nowhere, meaning nothing, meant for no one. I've seen plenty of them cry at funerals though, which suggests they think *something* is sacred.

Recall that night in the woods; it was Cheez, a person who could be considered the essence of and exact definition of what a juvenile delinquent embodies—who told me while dosed out on serious drugs—about the book that just happened to be sitting on the shelf there at rehab, and that I'd been flipping through during naptime when my savior appeared and the angels uplifted my soul. Explain it. I can't, other than just "God," which is all that I really need for myself to make any sort of sense out of any of this. This was a kid who'd been hurt by the ones who had 'raised' him and he'd sought to make sense of it all in the library stacks; he then turned to drugs like so many of us and somehow enlightened me just enough that I remembered his words that he spoke from a log in the woods fifteen years later in the midst of the darkest place I had ever been.

There was also James. He was in so many ways about the worst possible influence on my life back in high school and college. He was awful at parties, a total embarrassment who insisted on tagging along. He lied and he cheated and stole, was obnoxious, rude and inconsiderate. He was so many things that society could do without, but ended up being for me, an avenue to redemption. The fact that I remembered his number, that he got the message I left, and that he went out of his way—probably knowing exactly what was up with me—to nurse my sick soul and carry a message of recovery to my aching spirit is indicative, to me at least, of there being some sort of guiding intelligence at play in all of this, and that it's eternal and beyond time and space.

Call It whatever you'd like.

And what if my leg hadn't broken? What if, when the guys asked me to shoot hoops, I'd have said "Nah" and relaxed in the sun. What if I hadn't gone for the rebound? Who was driving the bus there? God had to get me to California, to begin the slow and arduous process, via cycling and surfing for nine years in Chicago, to eventually and inevitably land me in Encinitas to experience the ultimate freedom on faces of waves.

You might call it grace or good karma. Perhaps lifetimes ago I was saintly and kind, scrubbing feet and dressing sores. Maybe I lived as a monk and did nothing but good. For lifetimes perhaps I was Holy and pure, accumulating points of good merit—saving a Heavenly cache of goodness which afforded some future life "slips," (as we might euphemistically refer to the antics contained in this volume). Maybe this is why God came and saved me from gangsters and death, judges, jails, and asylums.

So in this life I get a pass—no prison, no tragic death, no weeping mother who wished she'd done better—on the agreement I keep the rest of this one squeaky and clean, making spiritual progress to the best of my ability.

All of it's interconnected. Every little thing is connected to every other thing, and I cannot explain the horrific things that have happened in this world and that will continue to happen. Some things are beyond understanding and human comprehension. All that I have is my own personal experience and the power that comes from sharing it all.

The entire story is just a tiny, somewhat significant speck unfolding inside of one particular expression of evolving consciousness which existed for just one tiny moment inside of an eternal span of forever. My journey, which is now part of yours, was one that required some luck, lots of love, some others who'd also been saved, and a dream which was wrapped up in willingness to do anything other than the things I was doing. The "anything" for me just happened to be a very specific, time-tested and traditional path of recovery.

Here's an American story: some well-meaning people give birth. They do their best, loving their child in all the best ways that they can; the best schools, the nicest clothing, a country-club sort of existence. The child goes out to a party one night fifteen or so years later, takes pills, gets addicted, and after a decades-long tragic and harrowing tale, the son or daughter finally OD's after three or four trips to rehab. Happens all the time. Nobody talks. Here's a different one: some kid gets addicted to drugs. He doesn't know why, but they seem to fix something inside, something he didn't know broke in the first place. He's just a kid; he knows nothing of girls, sex, or death. He's basically totally innocent and just going along with the trends of his day, doing what other kids do. But then suddenly he has a problem. The thing that will save him is God, but God is something too far off to even consider for such a young mind, so he settles for drug life instead, because drugs make him *feel*, like really feel life in this magical, mysterious way. It gives him a complex of sorts, like those who see God might develop, and sets him apart and down a cruel road. In the end he finally makes it through. He can't explain why it worked out, only that it did. He and others around him all call it a miracle. He attributes his new life to something that's greater than him.

And another: a kid sees other kids doing drugs. His parents not only loved him but communicated to him in a way that he or she really listened, he or she listened so much that when the drugs finally showed up, at a party fifteen years later, he "passed on the grass."

Either way you look at it, someday in some way, drugs will show up, and your kids and your loved ones, your brothers or sisters or spouses or parents, will have chances to someday get hooked. So how do we fix this? What is the pathway that helps with destruction's prevention? How do we cope with this problem of epic proportions?

We balance ourselves. We free ourselves from the things that we carry along, up through lifetimes we've lived unaware. We look at the problems that face us, square in the eye, and take responsibility. You find some way to work with something that's bigger than you. Start with whatever. Make it a doorknob if you want, but start out by reaching toward something, anything outside of you. Pick up a Bible if you think it might help you. Go to a church. Look up one of the twelve-step fellowships and check it out. Get some therapy *before* things hit crisis mode, as upkeep instead of disaster control—you'd be amazed at the power of talking things out and of being deeply listened to. It's just a matter of beginning to *want* what you *need*, or to surrender to the fact that your soul is begging your ego to set its preferences aside for a moment and move toward the deep sense of peace you have always desired. You have to handle you, first and foremost, if you want to handle everything else. Pray. Meditate. Challenge your preconceived notions of how you believe things should be. Give up your pride for a moment; choose from a good which is greater, one that will challenge you to grow in uncomfortable ways and will serve you in the long run. Answer a calling.

The Midwest (where much of the book was set) is a funny place, because nobody talks. There are all of these drugs and all of these kids dying from fentanyl and heroin and crack, and no one is actually *talking*. There are four other families close to my parents, all roughly the same age and all with two or three kids. EVERY family has a kid who became a junkie. I once asked my mother if any of them had ever had an actual discussion about it. "No" was her only response. The tone of the word, of the one syllable it embodied, spoke volumes. Granted, the later generations are more apt to discuss these types of issues without shame, but I know that I am deeply ashamed to even broach the subject with those older than me, particularly with those from the Midwest.

My friends were thirteen when the drugs started making their rounds in our school. I rode a skateboard instead, and because this older skater kid named George thought that drugs were stupid, I thought they were stupid as well and went along, until the same kid started dropping acid a few years later, along with a few of the other kids I skated with. The rest was downhill. Throw in the cultural phenomenon of the Grateful Dead, a culture which more or less promoted drug use to children in the 80's and 90's, drug use that began in the 60's, and a problem of epic proportions unfolded, one which had little choice but to unfold in exactly the way that it did. Again, ALL of the story had to happen or none if it could have happened, and all of it sat in a sort of remission, to be reborn until I chose to once and for all "handle the scandal" which was plaguing my soul.

Something was watching, gentle and patient, tugging the strings just enough. And I must have been listening. Again, just enough, my soul clawing outwards toward glory, begging to rise up beyond the sick mess that became me. Just enough. Just enough life to beat death. Just enough good over evil. Just enough. I can't explain *any* of it all without explaining *all* of it. All of it matters or none of it does.

You picked this book up for a reason. What was it? Perhaps it was to indulge in pornographic drug fantasies. To feel the gore. To get sucked into something you don't have the guts or stupidity to actually experience for yourself. To feel the stick of your own personal needle in a way that makes things feel not as bad as they actually are, or could be.

Perhaps I'm inspiring to you. I hope that you're walking away having learned a few lessons, in surrender and whatever that word might mean to you, and whatever other things this work may have transmitted into your soul. What is surrender after all, except a list of things that you don't want to do? It rarely involves anything passive. You've got to get up and do it when it's time to surrender. What are you fighting right now? What is the thing that you're doing, that if you stopped doing it, your entire existence would change? *What does opposite day look like for you?*

297

There has to be something, something that makes it distinct.

What could you change right now that would lead you to a future you'd love to live into?

So go out and make something happen. Be an Undercover Angel.

Made in the USA
Monee, IL
22 September 2023

43145299R00184